D1188340

TOLERATION AS RECOGNITION

In this book, Anna Elisabetta Galeotti examines the most intractable problems which toleration encounters and argues that what is really at stake is not religious or moral disagreement but the unequal status of different social groups. Liberal theories of toleration fail to grasp this and consequently come up with normative solutions that are inadequate when confronted with controversial cases. Galeotti proposes, as an alternative, toleration as recognition, which addresses the problem of according equal respect to groups as well as equal liberty to individuals. She offers an interpretation that is both a revision and an expansion of liberal theory, in which toleration constitutes an important component not only of a theory of justice, but also of the politics of identity. Her study will appeal to a wide range of readers in political philosophy, political theory, and law.

ANNA ELISABETTA GALEOTTI is professor of political philosophy at the Università del Piemonte Orientale, Vercelli, Italy. Her publications include *Tolerance: A Pluralist Proposal* (1994), *Philosophy on Identity Conflict* (1999), and a number of journal articles.

TOLERATION AS RECOGNITION

ANNA ELISABETTA GALEOTTI

Università del Piemonte Orientale

CAMBRIDGE
UNIVERSITY PRESS

PUBLISHED BY THE PRESS SYNDICATE OF THE UNIVERSITY OF CAMBRIDGE
The Pitt Building, Trumpington Street, Cambridge, United Kingdom

CAMBRIDGE UNIVERSITY PRESS
The Edinburgh Building, Cambridge CB2 2RU, UK
40 West 20th Street, New York, NY 10011-4211, USA
477 Williamstown Road, Port Melbourne, VIC 3207, Australia
Ruiz de Alarcón 13, 28014 Madrid, Spain
Dock House, The Waterfront, Cape Town 8001, South Africa

http://www.cambridge.org

© Anna Elisabetta Galeotti 2002

First published 2002

Printed in the United Kingdom at the University Press, Cambridge

Typeface Baskerville Monotype 11 / 12.5 pt.   *System* LATEX 2ε [TB]

A catalogue record for this book is available from the British Library

Library of Congress cataloguing in publication data
Galeotti, Anna E.
Toleration as Recognition / Anna Elisabetta Galeotti.
p.   cm.
Includes bibliographical references and index.
ISBN 0 521 80676 3
1. Toleration.   2. Pluralism (Social sciences)   3. Equality.   I. Title.
HM1271 .G35   2002
303.3′85 – dc21   2001043624

ISBN 0 521 80676 3

To Giulio and Ada,
and to the memory of their father

Contents

Acknowledgments

This book is the final result of work which started in 1989. During the past eleven years I have written two books in Italian and many essays and papers on the topic of toleration in both Italian and English. A shorter version of the Introduction is published as "Contemporary Pluralism and Toleration" in *Ratio Juris*, 10, 1997, pp. 223–35. The first three chapters of the book correspond to a revision and expansions of chapters 2, 3, and 4 of my *La tolleranza. Una proposta pluralista* (Naples: Liguori, 1994). An earlier version of chapter 4 appears in *Political Theory*, 21, 1993, pp. 585–605 and is now also published in German, in a collection of essays entitled *Toleranz* edited by Rainer Forst (Frankfurt: Campus Verlag, 2000, pp. 231–356). Chapter 5 appears in my *Multiculturalismo. Filosofia politica e conflitto identitario* (Naples: Liguori, 1999), Chapter 6 has never been published. A somewhat different version of chapter 7 also appears in my *Multiculturalismo*.

Many people have contributed to my work on this book, both by reading and commenting on drafts and parts of drafts, and by discussing the basic ideas in the text with me. The first person I wish to thank is my late husband, Franco Ferraresi, who supported me, discussed my ideas, helped me to work them out, and read the manuscript at various stages of its development. Reading my manuscript was actually the last work he did; to him, and to our children, the book is dedicated. I am indebted to the Institute for Advanced Study, at Princeton, for the opportunity of a wonderful year of work in 1991–2 and to the Mellon Foundation for financial support. Among the people who read and commented on my work at various stages of its development are: Alan Ryan, Bernhard Peters, Joan Scott, Albert Hirshman, Luc Boltanski, Andrew Aisenberg, Antonella Besussi, Giampoaolo Ferranti, Giovanna Zincone, Roberta Sala, Richard Bellamy, and Martin Hollis. Special thanks should go to several friends who have been constant and encouraging interlocutors: Salvatore Veca, Sebastiano Maffettone, Steven Lukes, and Michael Walzer.

Introduction

In this book I discuss the theory and practice of toleration, and ask whether liberal doctrine is sufficiently well equipped to address all those contemporary situations that give rise to issues of toleration. These issues arise whenever an individual or a group attempts to check or to interfere with the behavior or practices of others which they dislike or of which they disapprove. They also arise when an individual or group resists the interference and control of others regarding their own behavior. These questions acquire a political dimension when two opposing parties fail to find an accommodation, either by tolerating each other's views, or by means of repression. If neither party gives in, political authority is called upon to solve the conflict. Questions of toleration become directly political when the third party is a government or a political agent.

For this kind of issue, which we can recognize as pertaining to toleration, the liberal tradition has developed a well-defined interpretive framework and a highly refined normative doctrine. This has been implemented through the establishment of legal rights which have been constitutionally granted and which are firmly entrenched in the culture and practice of liberal democracy. Consequently, it is not clear why any politically relevant problem of toleration should arise in a liberal democratic regime. The first part of this book focuses on this question: why is toleration still a problem in the world of liberal democracy?

While the absolute states of the sixteenth and seventeenth centuries needed to formalize a principle of toleration as a solution to religious conflicts, in liberal democracies toleration is generally recognized as the ethically proper means of accommodating differences in values and lifestyles. Genuine (non-trivial) questions of political toleration – those which involve a political authority, which is faced with the decision as to which practices or behavior it should either ignore or positively protect – are

I

typical of totalitarian or authoritarian states, where dissent from authority can challenge the system as a whole. In any specific case of dissent, such
a state needs to decide whether the best policy is repression or toleration.
Within liberal democracies, on the other hand, principles of political
toleration should already be enshrined in the constitutional framework
of the state. Political dissent is recognized as a fundamental and positive
characteristic of democratic life, whereby the government is checked by
an opposition. Whether or not to tolerate an opposition in principle
is not an open question; rather toleration is a constitutive part of the
rules of the game. The liberal state has been built around the ideal of
toleration which emerged during the religious conflicts of the sixteenth
and seventeenth centuries. Generally speaking, the idea that differences
in matters of religion, lifestyles, moral and aesthetic values, and so on do
not constitute legitimate possible objects of direct political intervention,
but belong to the individual's sphere of liberty, is embodied in liberal
constitutions and translated into a system of rights. The inclusion of
the ideal of toleration in constitutional rights as a means of protecting
individual freedom of conscience, expression, and association seems to
render the very notion of toleration superfluous. If everyone is granted
the right to entertain and to pursue his or her own conception of the good
and its corresponding lifestyle, as long as no harm to any third party is
produced, the state has no right to tolerate any different behavior, ideas
or morality, since it has no right to "tolerate" (in the strict sense) what it
has no entitlement to forbid in the first place.

As Thomas Paine remarked about the 1791 French constitution, when
universal rights are recognized, there is no longer any reason to practice
toleration:

The French constitution hath abolished or renounced toleration, and intoleration also, and hath established universal rights of conscience. Toleration is
not the opposite of intoleration, but it is the counterfeit of it. Both are despotism.
The one assumes to itself the right of withholding liberty of conscience, and the
other of granting it. The one is the pope, armed with fire and faggot, and the
other is the pope selling or granting indulgences. The former is Church and
State, and the latter is Church and traffic.[1]

A similar understanding of the connection between toleration and despotism is implied by Kant in *An Answer to the Question: What is Enlightenment?*,
commenting on the attitude of Frederick the Great about religious

---

[1] Thomas Paine, *The Rights of Man*, Part 1 [1791], in *Political Writings*, ed. Bruce Kuklick (Cambridge:
Cambridge University Press, 1989), p. 94.

freedom.[2] Kant points out that the enlightened king has acknowledged that it is his duty to refrain from any interference in the religious choices of his subjects and to grant them full liberty in this matter. In doing this, Kant remarks that Frederick has given up toleration, adopting instead the principle of free-thinking. Thus, both Kant and Paine state that the practice of toleration is always the counterpart of an arbitrary power, while the bill of rights of liberal politics provides a more proper solution to the problem of pluralism, insofar as it offers a universal answer and preempts questions of toleration.

In liberal democracies, infringements of toleration can occur, even frequently, but, regrettable as they are, they do not usually raise genuine theoretical and political problems, as the theory and the practice of toleration is generally equipped to answer them. Cases involving issues of toleration often arise in everyday interactions: in relations between neighbors, between fellow travelers on a train, or between colleagues in the workplace, for example. But such familiar problems do not fall into the category of political toleration. Apart from occasional infringements of the principle and politically irrelevant cases that arise in everyday life, there is prima facie no room for genuine issues of toleration in a world where it is already a shared value.

However, even though toleration appears to have become an inalienable hallmark of the liberal order, questions do still arise. In the last decade of the twentieth century, in particular, some important issues acquired a prominent position in liberal politics, engendering a corresponding theoretical interest in the topic of toleration. I define a genuine, non-trivial case of toleration as one in which the issue is not only perceived by the general public as highly controversial but as one which also requires the intervention of the state to settle it, either by means of checking intolerance or by defining the limits of toleration. In genuine cases, the intolerance which is encountered is not merely residual, according to liberal doctrine, as, for instance, in the case of personal disapproval of unorthodox sexual behavior which does not harm a third party. In such instances, the liberal theory of toleration provides a pretty straightforward solution, no matter how much it is resisted in practice,

---

[2] Immanuel Kant, *An Answer to the Question: What is Enlightenment?* [1783], in *Political Writings*, ed. Hans Reiss (Cambridge: Cambridge University Press, 1991): "A prince who does not regard it as beneath him to say that he considers it his duty in religious matter, not to prescribe anything to his people, but to allow complete freedom, a prince who thus even declines to accept the presumptuous title of tolerant is himself enlightened" (p. 58).

and intolerance is to be imputed to bigotry and a failure to live up to liberal principles. By contrast, when genuine, non-trivial cases are to be addressed, the usual solutions, drawn from liberal views of toleration, are largely inadequate and seem unsatisfactory no matter what decision is reached – that is, either alternative – taking a tolerant stance and imposing limits on toleration – seems unsatisfactory. Examples of genuine cases include such controversial matters as the wearing of the Islamic headscarf in public schools, the admission of gays into the army and regulations regarding speech that incites violence or hatred. Given that the theory and the practice of toleration are solidly entrenched in liberal politics, why is this so? Are such contemporary instances simply failures to live up to the ideal, or, rather, do contemporary expectations of toleration stretch the limits of what is tolerable?[3] Or is toleration an impossible, elusive virtue, which basically has no meaning outside interpersonal relationships?[4] Alternatively, it may be simply an outdated means of coping with the opposing views and different levels of acceptance of social differences that are present in contemporary liberal democracies.[5]

These hypotheses have all been considered in contemporary discussions on toleration and pluralism within moral and political theory. Different though they are, the explanations that emerge basically agree on one point: they apparently assume the inability of liberal toleration to deal with contemporary controversial cases, either because they are deemed incompatible with the limits of toleration, or because they fall outside its usual domain.

I shall advance a different answer, and one that could be the starting point for a fundamental revision of liberal toleration, which would adapt it to deal with contemporary genuine cases. My argument will be concerned primarily with the interpretive framework underlying all versions of liberal toleration, which, in my view, provides an insufficient understanding of what is at stake in contemporary cases. The normative solution turns out to be inadequate, not so much because of any shortcomings in the normative argument itself, as because it is the answer to a different question.

---

[3] See, for example, Mario G. Losano, "Contro la società multietnica," *Micromega*, December 1991, pp. 7–16; Alon Harel, "The Boundaries of Justifiable Tolerance: A Liberal Perspective," in D. Heyd, ed., *Toleration: An Elusive Virtue* (Princeton: Princeton University Press, 1996), pp. 114–16.
[4] See Bernard Williams, "Toleration: An Impossible Virtue", in Heyd, ed., *Toleration: An Elusive Virtue*, pp. 3–18.
[5] See Ermanno Bencivenga, *Oltre la tolleranza* (Milan: Feltrinelli, 1991); Joseph Raz, "Multiculturalism: A Liberal Perspective," *Dissent*, Winter 1994, pp. 67–79; Barbara Herman, "Pluralism and the Community of Moral Judgment," in Heyd, ed., *Toleration: An Elusive Virtue*, pp. 60–80.

THE LIMITS OF LIBERAL TOLERATION

Liberal theory understands toleration in terms of disagreement and conflict about values, religion, culture, etc. It is a conflict produced by differences which ultimately pertain to individual choice. For this kind of conflict, usually described as unadjudicable and non-negotiable, the political solution provided by toleration consists in acknowledging that individual choice is sovereign in certain matters where uniformity is neither possible nor necessary, and perhaps not even desirable. In other words, toleration amounts to granting every citizen a free choice concerning religious, moral, and personal choices, and exercising a "public blindness" when it comes to forming policy.[6] In this way, toleration sits comfortably with pluralism, based on the coexistence of freedom of choice and non-discrimination.

I will propose an alternative interpretation of the circumstances in which toleration becomes a pressing issue. Although opposing opinions in conceptions of the good or in world-views exist in the most controversial cases at the present time, they are not the only conflictual aspect, nor are they the most salient. Though we actually recognize such cases as being about toleration because they involve attempts to control unpopular behavior which is considered incompatible with an orderly social life, what gives rise to most genuine contemporary issues of toleration are, in fact, differences between groups rather than between individuals. This is crucial. Group differences normally have an ascriptive nature, in that, unlike the cases discussed by classical theorists of toleration, they do not involve choice. Moreover, members of groups whose differences raise issues of toleration have usually been excluded from full citizenship and from the full enjoyment of rights, either because they are latecomers on the scene, or because they were previously oppressed and/or invisible. Within the pluralism of groups, cultures, and collective identities, the salient conflict does not concern moral disagreement, at least not primarily, but rather concerns asymmetries in social standing, status, respect, and public recognition, which then sustain ideological and cultural contrasts.[7]

---

[6] This is the liberal argument for toleration as a political principle; but toleration is also defended by a different liberal argument, at the social and interpersonal level, as a social and moral virtue. See for example, Bernard Williams, "Toleration, a Political or Moral Question?," *Diogenes*, 44, 1996, pp. 35–48 and chapters 1 and 2 below.

[7] That conflicts around recognition of identities are crucial in contemporary democracy is underlined by Alessandro Pizzorno, *Le radici della politica assoluta* (Milan: Feltrinelli, 1993), pp. 187–203, who presents an interesting typology of social conflicts. In a different way, Charles Taylor also

In other words, it is the exclusion or the unequal and incomplete inclusion of various groups into democratic citizenship which sharpen cultural differences.[8] Issues of toleration then break out when cultural differences, perceived by the majority as being at odds with societal standards, are publicly exhibited, implicitly claiming legitimacy. In the stand-off which usually follows, toleration is generally invoked as a first step towards inclusion, as a form of public recognition of the collective identity of a marginalized, oppressed, or invisible group.

If what is really at stake in contemporary issues of toleration is equal respect and social standing for minority groups, rather than equal liberties for individuals, then the issue of public toleration must be addressed not simply in terms of the compatibility between liberal institutions and various cultures or practices, but in terms of contests over the inclusion of distinct identities and their bearers in the polity via the public recognition of their differences. This revised understanding of contemporary issues of toleration does not, however, resolve the problem of compatibility, which plays the role of a secondary constraint, rather than of the main condition for toleration.

This interpretation of the nature of the problem will gradually emerge in the course of the reconstruction of the liberal doctrine of toleration, which I undertake in the first part of this book, when we see how it fails to address contemporary cases. Viewing social differences merely as different beliefs and opinions to be considered neutrally in the public sphere, as liberal theory does, fails to recognize any asymmetry between them. All differences, being individual attitudes and preferences, are, from the political standpoint, treated equally. The problem is that, reversing Orwell's well-known phrase, some differences are more different than others. Some differences – notably race, ethnicity, sexual orientation, and culture – are markers of oppressed or excluded collective identities, to which various kinds of disadvantage are attached, amongst which non-membership or second-class membership in the polity are especially prominent.

underlines the central role of recognition in contemporary politics. See Amy Gutmann, ed., *Multiculturalism and "The Politics of Recognition"* (Princeton: Princeton University Press, 1993). On a line of inquiry similar to that of Pizzorno, see M. Gianni, "Le 'fait' du multiculturalisme: Quelques implications concernant la théorie normative de la citoyenneté," mimeo, Geneva, 1994.

[8] That the notion of citizenship cannot be limited to its formal, legal meaning, but implies something more substantial, such as actual functioning as a citizen and the enjoyment of rights, is a view shared by Giovanna Zincone, *Da sudditi a cittadini* (Bologna: Il Mulino, 1992), pp. 187–8, by Judith Shklar in *American Citizenship: The Quest for Inclusion* (Cambridge, Mass.: Harvard University Press, 1991), and, more recently, by P. Johnston Conover and D. D. Searing, "Citizens and Members: Dilemmas for Accommodation for Cultural Minority," mimeo, Bordeaux, 1995.

Once the issue of social differences as markers of special disadvantages is grasped, some would claim that it can be dealt with by some form of compensatory distribution, thus dispensing with the need for toleration altogether. In this way, contemporary issues of toleration would be reduced to a matter of distributive justice. However, the liberal theory of justice would have to face a thorny problem, because the subjects of distribution are not individuals but groups, whose members do not share the disadvantages equally.[9] But leaving this issue aside, the problem underlying contemporary cases of toleration would then be recaptured within a well-known line of inquiry of liberal thinking, i.e. the distributive paradigm. The latter may be hard pressed when dealing with groups instead of individuals, but it has already confronted the controversial issue of preferential treatment,[10] and is, in principle, equipped with conceptual tools capable of dealing with differences (for example, the well-known difference principle advanced by John Rawls).

Equating contemporary questions of toleration with issues of distribution, dealt with by the appropriate extension of the distributive paradigm, would leave liberal toleration intact as the solution to religious, moral, and metaphysical pluralism. Moreover, it would avoid questioning the principle of state neutrality and it would neutralize the risk that particular memberships and collective identities might trespass into the public domain of citizenship. This latter should remain the area of common ground for citizens, the ground, indeed, of democratic legitimacy, of the overlapping consensus and of public reasons for the liberal democratic order to be preserved. And if the distributive paradigm could be stretched far enough to compensate for asymmetries in public respect, social standing, and opportunities linked to membership of disadvantaged groups, then the liberal ideal of toleration would be properly fulfilled. On the one hand, full freedom of expression for individual and group differences in terms of religion, culture, morality, and lifestyle would be granted and, on the other, people would be freed from the burden of their differences and from the disadvantages suffered as members of certain groups. From this viewpoint, John Rawls's political theory would appear to be the most advanced one available: it establishes a link between toleration and justice and proposes that questions of toleration can be answered by the straightforward application of distributive principles.[11]

---

[9] See Douglas Rae, *Equalities* (Cambridge, Mass.: Harvard University Press, 1981).
[10] See M. Cohen, T. Nagel, and T. Scanlon, eds., *Equality and Preferential Treatment* (Princeton: Princeton University Press, 1977).
[11] John Rawls, *A Theory of Justice* (Oxford: Oxford University Press, 1971), ch. 4, §§ 32, 33, 34, 35, pp. 201–21 (hereinafter abbreviated to *TJ*).

Yet this reduction of toleration to distribution leaves something out. Although social differences are considered,[12] it is only as disadvantages. This is probably not the best strategy for addressing the inequalities in respect and consideration that are experienced by different groups. Moreover, and more importantly, the distinction between what is defined as "different" and as "normal" is completely ignored. In fact, not only do some differences carry more burdensome disadvantages than others, but in a given society only certain human traits, habits, opinions, practices, and ways of life are specifically considered "different," and only a few of them mark out their bearers as having a "different" received identity. For example, "whiteness" is not considered a "difference," and being white, like being Christian, heterosexual, etc., is not seen as being "different" or "other." What is defined as different is in fact what is perceived as such from the standpoint of the majority in a society. They have the power to define people, cultures, languages, or practices as "different," implying that they themselves are normal. And whether one belongs to the "normal" group or to another group results in something more than an unequal distribution of resources or opportunity; it defines one's ability to be either a full or a second-class citizen.[13] In other words, the distinction between what is normal and what is different in a given society is crucial, defining the inclusion and exclusion of its members. Inclusion and exclusion here do not refer simply to the enjoyment of legal rights, but to public consideration as members of the political and social community. This consideration should be accorded not despite one's origin, culture, skin color, or sexual preference, but precisely because of such features.[14] Being the bearer of a different identity which is socially invisible, despised or stigmatized constitutes a special barrier to becoming a functioning citizen and a social actor. As I have mentioned, it is not just a matter of enjoying fewer resources and opportunities, though this is often the case, but a matter of having fewer capabilities to make use of them.[15] It means having lower aspirations and expectations than

---

[12] In this way, liberal theory, which typically disregards social differences, extends beyond its usual boundaries, but always with a view to eliminating differences in matters pertaining to politics and public policy. See Ronald Dworkin, "Liberalism," in *A Matter of Principle* (Cambridge, Mass.: Harvard University Press, 1985), pp. 181–204.

[13] The concept of capability has been advanced by Amartya Sen as a necessary supplement to the notion of acquisitions, be they resources, opportunities, or goods, in order to define the individual's well-being and his or her functioning. See A. K. Sen, "Well-Being, Agency and Freedom," *Journal of Philosophy*, 82, 1985, pp. 169–221.

[14] See A. E. Galeotti, "La differenza: politica, non metafisica," in S. Maffettone and S. Veca, eds., *Filosofia, politica, società* (Rome: Donzelli, 1995), pp. 19–35.

[15] Sen, "Well-Being, Agency and Freedom."

others.[16] Those whose collective identity is despised, or who are subject to prejudice and stereotyping, usually experience a lack of confidence or self-esteem and various forms of self-hatred which, *ceteris paribus*, make it much harder for them to become fully functioning social agents and citizens.

If having a different identity is equated with failing to reach a certain threshold of developing capabilities, then, quite apart from any actual scarcity of resources or opportunities, this is a problem that cannot be addressed simply by making adjustments in the distributive structure of society. The distributive paradigm is designed for a fair social allocation of opportunities and resources, of rights and goods; in this case, however, what is at stake is the negative social perception of certain collective identities marked as different, a perception which affects the hopes and aspirations of the corresponding group's members. The majority's perception of social difference is politically relevant in two senses: first, it constitutes a particular disadvantage for those who are different, making it harder for them to acquire resources and opportunities, and as a result it causes social injustice. Second, it excludes minorities from certain preconditions for full participation in democratic citizenship. The feeling of shame, humiliation, and self-hatred experienced in connection with their differences, reinforced by the required public invisibility of their identity, prevents people from developing an adequate level of self-respect and self-esteem,[17] both of which are necessary for developing a voice and for making it heard, as well as for enjoying rights and for participating fully in the polity.[18]

In conclusion, the reinterpretation which I am proposing of the circumstances in which genuine questions of toleration arise resists the widespread contemporary attempt to reduce questions of toleration to questions of distribution,[19] and requires, rather, a general revision of the concept of toleration.

---

[16] Owen Fiss, "Groups and the Equal Protection Clause," *Philosophy and Public Affairs*, 5, 1975–6, pp. 107–77.

[17] A mention of Rawls's inclusion of self-respect and self-esteem among the primary goods to be socially distributed is in order here. *TJ*, p. 62 and pp. 440–6.

[18] On this point, see the argument by Susan James in "Cittadinanza femminile e indipendenza," in A. E. Galeotti, ed., *Individui e istituzioni* (Turin: La Rosa, 1992), pp. 175–205.

[19] Somewhat similar anti-reductionist positions are held by Iris Young, *Justice and the Politics of Difference* (Princeton: Princeton University Press, 1990), who criticizes the dominance of the "distributive paradigm" in political theory and highlights the problem of oppression and domination as non-reducible to distributive devices, and, more recently, by Nancy Frazer, "From Distribution to Recognition? Dilemmas of Justice in a 'Post-Socialist' Era," *New Left Review*, 212, 1995, pp. 68–93.

TOLERATION AS RECOGNITION

The second part of this book offers a general reconsideration of toleration, starting from the understanding of pluralism and diversity which I have briefly sketched above. Toleration will appear to be founded on considerations of justice, though not distributive justice, representing the first step in a strategy for the full inclusion of members belonging to oppressed and marginal minorities. In order to play that role, toleration will be conceived of as a form of recognition of different identities in the public sphere. In this way the conception of toleration I propose in chapter 3 implies a double extension of the liberal notion: first, a spatial extension from the private to the public domain, and, second, a semantic extension from the negative meaning of non-interference to the positive sense of acceptance and recognition.[20] At first glance, both extensions look troublesome for liberal theory, because they seem to call into question the central notion of a neutral and impartial sphere. Yet such liberal worries will be shown to be misplaced insofar as toleration as recognition turns out to be compatible both with a revised notion of neutrality and with impartiality.

Briefly, the outline of the argument for toleration as recognition is the following. If we take pluralism to be the presence of several groups and cultures within the same society – occupying unequal positions in relation to social standing, public respect, social and political power – circumstances in which toleration is required are reconceived as being produced by the majoritarian (negative) perception of traits, habits, and practices of minority groups which are singled out as "different" and excluded from what the majority defines as standard forms of behavior. Such situations of cultural domination then develop into contests over the public toleration of differences. This occurs when the appearance of minority groups in some public/political space is perceived as vociferous and provocative, and hence as an invasion of the political domain by particular identities and a plea for special consideration which cannot be ignored. In such cases, I defend toleration of differences in the public sphere not on the grounds of an argument showing the compatibility of the recognition of differences with neutrality, but on the grounds of justice. Indeed, the public exclusion of differences is unfair, because it

---

[20] On the shift from the negative to the positive meaning of toleration, see Otto A. Apel, "Plurality of the Good? The Problem of Affirmative Tolerance in a Multicultural Society from an Ethical Point of View," *Ratio Juris*, 10, 1997, pp. 199–222.

treats members of minorities differently from members of the majority, whose identity is openly visible everywhere in the political domain. It unjustly keeps minorities in a marginal position of second-class citizenship. Toleration can be seen as responding to and satisfying these requirements of justice if it is understood as a recognition of excluded, marginalized, and oppressed identities. It can, however, work as a form of recognition only if it is considered symbolically as a public gesture intended to legitimize the existence of differences and place them on the same footing as the habits and practices of the majority.

A brief illustration of the literal and symbolic sense of toleration is in order here.[21] Let us consider such controversial cases as the acceptance of the Islamic veil in schools, or the admission of gays into the army. In these instances, toleration literally involves nothing more than granting the liberty to express one's culture and identity in a given public space. This is not significantly different from traditional toleration, which is precisely why we recognize such hard contemporary cases as pertaining to toleration. In the literal sense, contemporary toleration consists of an extension of personal liberty from the private to the public sphere, an extension which is generally argued on the basis of the non-discrimination principle. This literal meaning of toleration is in line with liberal doctrine and most of the present discussion is concerned with it, especially with reference to its acceptable limits. Yet it by no means exhausts the meanings of toleration in pluralistic democracy.

Genuine cases of toleration do still arise in liberal democracy, despite the fact that individual rights are already granted, because what is at stake is something beyond freedom of conscience, freedom of expression, and privacy. If what underlies contemporary claims for toleration is a quest for the public recognition of different identities, then the claimant's goal cannot be simply the acquisition of an extra piece of liberty. Take the example of gays in the army: if it were simply a matter of access to the army for homosexuals, the compromise policy "don't ask, don't tell" should be sufficient. But such a policy, which is de facto tolerant, cannot be satisfactory for an oppressed minority struggling for visibility and public acceptance, because it lacks the symbolic official gesture or act of public recognition that makes that difference legitimate.

---

[21] The idea of the symbolic aspect of toleration was suggested to me by Steven Lukes' comment on my work, *La tolleranza. Una proposta pluralista* (Naples: Liguori, 1994). See Steven Lukes, "Toleration and Recognition," *Ratio Juris*, 10, 1997, pp. 213–22.

Thus, while de facto tolerance satisfies the demand for toleration in its literal sense – opening up new spaces of liberty for the tolerated – it fails utterly to satisfy the symbolic demand, which is the real reason why toleration in that instance is pursued and is considered important.[22]

The meaning of toleration, be it literal or symbolic, is strictly dependent on the reasons sustaining it. Only the reasons that derive from a concern for justice, which I have mentioned above, support the symbolic meaning of public recognition. By contrast, grounding toleration on the wrong reasons prevents any symbolic meaning from being attached to it: it becomes only non-interference. In this sense, liberal toleration, proceeding from an argument about compatibility, precludes the assigning of a symbolic meaning to toleration, and hence does not constitute a normatively adequate response to the real issues about toleration that arise in contemporary society.

The reason why the symbolic meaning of toleration is so important for the settlement of genuine contemporary cases depends on a conjectural causal chain linking the lack of public visibility of "different" identities with the lack of public respect for their bearers and their consequent incapacity to develop adequate self-esteem. Given the public invisibility of their identity and its social stigmatization, self-esteem is often pursued at the price of rejecting difference, resulting in humiliation and the loss of self-respect. If this causal chain holds, and if public toleration of a certain trait symbolically entails public acceptance and the legitimization of the different identity, then this very gesture of symbolic toleration will signify public respect and consideration for minorities as well as for the majority. This, in turn, should help members of minorities to build up an adequate reserve of self-esteem and self-respect; in this way the preconditions for full citizenship would be fulfilled. If this hypothesis stands, then the symbolic aspect of toleration will contribute to the peaceful coexistence in a pluralist democracy of various groups who *all* show one another mutual respect. In such a society the individual members will, in principle, be able to choose the terms of their membership.

---

[22] This account of the symbolic aspect, besides the literal meaning of toleration, is in line with that stated by Sheldon Leader in "Three Faces of Toleration in a Democracy," *Journal of Political Philosophy*, 4, 1996, pp. 45–67. Leader holds that the laissez-faire view of toleration is at the same time too narrow and too broad, because it does not take into account that in contemporary democracies the demands of toleration comprise, in fact, three different claims: (i) claims for non-interference; (ii) claims for fair access (which correspond to claims for a public recognition of identity); and (iii) claims for the interference with others in the course of securing fair access. I shall come back to this last point later.

A question may arise at this point: how can arguments that toleration should be restricted in cases such as pornography and hate speech fit into this conception?[23] Should they be considered as no more than residual demands for censorship and for the enforcement of morals that have nothing to do with toleration as recognition of differences? I do not think so. I think these arguments can be straightforwardly situated within the interpretive framework which I have outlined, although answering liberal objections to them could prove much harder to effect. At issue here are limits to individual freedom in connection with practices and behavior which allegedly have the effect of offending and damaging the identity and the social perception of minorities and oppressed groups. Though the actual content of these demands runs counter to that of claims for toleration of differences,[24] the circumstances in which these demands arise as well as what is at stake are similar for both categories: differences and collective identities, linked to oppressed, marginalized, or excluded groups who demand full inclusion in the liberal society via recognition and the protection of their identity. Demands to restrict offensive practices can in fact be seen as the second step in the process of inclusion of members of minority groups.[25] Once different identities have been legitimated in the public sphere by means of toleration, their public presence still needs to be stabilized over time. Members of minority groups are still targets of prejudice, stereotyping, and discrimination, and their inclusion is thus undermined. In these circumstances, arguments

[23] On the theme of whether hate speech or pornography should or should not be tolerated, there is a vast literature, reflecting the ongoing public discussion. As examples, on hate speech see Mary Matsuda, "Public Response to Racist Speech: Considering the Victim's Story," *Michigan Law Review*, 87, 1989, pp. 2329–59; Andrew Altmann, "Liberalism and Campus Hate Speech: A Philosophical Examination," *Ethics*, 193, 1993, pp. 302–17; Ross Harrison, "Tolerating the Offensive," in J. Horton and P. Nicholson, eds., *Toleration: Theory and Practice* (Aldershot: Avebury, 1992), pp. 14–27; Jennifer Jackson, "Intolerance on the Campus," in ibid., pp. 28–46; M. Matsuda and C. L. Delgado, *Words that Wound* (San Francisco: Westview, 1992); on pornography see Andrea Dworkin, *Men Possessing Women* (New York: Periggee, 1980); Catharine MacKinnon, "Sexuality, Pornography and Method: Pleasure under Patriarchy," *Ethics*, 99, 1989, pp. 314–46; Catharine MacKinnon, *Only Words* (Cambridge, Mass.: Harvard University Press, 1993). On the liberal side, see Ronald Dworkin, "Do We Have a Right to Pornography?," in *A Matter of Principle*, pp. 335–72 and Ronald Dworkin, "Women and Pornography," *New York Review of Books*, October 1993, pp. 36–42.

[24] Some consider these claims as incompatible with claims for toleration as recognition. See, for example, Harel, "The Boundaries of Justifiable Tolerance: A Liberal Perspective," p. 114.

[25] A similar view is held by Sheldon Leader, "Three Faces of Toleration." He argues that in the process of getting fair access to democratic society, previously excluded or oppressed groups claim for themselves the power to interfere with the behavior and practices both of their own members and of members of other groups which stand in their way. This kind of argument belongs to what is demanded as toleration in contemporary democracies.

against pornography and hate speech aim to achieve public protection for identities that are still weak; this is a further step towards stabilizing their public acceptance as legitimate. It is argued that the restriction of some people's liberty is necessary to allow for the full toleration of differences which are the target of discrimination and prejudice. Though these claims can thus be understood within the same interpretive framework as claims for the public protection of differences, the argument for restricting offensive practices is much more complex than that in favor of toleration as recognition of differences. Apart from all pragmatic considerations, two main obstacles of principle should be mentioned: the first is represented by special treatment, which is implied in the demand for a special public protection beyond that normally granted by liberal institutions; and the second consists of the conflict between special protection for given identities and free speech. I will postpone this discussion to chapters 3 and 4. For the moment I simply want to stress that the conception of toleration as recognition does capture these cases in its theoretical grid.

RECOGNITION, LIBERALISM, AND IDENTITY POLITICS

So far the argument for toleration as recognition has been shown to be grounded on principles of liberal justice, namely non-discrimination, equality of respect, and inclusion. Yet some may object that public recognition implies a conflict with liberal principles – that is, with neutrality, universality, and impartiality. Recognition in fact seems to imply that the content of differences should be considered and should be evaluated; in doing so, the state and its officials would have to refer to some ideal of the good as the criterion. But then the liberal state would surrender its anti-perfectionist stance.[26] Moreover, an institutional or public recognition of differences cannot be granted universally, but must always be a specific measure, and only for such differences as had been certified as having passed some test for recognition. Thus, impartiality too would be sacrificed in the name of identity politics. To sum up, public recognition of differences, even though justifiable in terms of liberal justice, would then turn out to be incompatible with other principles to which liberal justice is also committed.

I contend, however, that this objection depends on a questionable conception of recognition. Recognition is interpreted here as acknowledging,

---

[26] On perfectionism and anti-perfectionism, see below, chapters 1 and 2.

or even endorsing, the intrinsic value of the difference in question.[27] On this strong interpretation, recognition definitely ought not to be extended by democratic institutions to particular forms of life. But public recognition of differences admits of another less problematic meaning. Differences can be recognized not for their intrinsic value, which it is not up to the political authorities to determine, but instrumentally, for the value they have for their bearers. To be more precise, differences can be acknowledged to have the same value for their bearers as that which "normal" characteristics and practices have for the majority. In other words, the institutional recognition of differences, achieved as the symbolic side-effect of public toleration of different behavior or of some aspect of a different practice, has nothing to do with the public appreciation of a difference or with the declaration of its value, or its public endorsement. Here, the notion of public recognition more modestly means the acceptance, and hence the inclusion, of a different trait, behavior, practice, or identity in the range of the legitimate, viable, "normal" options and alternatives of an open society. It is an indirect negation of the majoritarian definition of something as different, but it stops short of evaluating the actual content of this "different" option. In this respect an institutional recognition of differences which are considered independently from their content is in fact compatible with public neutrality. Indeed, it requires no assessment and no evaluation of the many differences present in a pluralist democracy, but simply an opening up of society, widening the range of viable alternatives to include the different ones on the same footing as the normal, familiar, and traditional menu.

The notion of neutrality with which toleration as recognition can be reconciled is, however, one that has been revised vis-à-vis its normal interpretation. For example, the idea of a neutral public sphere in which differences and particularities are disregarded, as implied in the ideal of the secular state, has to be reconsidered. It is not the fact that particular identities are overlooked (something that has never applied to the identity of the majority) that makes liberal politics truly general, non-discriminatory and impartial, but rather the use of public reasons in political argument and decisions.[28] Similarly, the indifference shown by the majority towards the different, as captured in the idea of

---

[27] See: Charles Taylor, "The Politics of Recognition," in Gutmann, *Multiculturalism and "The Politics of Recognition,"* pp. 25–73.

[28] On the notion of public reasons, see Onora O'Neill, "The Public Use of Reason," *Political Theory*, 14, 1986, pp. 523–51, and John Rawls, "The Idea of Public Reason," in *Political Liberalism* (New York: Columbia University Press, 1993), pp. 213–54 (hereinafter abbreviated *PL*).

"public/institutional blindness," can be revised without giving up the constitutive core of neutrality. If differences have been the markers of invisibility and exclusion, then, as compensation, positive public attention and consideration is precisely in line with what neutrality stands for. A revised neutrality, which makes room for the public recognition of differences, should not aim at cancelling out all differences by compensating for the disadvantages that are attached to them, but should make all citizens feel positively at ease with their particular identity in public as well as in private.

If public recognition can be reconciled with a revised notion of neutrality, it can also be reconciled with impartiality. Though recognition works only if it is granted to particular identities, this does not mean singling out and favoring any group in particular, and thus giving up the principle of universal justice. Symbolic recognition is not exclusive; i.e. it is not a scarce commodity, posing problems of distribution. As long as the difference in question does not infringe any right, public recognition, though it must be granted to each difference separately, can be generalized to all claimants.

The third part of the book is concerned with testing the general argument of toleration as recognition in a discussion of certain controversial cases and issues. These cases are treated as examples in a philosophical argument, and their theoretical and normative implications for toleration are discussed. No attempt is made to provide historical, sociological, or political interpretations, which are not relevant to my argument.

The first case which I consider in chapter 4 constitutes a typical example of toleration as recognition; it is a widely debated and highly controversial case, also known as *l'affaire du foulard*, relating to the contested use of the Islamic headscarf in state schools in France. Discussion of this case allows me to show how liberal toleration is insufficient in confronting claims for public visibility and acceptance of cultural differences, mainly because it does not allow one properly to understand what is at stake. As a consequence, any normative response based on the liberal understanding of tolerance will be inadequate. Toleration, if adopted, will follow for the wrong reasons, preventing the symbolic meaning of public recognition from being expressed. Equally, intolerance, espoused as a means for protecting secularism and universalism from tribalism, would prove unjustified. Toleration as recognition of the Islamic differences would emerge as the only response which takes seriously the problem of how the state might include immigrants fairly in the democratic process, while demanding in return loyalty to its institutions.

I will then consider the issue of whether racism can ever be tolerated (see chapter 5). This question will be addressed through a number of examples taken from different countries and cultural contexts: from hate speech regulations in the United States to the decision of the German Supreme Court to outlaw historical revisionism, to the question of whether or not Nazi marches should be forbidden and fascist organizations banned in Italy and in the United States. All of these cases concern the question of whether there are limits to the toleration of certain forms of behavior and practices which are allegedly offensive to the identity of previously oppressed and excluded groups. As I have said, the argument for limiting toleration of offensive behavior is much harder to establish than the argument in favor of toleration as recognition of differences, because it involves both a conflict with free speech and with differential treatment. Yet whether racism is tolerable or not is a particularly intriguing question, given that it is universally regarded as morally wrong, and is also held to be the exact opposite of tolerance; it would seem to be the perfect case to which the principle that toleration should not be extended to intolerance should apply. But this principle appears dramatically inadequate when confronted with actual instances. I will try to sort out the different modes of presentation of racism – ideas, political organizations and activity, individual acts and attitudes, insults, ideology, and theory – and for each of them I will ask whether any limit to toleration can be justified. The discussion will show that liberal toleration and toleration as recognition can fruitfully interact and that the latter is not a substitute for liberal toleration, but, it is hoped, a useful supplement.

Lastly, in chapter 6, I will take up the issue of gay marriage, taking into account the ongoing discussion in the United States, after the State of Hawaii's decision in 1991. I see the case of same-sex marriage as a crucial example of the implications of toleration as recognition. If the invisibility which has always surrounded the minority of gay and lesbian citizens is lifted, if differences in sexual orientation are recognized as a legitimate option in an open society, then societal standards and conventions need to be redrawn accordingly. One of the most prominent social institutions is the family, which, notwithstanding its many transformations through human history, is considered by the moral majority to have a definite, biologically fixed boundary in the heterosexual couple. The issue of same-sex marriage, then, is particularly interesting because it unveils the special connection between invisibility and intolerance which normal liberal views of toleration are not equipped to tackle. In contrast to immigrants and cultural minorities, homosexuals are not excluded from citizenship rights or from the opportunity to make use of them, as long as their sexual orientation is kept in the closet. Their incomplete inclusion becomes evident when their sexual orientation is a significant factor in making a life decision such as forming a recognized partnership or raising children. This option precludes homosexuals, while it is open to those who pretend to be straight. In discussing this example, the relationship between liberal toleration and toleration as recognition will be clarified. On the one hand, the specificity of toleration as recognition will become apparent insofar as it does not simply require that the right of privacy be granted to anyone, whatever their sexual orientation, nor does it demand merely that areas such as the military, formerly closed to homosexual citizens, be open to all. Rather it also requires that the boundaries of traditional practices which exclude minorities be redrawn in order that everyone may partake fully in social and political life in their different ways without stigma. On the other hand, toleration as recognition will thus prove to be the proper fulfillment of liberal toleration taken at its best. After all, equal liberty can be interpreted in many ways, but I take it here to mean the comparable absence of obstacles that would block making effective use of opportunities to shape a meaningful life.

Finally, I conclude by considering toleration as recognition as part of what is often called the politics of recognition or, alternatively, identity politics, which groups together a cluster of claims and demands aimed at the public assertion of the collective identities of oppressed and excluded groups and at securing public protection and support for them. This kind of politics, associated with the ideal of a multicultural society where various groups can coexist and interact free from cultural domination and without giving up their identity, exhibits a number of well-known problems which seem to undermine the pillars of liberal justice and social cohesion. Preferential treatment, treating groups instead of individuals as distributive units, and protection for certain cultures (seen as a poten- tial danger to the protection of individual rights) are just a few of the controversial issues that emerge in identity politics. In order to face these issues effectively, we must not reject the politics of recognition altogether. If, as I have suggested, demands for the public recognition of identity are to be seen as moves in a strategy towards the even-handed inclusion of members of minorities in democratic citizenship, there is good reason to consider these claims seriously (and also to see them as less threatening to social unity). Moreover, given that each of them raises a special problem, there is good reason to consider them separately. One such demand is for affirmative action, another for the reform of school curricula, and yet another is for the public financing of bilingual schools. Even if the general argument for public recognition is granted, it does not follow that all demands are to be met and on their own terms. Some may be supported by more substantial reasons, such as evidence of persistent discrimination; some may imply no direct conflict with liberal politics – as I argue is the case for claims of public toleration. Others still may conflict with some rights or with liberal institutions.

In general, I will argue that what is at stake in all arguments for recognition is the symbolic value of being accepted, included, and supported, above and beyond the actual provision or measure which might constitute the symbolic expression of such recognition. If my reading is correct, then even though identity politics is typically defined as non-negotiable, the content of particular demands made by minority groups is open to negotiation and pragmatic accommodation once the symbolic expression of their right to toleration is ensured. Thus, on the one hand, toleration can be seen as pertaining to the politics of recognition, but without implying any significant conflict with liberal politics, and, on the other, identity politics can appear less intractable than is usually supposed and ultimately open to negotiation.

Chapter 7 places the conception of toleration within the context of the politics of recognition in general. This demonstrates how it is possible to obviate criticisms of affirmative action or group rights, for example, as being unjust extensions of toleration, but also to stress that toleration, in my view, constitutes a component of multicultural politics. In this respect, toleration as recognition, though well rooted in liberal justice and not violating the principles of liberal neutrality and impartiality, exceeds the role which liberal theory has traditionally assigned to it. Yet, under a different description, it constitutes the proper fulfillment of the ideal of toleration; it aims at freeing everyone from the burden of his or her religion, morals, lifestyles, and customs, whether inherited or individually chosen, while keeping that part of them that the individual considers important and valuable. In this way, personal and social identities are made consistent and everyone becomes a proper member of society, fully partaking of the benefits and costs of social cooperation on an equal footing.

Liberal theories of toleration

THE CONCEPT OF TOLERATION

Toleration is the social virtue and the political principle that allows for the peaceful coexistence of individuals and groups who hold different views and practice different ways of life within the same society.[1] This very general definition indicates that the conditions under which toleration is required are situations in which social differences exist which do not naturally coexist harmoniously; if they were to do so, there would be no need for any such principle.[2] Potential or actual causes of conflict are required for toleration to be necessary in order to bring about social order and peace. As long as peace is a political value, toleration will be valued as well. However, toleration also exhibits a particularly problematic aspect: if its precondition is the presence of conflicting social differences, this implies that the bearers of such differences do not welcome what they see as being incompatible with their views and forms of life. In order to become tolerant they first need to dislike or disapprove of the different

[1] In recent studies in moral philosophy, the concept of toleration has been explored extensively. In particular, the Morell Toleration Project hosted by York University has made available a wide-ranging analysis which has been published in various volumes: S. Mendus and J. Horton, eds., *Aspects of Toleration* (London: Methuen, 1985); S. Mendus and D. Edwards, eds., *On Toleration* (Oxford: Clarendon Press, 1987); S. Mendus, ed., *Justifying Toleration* (Cambridge: Cambridge University Press, 1988); S. Mendus, *Toleration and the Limits of Liberalism* (London: Macmillan, 1989); J. Horton and P. Nicholson, *Toleration: Theory and Practice* (Aldershot: Avebury, 1992); J. Horton, ed., *Liberalism, Multiculturalism and Religious Pluralism* (London: Macmillan, 1993); J. Horton and S. Mendus, eds., *Toleration, Identity and Difference* (London: Macmillan, 1999); S. Mendus, *Politics of Toleration: Tolerance and Intolerance in Modern Life* (Edinburgh: Edinburgh University Press, 1999). Other important recent works exploring the topic are: Heyd, ed., *Toleration: An Elusive Virtue*, and the issue of *Ratio Juris*, 10, 1997; Rainer Forst, ed., *Toleranz* (Frankfurt: Campus Verlag, 2000); the issue of *Res Publica Beyond Toleration?*, 2001.

[2] A detailed discussion of the conditions and circumstances under which toleration comes to be an issue can be found in P. King, *Toleration* (London: Allen and Unwin, 1976); A. Weale, "Toleration, Individual Differences and Respect for Persons," in *Aspects of Toleration*, pp. 16–35; P. Nicholson, "Toleration as a Moral Ideal," in *Aspects of Toleration*, pp. 158–73; M. Warnock "The Limits to Toleration," in *On Toleration*, pp. 123–39; D. Heyd, "Introduction," in *Toleration: An Elusive Virtue*, pp. 3–17; J. Horton, "Toleration as a Virtue," in *Toleration: An Elusive Virtue*, pp. 28–43.

practices which are at odds with their own, and then to overcome such feelings, giving way to toleration. Yet this is puzzling: how can toleration be good if it involves putting up with what is disliked or disapproved of? In this light, toleration seems to be more a disposition that results from a compromise than one which could count as having positive ethical and political value in its own right.[3]

In its turn, this question raises another problem: what does toleration properly consist in – letting go, putting up with, non-interference or, maybe, even acceptance? Whether toleration is given a negative or a positive meaning has consequences for its value. The merely negative meaning would imply that being tolerated is better than being coerced into or prevented from doing something, but that it is far from being an ideal condition of social and political life, and this looks more like a modus vivendi than a principled solution to the conflicts of pluralism. By contrast, a positive interpretation of toleration as acceptance makes it seem more attractive and more wholeheartedly valued; yet, if its premises are disapproval and dislike, the positive meaning does not seem easily available. Much of the current analysis of toleration deals with these two correlated points: on the one hand, it focuses on the reasons for exercising toleration despite the initial disapproval or dislike which it presupposes and apart from mere prudential motives. The intention of this approach is to overcome the so-called ethical paradox of toleration. In this respect, a number of answers have been put forward, amongst which the most prominent are theories emphasizing the value of pluralism, or of autonomy, or of respect for other people, or all of these.[4] On the other hand, contemporary reflections on toleration ask whether the concept can also be intended in a positive sense as active acceptance, so that its social and political value can be strengthened beyond that of a mere modus vivendi.[5] Here, students of toleration are divided: those who admit only a negative meaning come to the conclusion that toleration is an insufficient principle for dealing with the problems of contemporary pluralism; a positive conception of toleration, on the other hand, can be seen as a useful tool, though not the only one, for dealing with the social differences of contemporary pluralism. The point is that the adoption of

---

[3] This puzzle is also known as a paradox: see B. Cohen, "An Ethical Paradox," *Mind*, 76, 1967, pp. 250–9; G. Harrison, "Relativism and Tolerance," in P. Laslett and J. Fishkin, eds. *Philosophy, Politics, Society* (Oxford: Blackwell, 1979), pp. 273–90; Williams, "Toleration: An Impossible Virtue," and Williams, "Toleration: A Political or Moral Question?"

[4] A useful survey of the main arguments for toleration can be found in Mendus, "Introduction," to *Justifying Toleration*, pp. 1–20.

[5] On this point, see Apel, "Plurality of the Good?"

a negative or a positive view of toleration depends on the understanding of the circumstances under which issues of toleration arise, as we shall see later on. In any case, toleration, be it a negative or a positive attitude, seems to imply some power of interference with or hindrance of what is disliked in the first place; otherwise we would more properly talk of acquiescence. In turn, this suggests that the relationship between the tolerator and the tolerated is generally asymmetrical, and that even if each party dislikes that which is "different" about the other, only one, the tolerator, enjoys significant power over the members of the other party; it is the restraint of this power which results in toleration. The weaker party, on the other hand, the person or persons who are tolerated, cannot but acquiesce.[6] To sum up, toleration is the principle of peaceful coexistence where there are conflicting, incompatible, and irreducible differences in ways of life, practices, habits, and characters. Incompatibility emerges from a mutual disapproval or dislike or, at least, a suspicion of differences, which can give rise to social conflict and to the suppression or prohibition of certain practices by the stronger party, or by the state if it becomes involved in the stand-off. Toleration occurs when dislike or disapproval is overcome in the name of some other, stronger reason (e.g. the values of pluralism, autonomy, or respect for others), and when the stronger party consequently refrains from interference with the form of behavior which is disliked. An account of the circumstances in which toleration comes to be an issue – that is, which differences count, how they are construed, and when they give rise to a stand-off – is crucial for determining whether the concept of toleration should have negative or positive connotations, or both. However conceived of, it is clear in any case that toleration must have limits, because there are some deviant forms of behavior and practices that cannot be tolerated; for example, homicide, rape, and robbery are obviously not candidates for toleration. In general, it is widely agreed that the Millian harm principle and the Lockean self-defense principle constitute limits for toleration, though in

---

[6] The distinction between tolerance and acquiescence has been drawn by King, *Toleration*, p. 62, and revisited by Weale in "Toleration, Individual Differences and Respect for Persons," in *Aspects of Toleration*, pp. 16–35. In particular, King stresses power asymmetry as one of the conditions for the existence of toleration: "When individuals or groups exercise a roughly equal power within some larger context, the grounds exist for anarchy or accommodation, but not for tolerance or intolerance," p. 67. A further distinction that is held to be important for defining the concept of toleration is that between tolerance and indifference. This distinction concerns the significance of the difference which is the potential object of toleration: if the difference is not really important for either party, then one has a case of indifference. See Bernard Crick, "Toleration and Tolerance in Theory and Practice," *Government and Opposition*, 6, 1971, pp. 144–71; King, *Toleration*, and Nicholson, "Toleration as A Moral Ideal."

practice it is difficult to define what counts as harm to a third party and what puts the political order and peace at risk. This is a very sketchy presentation of a very complex concept, which contemporary philosophy has analyzed in depth, highlighting its problematic features and suggesting ways of dealing with its paradoxical features. But, for the purpose of this work, which is focused on toleration in the context of political theory, this brief account must suffice as an introduction to the liberal versions of toleration, although some further points will be discussed in the outline of the argument for toleration as recognition. The fact is that the philosophical discussion on toleration as a moral disposition is of little consequence for dealing with the political issue of toleration: one thing it is to understand how permitting wrongdoings can be a virtue, and another to understand how difficult and conflicting ways of life can peacefully coexist and express themselves freely.[7] The question I am going to raise is, rather, how toleration works as a political principle within the wide tradition of liberalism. To put it more precisely, how does it provide a proper solution to the problem of conflicts of religious, moral, and cultural pluralism, while allowing for liberty and diversity?

RELIGIOUS CONFLICT, TOLERATION, AND LIBERALISM

As a political principle, toleration is strictly intertwined with liberalism, both from a historical and from a theoretical point of view. Historically, the theory of toleration emerged as the solution to the challenge posed by the religious wars which devastated early modern Europe after the Reformation, and it constituted the first step towards a liberal politics. Theoretically, toleration provides a strategy for making the liberty of each individual in matters of beliefs, values, and ways of life compatible with the liberty of everybody else, and for minimizing state coercion. Given that the main goals of liberalism, under any possible description, are the protection and the fostering of individual freedom and the limitation of justifiable coercion on the part of the state, toleration constitutes an essential element of the liberal project. However, liberal theory comprises

---

[7] On the discontinuity between the virtue of tolerance and the political principle of toleration, see my "Do We Need Toleration as a Moral Virtue?" *Res Publica*, 2001. On the harm principle, with reference to toleration, see S. Mendus, "Harm, Offence, Censorship," pp. 99–112, J. Horton, "Toleration, Morality and Harm," pp. 113–35, and P. Jones, "Toleration, Harm and Moral Effect," pp. 136–57, all of which are in *Aspects of Toleration*; and J. Raz, "Autonomy, Toleration and the Harm Principle," in *Justifying Toleration*, pp. 155–75. The principle of self-defense has not been directly analyzed to the same extent, though implicitly the great question of the compatibility of liberal democracy and fundamentalism rests on the correct analysis of this principle.

many varieties and the conception of toleration varies accordingly. I shall start with a conjectural reconstruction of the theoretical itinerary from the religious wars to toleration and the emergence of the liberal secular state.

After the religious Reformation and its devastating effects, the idea of toleration emerged slowly from the convergence of a number of lines of thought.[8] Even though the arguments in favor of toleration varied, ranging from humanist skepticism to the impossibility of forcing the true faith,[9] its way of working for peace and civil coexistence exhibited a common pattern.[10] It basically consisted in making a strict demarcation between matters pertaining to the political order and public affairs, on the one hand, and, on the other, matters unrelated to the political order; primary among the latter were religious convictions.[11] This demarcation divided society into two areas: the first, built around matters that were relevant to order and peace, constituted the political sphere, a domain subject to the political authorities and public regulation; the second,

---

[8] In the extensive historical literature on toleration, see, for example, R. H. Bainton, *Studies in the Reformation* (Boston: Beacon Press, 1963); E. M. Beaume, "The Limits of Toleration in Sixteenth Century France," *Studies in the Renaissance*, 16, 1966; I. Mereu, *Storia dell'intolleranza in Europa* (Milan: Mondadori, 1979); C. Vivanti, "Assolutismo e tolleranza nel pensiero politico francese del Cinque–Seicento," in L. Firpo, ed., *Storia delle idee economiche, politiche e sociali*, vol. iv (Turin: UTET, 1986), pp. 13–93; J. G. A. Pocock, "Religious Freedom and the Desacralization of Politics: From the English Civil Wars to the Virginia Statute," in M. D. Peterson and R. Vaughan, eds., *The Virginia Statute for Religious Freedom* (Cambridge: Cambridge University Press, 1988), pp. 43–73; S. Mendus, ed., *The Politics of Toleration in Modern Life* (Durham, N.C.: Duke University Press, 2000).

[9] One of the first arguments for toleration focuses on the folly of persecution: see Sebastian Castellion, *Concerning Heretics: Whether They Are To Be Persecuted and How They Are To Be Treated* [1553] (New York: Columbia University Press, 1935). Humanist skepticism is represented by Erasmus, *In Praise of Folly* [1511] (Princeton: Princeton University Press, 1970). The impossibility of forcing people to embrace the true faith is defended in John Milton, *Areopagitica* [1644], ed. R. M. Lea (Oxford: Clarendon Press, 1973), and John Locke, *A Letter Concerning Toleration*, ed. J. Horton and S. Mendus (London: Routledge, 1991). Among the secondary literature, see Reinhard Koselleck, *Kritik und Krise: Eine Studie zur Pathogenese der bürgerlichen Welt* (Frankfurt: Suhrkamp Verlag, 1973); Alan Ryan, "Hobbes, Toleration and the Inner Life," in David Miller and Larry Siedentop, eds., *The Nature of Political Theory* (Oxford: Clarendon Press, 1983), pp. 197–218; Gary Remer, "Rhetoric and the Erasmian Defence of Religious Toleration," *History of Political Thought*, 10, 1989, pp. 377–403; Richard Tuck, "Scepticism and Toleration in the Seventeenth Century," in *Justifying Toleration*, pp. 21–35; Jeremy Waldron, "Toleration and the Rationality of Persecution," in *Justifying Toleration*, pp. 61–86.

[10] Indeed, toleration finally won, though in a limited way, because the war could not be stopped and toleration appeared to be the only political solution that would lead to a stable peace. It was the doctrines of the French "politiques" during the sixteenth century that affirmed that religion should be politically neutralized as the only way to maintain peaceful coexistence in a religiously divided society. See Bainton, *Studies in the Reformation*, and Vivanti, "Assolutismo e tolleranza." The champion of toleration for the sake of peace is Thomas Hobbes: see Alan Ryan, "A More Tolerant Hobbes?," in *Justifying Toleration*, pp. 37–59.

[11] Koselleck, *Kritik und Krise*.

concerned with issues that were irrelevant to order and peace, defined the private realm as one in which the state had no business and hence no reason to intervene with coercive action. This protected area, where political interference was to be suspended, constituted the proper object-domain of toleration.[12] The principle of toleration thus relied on and worked through the public/private distinction and, as a result, had a double effect: it created protection against state intervention in matters of faith, and it circumscribed religion within a politically neutralized area, the private realm of conscience, hence preventing churches and religious movements from interfering with political decisions.[13] Thus, toleration engendered a lengthy and highly contested process by which church and state became increasingly autonomous in their respective spheres. The political neutralization of religion, i.e. its privatization, did not in fact originally entail the religious neutralization of politics.[14] In other words, originally toleration meant both the absence of political coercion in matters of faith and conscience and the delegitimation of religious interference in politics. But the political authorities felt no compunction in favoring a particular church or endorsing a state religion, as long as other churches and creeds were not persecuted. For example, it depended upon political convenience whether the privileges enjoyed by the majority church and by religious orders were suspended or not. In the seventeenth and eighteenth centuries the absolute state did not need to be secular in order to be tolerant.[15]

It was only when toleration was transformed by the liberal state into a universal right to free conscience and free association that the idea of a religiously neutral state – the secular state – could be advanced. From a theoretical viewpoint, it is easy to see that, if everyone is granted an equal right to a free conscience, then the state has no right to favor or to give public support to any one view or church, because that would be an illegitimate interference in matters outside the sphere of politics. Moreover, it would mean giving more weight to the choice of some citizens than to

---

[12] Locke's *Letter* is paradigmatic in this respect.

[13] Koselleck, *Kritik und Krise*.

[14] This reading is close to the interpretation given by Koselleck, whose notion of neutralization is indebted to Carl Schmitt's concept of the political. (See C. Schmitt, "Der Begriff des Politischen," *Archiv für Sozialwissenschaft und Sozialpolitik*, 53, 1927.) A similar view, though embedded in a different historical approach, is given by Pocock in "Religious Freedom and the Desacralization of Politics."

[15] Joseph Charles Heim, "The Demise of the Confessional State and the Rise of the Idea of a Legitimate Minority," in *Majorities and Minorities* (New York: New York University Press, 1980), pp. 11–23.

that of others, thus opening the way to religious discrimination. Finally, it could lead to a hidden influence of the favored church in state affairs. In this way, the generalization of the ideal of toleration in the liberal state, by means of universal rights of liberty, made possible the notion of the religiously neutral secular state, conceptualized in the liberal doctrine of the separation of church and state.[16] In that context, the principle of neutrality could be developed, though the actual term is in fact a recent one.[17]

While toleration is the suspension of the political power of interference in individuals' religious and moral views, neutrality means not favoring any one set of such views, or their holders, over others in the public sphere. The principle of neutrality introduces a further requirement for the definition of legitimate political action.[18] Whereas toleration simply removes some areas, declared as private, from the domain of legitimate political intervention, neutrality provides a positive guideline for public action, which is henceforth to be consistent with the independence of the political sphere from religion. With reference to citizens, then, while toleration grants them freedom of conscience, neutrality grants them the right not to be discriminated against because of their conscience. At the same time, while originally the differences to be tolerated had to be declared irrelevant from the point of view of order and peace, with the rise of the concept of neutrality, the political irrelevance of differences is transformed into political indifference and blindness towards them. So while social differences, well protected by individual rights, are to be tolerated in the private sphere, in the public sphere they should simply be ignored. In addition to this indifference, the principle of neutrality also engendered a conceptualization of the public sphere as a neutralized area from which social differences were irrelevant, a purified space of equals where only merit should count as a differentiating principle. Thus, even though neutrality does not require citizens to hide their differences

---

[16] See Robert Audi, "The Separation of Church and State and the Obligation of Citizenship," *Philosophy and Public Affairs*, 18, 1989, pp. 258–96; J. P. Day, *Liberty and Justice* (London: Croom Helm, 1987).

[17] The expression, though not the concept of "liberal neutrality" is, indeed, fairly recent, introduced by Gerald Dworkin in "Non-Neutral Principles," *Journal of Philosophy*, 71, 1974, pp. 491–506, and Alan Montefiore, ed., *Neutrality and Impartiality. The University and Political Commitment* (Cambridge: Cambridge University Press, 1975).

[18] That such a further stage in the doctrine and in the practice of liberal toleration is needed is acknowledged by Joseph Raz in "Multiculturalism," when he draws distinctions between various liberal attitudes towards social differences. The first stage is toleration, meaning non-interference with the beliefs and practices of the minorities; the second is non-discrimination, based on universal individual rights requiring public blindness toward social differences; the third, which is more an ideal to be realized, is multiculturalism corresponding to non-discrimination, but without the individualistic bias which has so far characterized public blindness.

in the public sphere, but only that public officials be blind to them, an influential interpretation – embodied in the continental ideal of *laicité* – has equated neutrality with a public sphere to which everyone belongs qua citizen, and where no particular loyalty, identity, or group that might threaten the general will is allowed.

Insofar as neutrality means a general tendency in the direction of a lack of discrimination in the public sphere, whatever one's beliefs, practices, culture, or affiliations, it is part of the liberal tradition in general, being, on the one hand, the generalization of the principle of toleration and, on the other, embodied in the individual basic rights to freedom of expression, association, and privacy. Within contemporary liberalism there is, however, disagreement (a) on the best way to satisfy the principle of non-discrimination, that is, whether it is best to disregard differences or to take them into account so as to counter the different weight and value that is socially attached to them, and (b) on the principle of neutrality, which is usually taken to imply something more than a lack of discrimination, namely the independence of liberal politics from any substantive moral outlook. In fact, it is the independence of liberal politics from any substantive conception of the good life that grounds a lack of discrimination in the public sphere, or so the supporters of liberal neutrality contend. Yet, as its opponents ask, can there be a political arrangement, which actually does away with any substantive moral, religious, and philosophical view?

The issue surrounding neutrality, which is widely debated in contemporary political philosophy, sorts liberal theories into two major groups: neutralist (or political, or deontological) versions and perfectionist (or ethical) versions. The disagreement about the best way to promote non-discrimination in general does not coincide with the neutralist/perfectionist divide, but is, rather, internal to neutralist liberalism, depending on different interpretations of neutrality. The two distinct views here are sometimes labeled as, respectively, intentional and causal neutrality.[19] But let us start by examining the neutralist/perfectionist debate with reference to the problem of toleration.

NEUTRALISM VERSUS PERFECTIONISM

As we have seen, neutrality originally arises as the generalization of toleration within the liberal state when freedom of conscience becomes a

---

[19] On this point, see Weale, "Toleration, Individual Differences, and Respect for People."

universal right. In its more general formulation neutrality means that public action should discount all personal differences that are politically irrelevant (from ethnic origin to affiliations, religious beliefs, moral values, skin color, and sexual preferences) so as to treat all citizens as equals. Thus, the ideal of neutrality is meant to fulfill the liberal principles of equal liberty, non-discrimination, and impartiality by means of an anti-perfectionist attitude. Anti-perfectionism entails that the state and political agencies have no business in trying to improve citizens according to any conception of what is valuable in life or how they should live.[20] Conceptions of the good and religious, moral or metaphysical views should be extracted from control by the political authorities and left to individual freedom and choice. Anti-perfectionism prescribes a public blindness to personal differences, and does so for two reasons: on the one hand, it inhibits the interference of religious and moral disagreement in political matters and, on the other, it prevents any particular set of convictions or way of life from being favored and thus giving rise to advantages in social position or standing. Peaceful coexistence and equal liberty are the two political goals pursued by liberal neutrality, while anti-perfectionism is the means by which such goals can be attained.

The ideal of neutrality, originally established as a guideline for public action when toleration became embodied in the doctrine of universal rights, has recently been generalized into a principle governing the political legitimacy of liberal institutions. An implication of the anti-perfectionist attitude has made this move possible. If liberal politics is indeed independent of any substantive religious, philosophical, and moral views, it means that all reasonable people, despite their different and conflicting conceptions of the good life, can endorse it because it is no more than the precondition for the maintenance of law, order, and justice. In this way neutrality is presented as the principle by means of which liberal institutions are legitimated, consistent with the actual fact of pluralism that characterizes contemporary society. Thus, not only should

---

[20] The term "perfectionism" was introduced by John Rawls, *The Theory of Justice* (Cambridge, Mass.: Harvard University Press, 1971) (hereinafter abbreviated *TJ*), II, 5, § 50, to designate the kind of teleological theory which asserts that morally good politics is politics aimed at attaining ethical ideals (while utilitarianism, for example, is a teleological theory which defines those actions as good which are aimed at fulfilling interests and needs). Classical liberalism, which emerged from the religious wars, is typically anti-perfectionist, since in general it conceives of politics as being instrumental to individual ends and purposes, and as a guarantee of rights and order. Yet, as some contemporary liberal thinkers have remarked, liberalism as a political ideal is not morally empty, but includes a set of distinctive virtues and purposes. The discussion between neutralist and perfectionist interpretations of liberalism has to do with the ethical content of liberal theory.

the liberal state be neutral with reference to 'private' social differences, but also, more importantly, toleration and neutrality are proposed as the normative devices in a constitutional argument for bringing about a consensus on the liberal principles which underwrite political legitimacy. And this further step is precisely what characterizes the position of neutralist liberalism.[21] Let us reconstruct this move, which represents the main point of discussion in the present debate.

The premise of neutralist liberalism is that pluralism is problematic, because the commitment to liberal democracy rules out a forced homogenization of the citizen body or a simple repression of irreducible differences. The distinctive feature of this liberal tradition, is that pluralism is conceived of as the plurality of the conceptions of the good, i.e. what each individual thinks worthwhile and valuable in life. The problem is that in contemporary societies there are many conceptions of the good and, often, they are not compatible. Indeed, since they have to do with ultimate values, final meanings, and basic principles, their diversity is a potential source of conflict.[22] Moreover, in many cases, they are incommensurable, since they embody alternative and irreducible interpretations of what is valuable and why. Finally, they cannot be adjudicated, insofar as there is no common, publicly accepted way of making a reasonable judgment about them, or of defining priorities. In a word, pluralism basically implies moral and metaphysical disagreement; such disagreement appears even more intractable than conflict of interests, since in this case some form of compensation can be arranged and compromise is more easily reached by means of negotiation. In the case of moral conflict, incommensurability and lack of a common procedure for adjudication make losses unredeemable.[23]

---

[21] See, for example, Peter de Marneffe, "Liberalism, Liberty and Neutrality," *Philosophy and Public Affairs*, 19, 1990, pp. 253–74, and Deborah Fitzmaurice, "Liberal Neutrality, Traditional Minorities and Education," in J. Horton, ed., *Liberalism, Multiculturalism and Toleration*, pp. 50–69.

[22] This picture of the problematic differences between the conceptions of the good is presented by John Rawls in "The Domain of the Political and Overlapping Consensus," *New York University Law Review*, 64, 1989, pp. 233–55, and analyzed by Henry S. Richardson in "The Problem of Liberalism and the Good," in R. B. Douglass, G. R. Mara and H. S. Richardson, eds., *Liberalism and the Good* (London: Routledge, 1990), pp. 1–28.

[23] This viewpoint is strongly underlined by Thomas Nagel as one which gives rise to issues about toleration:
Members of a society all motivated by an impartial regard for one another will be led into conflict by that very motive if they disagree about what the good life consists in, hence what they should want impartially for everyone . . . Such disagreements can be much more bitter and intractable than mere conflicts of interest, and the question is whether there is any method of handling them at a higher level which all reasonable people ought to accept, so that they cannot object to the particular result even if it goes against them (*Equality and Partiality* [Oxford: Oxford University Press, 1991], p. 154).

Given this description of pluralism, the issue is how to obtain the consensus of opinion, which is necessary for political legitimacy, given the fact of moral disagreement and irreducible differences about how life should be lived. The solution is provided by the ideal of toleration, as applied in what I will call "the constitutional argument." The constitutional argument proposes the hypothetical reconstruction of a way in which the members of a society could reach political consensus on basic principles and institutions; this consensus must be shown to result from collective choice by equal, free, and rational individuals, each having potentially conflicting interests and holding divergent conceptions of the good.[24] The constitutional setting may be interpreted in different ways; in any case, it is designed so as to consist of a fair procedure for collective choice, in which each party has equal liberty and power. Given a fair procedure, the constitutional choice is also fair, and the principles and rules, which are the outcome of the resulting agreement, are thus justified by the full consent of all parties. Toleration has ruled out force concerning moral and metaphysical beliefs and, at the same time, has circumscribed the effects these beliefs can have outside the realm of politics, neutralizing thereby the possible damage the clash of beliefs could have. Applying this ideal to hypothetical constitutional reasoning, the first result is that the political realm is reduced to a limited proportion of social life,[25] with the result that only a limited consensus, either on procedures and rules or on basic principles of justice, is required for political legitimacy. Yet this consensus should be found to emerge from different and divisive starting points, none of which, according to the principle of toleration, can be repressed. It is reasonable, therefore, to think that the content of the agreement – be it substantive principles or procedural values – has to be neutral, perhaps not absolutely, but with respect to the various conceptions of the good held by the parties,[26] since no one wants to see his or her own convictions disadvantaged. Neutrality

[24] I choose to refer to the constitutional argument instead of the contractarian argument, which is specific to John Rawls's *A Theory of Justice*. Since neutrality is what sustains liberal legitimacy, the analysis is developed at the constitutional level, but not all neutralists make reference to the social contract framework.

[25] Cf. Rawls, "The Domain of the Political and Overlapping Consensus." The resulting limits to the political domain lead to what Joseph Raz has called "epistemic abstinence" in political theory with the effect of excluding from the political agenda issues such as people's well-being. See J. Raz, "Facing Diversity: The Case for Epistemic Abstinence," *Philosophy and Public Affairs*, 19, 1990, pp. 3–46.

[26] Many authors have denied that neutrality can be absolutely neutral, as we will see when we consider the criticisms to liberal neutrality; however, Deborah Fitzmaurice has proposed an interpretation of neutrality which is absolutely neutral and which she has called procedural

is then a necessary result of this kind of constitutional argument, if it is constrained by toleration; in order to come to an agreement in a pluralist situation, what can be shared must be neutral; moreover, the outcome of the agreement also ought to be neutral, since neutrality results in a fair constitutional setting from the application of a fair procedure for dealing with irreducible moral and metaphysical differences. A problem arises about such a consensus in the context of trying to give a hypothetical construction of liberal legitimacy: how can (a neutral) consensus be reached, assuming it could be reached? The answers may vary but, in general, they can be grouped around two alternatives.

The first and more traditional solution is that of excluding all conflicting moral issues from the area of political legitimacy, so that what is left in common can serve as the neutral basis for political legitimacy.[27] In this case, the neutral consensus is produced on grounds which sustain liberal institutions as legitimate.[28]

The second solution is more ingenious, focusing on the notion of overlapping consensus, as spelled out by John Rawls.[29] The basic idea is that, in a pluralist society, agreement need not be based on a theory of political legitimacy, but, rather, on the political principles of justice embodied in liberal institutions (roughly corresponding to rights, opportunities, fairness and reciprocity in public life). There is more than one path that leads to the endorsement of liberal institutions, since the principles of

neutrality. It depends on a derivation of political principles from reason alone, independent of any conceptions of the good. This version of neutrality, corresponding to a Kantian formulation, and proposing principles which are universally rationally justifiable, may not be substantively neutral with reference to the actual conceptions of the good held by people, in the sense that some can be ruled out as irrational. However, Fitzmaurice acknowledges that current liberal theories usually refer to the substantive principle of neutrality, in the sense that political principles, whether they are procedural or substantive, are derived only from what is shared in common by all parties. And, in this sense, neutrality is always relative to the range of conceptions of the good which are considered. See Fitzmaurice, "Liberal Neutrality, Traditional Minorities and Education," pp. 52ff.

[27] See Bruce Ackerman, *Social Justice in the Liberal State* (New Haven: Yale University Press, 1980); Bruce Ackerman, "What is Neutral about Neutrality?," *Ethics*, 93, 1983, pp. 372–90; Thomas Nagel, "Moral Conflict and Political Legitimacy," *Philosophy and Public Affairs*, 16, 1987, pp. 215–40; Nagel, *Equality and Partiality*; Charles Larmore, *Patterns of Moral Complexity* (Cambridge: Cambridge University Press, 1987).

[28] It is not clear, though, whether "what is left in common" are mere values and principles contingently held by individuals in the constitutional setting, or principles of reason alone, and thus universally justifiable. Ackerman probably regards the dialogical procedure as a universal feature of human rationality, yet it presupposes a preference for peaceful accommodation which can be derived only by instrumental rationality.

[29] See: John Rawls, "Justice as Fairness: Political not Metaphysical," *Philosophy and Public Affairs*, 14, 1985, pp. 219–51; "The Idea of an Overlapping Consensus," *Oxford Journal of Legal Studies*, 16, 1987, pp. 1–25; "The Domain of the Political and Overlapping Consensus"; and *PL*.

liberal justice comprise only one of the components of a comprehensive conception of the good. It is, in fact, a component, which turns out to be compatible with many reasonable comprehensive views.[30] The prospective solution, therefore, is not to put aside one's conception of the good in order to find a common premise for grounding liberal legitimacy but, on the contrary, to find out the common liberal principles of justice which are included in different comprehensive views. Liberal principles of justice emerge first within Rawls's conception of the political, which he presents as freestanding, i.e. independent of metaphysical and ethical foundations. The content of political justice is primarily arrived at by applying the well-known original position argument and starting from the premise that the individuals who are the participants in discussion are free and equal. The plausibility of this premise is no longer rooted in human rationality alone, as it was in *A Theory of Justice*, but in the public culture of liberalism, hence in a well-defined historical tradition. But, in this way, the justification for principles of justice is internal only to the political conception, and this only *pro tanto*, as Rawls qualifies it.[31] In other words, it is justification for a citizen (i.e. for a person considered merely as a political agent with a view of the political world of which he or she is a part), but not for individuals (who will have their own broader views of a wide variety of topics in addition to politics). At this point, political principles, built up from premises rooted in the liberal democratic tradition, are shown to be common to, or at least compatible with, many of the comprehensive views that coexist within liberal democratic societies. Thus these principles come to represent the area of overlap between many conceptions, a neutral area shared by those who hold a variety of different beliefs, although the principles are held by different individuals for different reasons.[32] In this way, any individual citizen who finds an overlap between his or her comprehensive view and the political conception can work out

---

[30] In *PL*, Rawls introduces the notion of "reasonable pluralism," including that set of comprehensive views which are the outcome of the free use of reason. Human reason, being limited both in cognitive and in motivational terms, if left free, can take a number of different paths, all of them perfectly reasonable, since all of them are rationally undetermined. The outcome is reasonable pluralism, that is, a variety of world-views which, despite their potential conflict, are all compatible with the constraints imposed by reason. This notion strongly limits the extension of Rawls's pluralism.

[31] See: John Rawls, "Reply to Habermas," *Journal of Philosophy*, 92, 1995, p. 142.

[32] In Rawls's case it is more appropriate to speak of a "political" rather than a "neutralist" interpretation of liberalism: what is publicly shared is better characterized as "impartial" than "neutral" with reference to the comprehensive views which overlap in the common area. In fact, the common political principles are not independent of the whole set of comprehensive views, though they are not dependent on any one in particular.

another justification for principles of justice. This second kind of justification will be sustained by non-public reasons – that is, by reasons internal to any comprehensive view, thus bridging the gap between private convictions and public reasons. But, if private and public morality are thus made contiguous, the only principles that can legitimately be used in public discourse and actions are those included in the area of the overlapping consensus, which constitutes the basis of public reasoning in liberal society. This interpretation has the advantage of doing away with the exclusion of substantive moral views from participation in the process of discussion that leads towards consensus.[33] In the overlapping consensus picture, no one has to put aside his or her deep beliefs and values in order to find a reason in favor of the liberal order. Everyone can support liberal institutions for their own special reasons, according to their particular conception of the good.[34] The disadvantage is that not all comprehensive views turn out to be compatible with the liberal core of basic principles.[35] Only comprehensive views that are "reasonable," in Rawls's own formulation, can plausibly come to share the liberal conception of justice.[36]

In any case, both interpretations of the political consensus hold the view that the outcome lies in the restriction of the political realm vis-à-vis the domain of the social and in its neutrality vis-à-vis the many conceptions of the good of the pluralist society. In this way, toleration is not only a crucial liberal principle, built in to the liberal constitution, but is also the ideal that grounds liberal legitimacy; neutrality is not only a

---

[33] The exclusion of substantive ethical principles from the political domain, which corresponds to the demands of the "neutrality" view, is criticized not just by communitarians but also by perfectionists. See Dworkin, "Non-Neutral Principles"; Michael Perry, "Neutral Politics?," *Review of Politics*, 51, 4, 1989. However, this exclusion is also troublesome for liberals who are not perfectionists. See Amy Gutmann and Dennis Thompson, "Moral Conflict and Political Consensus," *Ethics*, 101, 1990, pp. 64–88 and Dennis Thompson, *Democracy and Disagreement* (Cambridge, Mass.: Harvard University Press, 1996).

[34] Rawls's position thus answers the questions asked, for example, by Kent Greenawalt in *Religious Convictions and Political Choice* (Oxford: Oxford University Press, 1988). How can a true believer find a ground which is neutral and does not depend on his deep convictions without compromising those very convictions? In the overlapping consensus picture, the true believer need not find public reasons that are different and distinct from his or her own religious view.

[35] See Patrick Neal, "A Liberal Theory of the Good?," *Canadian Journal of Philosophy*, 17, 1987, pp. 567–81.

[36] The only suggestion Rawls can make about unreasonable comprehensive views is that they should be objects of accommodation and compromise. He hopes that treating them in this way will increase the political stability of society and that the benefits of such stability will eventually induce those who hold unreasonable comprehensive views to become more reasonable and, eventually, even loyal to the democratic order. Yet this hope is only empirically based, and there is no particular theoretical reason to believe it will be vindicated.

guideline for public action, but also the distinguishing mark of the liberal political domain.

This position, as mentioned, can be elaborated out in different ways. Yet, despite this, a unifying premise underlies all defenses of neutrality: it is the rejection of the view that it is permissible to appeal to the alleged fact that certain ideas, values, or opinions are unreasonable, inappropriate, or immoral in order to justify using force to suppress them.[37] Given the rejection of coercion, the values of toleration and neutrality can be further justified by at least three different arguments. The first endorses a skeptical position: neutrality and toleration are required because there is no rational and shared way of adjudicating between different conceptions of the good.[38] Yet this justification shows three major weaknesses: (a) in order for toleration and neutrality to derive from skepticism, the latter must be supplemented by a preference for peace over war, which here is rather taken for granted.[39] Otherwise, from the lack of rational truths, one can as well derive a reason for conformity, rather than for toleration of diversity. (b) If skeptical arguments are taken to be the foundation for toleration and neutrality, it becomes impossible to give a coherent account of the compatibility of two attitudes both of which are deeply rooted in liberal thought. On the one hand, liberalism is committed to the farreaching protection of human differences (differences in values, convictions, and identities) from coercion, which seem to imply that they are inherently valuable; on the other hand, liberalism construes such differences as purely private, subjective matters[40] and thus reduces them to mere individual preferences, i.e. tastes and idiosyncracies, about which, by definition, "*non est disputandum.*"[41] (c) Finally, this form of liberal

---

[37] The argument against coercion in matters of faith belongs to the traditional doctrine of toleration, starting with Sebastian Castellion. In Locke's *Letter* we find a clear and complete formulation of it. Coercion is first of all unreasonable because beliefs, by their very nature, cannot be forced. Second, it is inappropriate because the value of faith is not independent of the way in which it is formed. Third, it is immoral because, just as it is generally acknowledged that no one has the right to impose on others their views about what food to buy and where to buy it, no one can claim the right to decide for another about salvation.

[38] The skeptical argument for liberal neutrality is endorsed by Bruce Ackerman in *Social Justice*. Many criticisms have been made of his conception: see issue 93 of *Ethics*, 1982–3 devoted to Ackerman's position. See, especially, B. J. Barber, "Unconstrained Conversation: Neutral or Otherwise," pp. 330–47; J. S. Fishkin, "Can There Be a Neutral Theory of Justice?," pp. 348–56; R. E. Flathman, "Egalitarian Blood in Skeptical Turnips?," pp. 357–66; B. Williams, "Space Talk: The Conversation Continued," pp. 367–71.

[39] See, for example, Brian Barry, "How Not to Defend Liberal Institutions," in Douglass, Mara, and Richardson, *Liberalism and the Good* (pp. 44–58) p. 47.

[40] M. Stocker, "The Schizophrenia of Modern Ethical Theories," *Journal of Philosophy*, 73, 1976, pp. 453–65.

[41] Albert Hirschman, "Against Parsimony," *Economics and Philosophy*, 1, 1985, pp. 7–20.

argumentation seems to be inconsistent when it begins with an appeal to moral skepticism and then moves on to assume that there will be easy, unproblematic public agreement on the procedures for conducting political dialogue.[42] Furthermore, the skeptical argument is not itself neutral, insofar as it is very controversial.[43]

The second argument in favor of liberal toleration and neutrality refers back to the value of pluralism: state neutrality and toleration are required in order to protect social variety. In its turn, pluralism is valued for a number of reasons, among which I mention only two for their traditional relevance to the issue of toleration. First, pluralism is a value in epistemological terms, insofar as it allows for experimentation and novelty out of which, eventually, truth will emerge.[44] Following this reasoning, however, toleration and neutrality are only instrumental, pragmatic values and, more importantly, they are limited to those issues that can be related to knowledge and truth. Second, the value of pluralism is made to rest on the value of personal autonomy: in order to have a free choice, individual members of a society should enjoy genuine options, which will be available only in a society characterized by pluralism of values, opinions, and lifestyles.[45] In this case, toleration is ultimately supported by the crucial value of autonomy,[46] but, then, all the many theoretical difficulties related to the latter concept will apply equally to toleration.

Finally, the third argument for liberal neutrality, which is the one which has been most influential in structuring the current debate, is based on fairness.[47] It runs approximately as follows: in a pluralistic society political support for one or some small number of the many conceptions of the good that coexist cannot fail to introduce moral

[42] Benhabib, "Liberal Dialogue versus Discourse Ethics."

[43] This position is held by Charles Larmore, who maintains that neutrality can be justified by arguments that are not absolutely neutral but merely neutral with reference to the moral and religious conflicts that it is supposed to solve. Skepticism is part of a world-view which is rejected, for example, by those who endorse objective ethics; hence it is inappropriate as a justification for neutrality. See Larmore, *Patterns of Moral Complexity*, pp. 53–4.

[44] This argument, coming from Mill, is shared by Karl Popper; see "Toleration and Intellectual Responsibility," in S. Mendus and D. Edwards, eds., *On Toleration*, pp. 17–34.

[45] Williams, "Toleration: An Impossible Virtue."

[46] This justification is advanced, for instance, by Will Kymlicka, *Liberalism, Community, and Culture* (Oxford: Oxford University Press, 1989).

[47] See Ronald Dworkin, "Liberalism," in Stuart Hampshire, ed., *Private and Public Morality* (Cambridge: Cambridge University Press, 1978), pp. 113–43; Ronald Dworkin, "Fondamenti filosofici per la neutralità liberale," in Sebastiano Maffettone, ed., *L'idea di giustizia* (Naples: Guida, 1993), pp. 57–71; Nagel, "Moral Conflict and Political Legitimacy"; Nagel, *Equality and Partiality*; Rawls, *TJ*, II, 4, § 33, § 34, § 35; "The Priority of the Right and Ideas of the Good," *Journal of Philosophy*, 1988, pp. 251–76. According to Larmore the argument for fairness is the only neutral justification of the ideal of neutrality, being independent of any conception of the good and referring only to the treatment of persons. See *Patterns of Moral Complexity*.

distinctions between persons and, consequently, to treat them with unequal respect. From any impersonal or impartial viewpoint toleration and neutrality are the obvious policies to be adopted with reference to conceptions of the good, because no one wants to live in a society in which his or her deepest convictions are given less than equal weight in the public arena. Hence, on the one hand, the common principles of justice should be neutral in order to be fair in relation to the many conceptions of the good that exist among the individuals and groups in the society. On the other, neutrality also should be the principal guiding public action in order to ensure fair treatment to all citizens irrespective of their conception of the good.[48] This line of argument seems to me to be the most original and promising of those that have been put forward in the recent discussion. It avoids the shortcomings of a skeptical or purely pragmatical foundation for toleration, characterizing instead the neutralist interpretation in ethical terms, but also avoids the difficulties of a perfectionist argument for toleration and the problematic distinction among differences, as we shall see below.

Perfectionist liberalism refers to various positions which, within the liberal tradition, take issue with neutrality.[49] Neutrality, perfectionists maintain, is an inconsistent, unattainable and, in the end, undesirable ideal.[50] Generally speaking, perfectionist positions criticize the view that

[48] This double role of neutrality, which is at the same time constitutive of liberal legitimacy and a constraint on public action, is acknowledged also by Joseph Raz, *The Morality of Freedom* (Oxford: Clarendon Press, 1986), p. 112, and by de Marneffe, "Liberalism, Liberty and Neutrality." Raz derives the fundamental ambiguity of the concept from this fact, while de Marneffe maintains that only the second role is central for the neutralist model. In fact the two roles are interdependent since the latter is the generalization of the former.

[49] Though arguments in favor of perfectionist liberalism can be found throughout the liberal tradition, for example in Kant's conception of liberty and autonomy and to some extent also in Mill's view of liberalism, this position has been most fully elaborated in contemporary liberal theory as a response to the prevalent interpretation of liberalism in terms of neutrality. An interpretation in terms of neutrality can also count on classical precedents such as Locke.

[50] Among the first liberal defenders of perfectionism are Brian Barry, *The Liberal Theory of Justice* (Oxford: Clarendon Press, 1973), and Vinit Haskar, *Equality, Liberty and Perfectionism* (Oxford: Oxford University Press, 1979). In the 1980s and 1990s, perfectionist positions were held by William Galston, *Justice and the Human Good* (Chicago: University of Chicago Press, 1980); Raz, *The Morality of Freedom*; Raz, "Facing Diversity: The Case for Epistemic Abstinence"; Larry Alexander and Maimon Schwarzschild, "Liberalism, Neutrality of Welfare vs. Equality of Resources," *Philosophy and Public Affairs*, 16, 1987, pp. 85–110; Richard Flathman, *Toward a Liberalism* (Ithaca: Cornell University Press, 1989); Jonathan Riley, "Rights to Liberty in Purely Private Matters," part 1: *Economics and Philosophy*, 5, 1989, pp. 1–121; part 2: *Economics and Philosophy*, 6, 1990, pp. 27–64; Jeremy Waldron, "Autonomy and Perfectionism in Raz, *Morality of Freedom*," *California Law Review*, 62, 3–4, 1989, pp. 1097–152; Barry, "How Not to Defend Liberal

the distinguishing feature of liberalism, as opposed to other political ideals, is its commitment to a set of rules and principles of justice with no moral content, that is, a set of principles which is neutral with reference to any ethical conception. By contrast, according to perfectionists, liberalism, like its rival political ideals, necessarily presupposes a conception of the human good, which is not simply procedural, but also ethically substantive. The liberal conception of the good is indeed rather specific, being focused on the values of human rationality, autonomy, self-reliance, and self-development.[51] In other words, the appeal of liberalism cannot and should not be like that of a hospitable empty box, in which any culture, tradition, form of life, or world-view is welcome and can pursue its dream.[52] For perfectionists, such a portrayal of liberalism is not only inaccurate, because liberalism exhibits a distinctive moral outlook, but it will also not help liberal institutions to gain the loyal support of members of alien cultural traditions. Those who have radically different cultural traditions would rather live in societies that endorse their own conception of the good, and are not easily persuaded of the superiority of liberalism as an impartial and neutral political order. Moreover, in pursuing an unattainable dream of universality, the neutralist picture of liberalism impoverishes the meaning of the liberal life. The liberal life cannot simply mean living so as to avoid conflicts and conceal disagreements, as some supporters of liberal neutrality seem to presume. Instead of defending liberalism

Institutions"; Stephen Macedo, *Liberal Virtues: Citizenship, Virtues and Community* (Oxford: Clarendon Press, 1990); Thomas Hurka, *Perfectionism* (Oxford: Oxford University Press, 1993); Simon Caney, "Antiperfectionism and Rawlsian Liberalism," *Political Studies*, 63, 1995, pp. 248–64; Simon Caney, "Liberal Legitimacy, Reasonable Disagreement, and Justice," in R. Bellamy and M. Hollis, eds., *Pluralism and Liberal Neutrality* (London: Frank Cass, 1999), pp. 19–36; Richard Kraut, "Politics, Neutrality and the Good," *Social Philosophy and Policy*, 16, 1999, pp. 315–32; Steven Wall, *Liberalism, Perfectionism and Restraint* (Cambridge: Cambridge University Press, 1988).

Neal, "A Liberal Theory of the Good?," and William Galston, *Liberal Purposes* (Cambridge: Cambridge University Press, 1991), define their own position as ethical liberalism, but reject perfectionism, since liberalism should not include a substantive ideal of human excellence, but only a formal ideal, i.e. autonomy. Yet it is arguable whether autonomy can be merely a formal principle.

For a survey of the discussion of perfectionism versus neutrality, see R. Goodin and A. Reeve, *Liberal Neutrality* (London: Routledge, 1987); Douglass, Mara, and Richardson, *Liberalism and the Good*; Richard Bellamy, "Defining Liberalism: Neutralist, Ethical and Political," *ARSP*, Beiheft 36, pp. 23–43; *Social Philosophy and Politics*, issue on human happiness and the human good, 1, 16, 1999; Bellamy and Hollis, eds., *Pluralism and Neutrality*.

[51] It is controversial whether such a conception implies the political project of trying to make people morally better. William Galston explicitly denies this. Given that the liberal conception of the good is open to the individual's definition of his or her own good, Galston rejects perfectionism. See, *Liberal Purposes*.

[52] See Barry, "How Not to Defend Liberal Institutions," pp. 48–53.

in negative terms for what it is not, perfectionists choose a more aggressive strategy, arguing for liberal values, purposes, institutions, and outlook in directly positive terms. In this way, the neutralist illusion of liberalism as a political ideal *sui generis*, based on moral parsimony and epistemological abstinence,[53] thoroughly universalist and potentially all-inclusive, is dispelled. In its place, perfectionist liberalism intends to provide a more robust and sanguine defense, which allegedly makes liberalism a more realistic competitor of communitarianism and, in a way, also of fundamentalism. As a consequence, a major concern for perfectionist liberalism is the proper definition of the liberal good, which must be shown to be consistent with pluralism, with the minimum use of coercion and with the right of each individual to define his or her own good[54] – in a word, with those features of the liberal order that are much emphasized also by neutralist liberalism, though in different ways. The liberal conception of the human good that focuses on the worth of human existence and human purposiveness and on the value of rationality, i.e. rational humanism, indeed meets these requirements.[55]

How do these two different interpretations of liberalism bear on the issue of toleration? The crucial difference lies in the role played by toleration in these two distinct perspectives. For perfectionist liberalism, toleration is basically considered as one of the liberal values and as a specific social virtue required for the flourishing of liberal society and its members, while political toleration is just a background condition for an open society. For neutralist liberalism, by contrast, toleration is construed as the political principle that grounds legitimate political order in a pluralist society: the emphasis is on its fundamental role in the constitutional design of liberal institutions. We have already outlined above the neutralist argument, starting from pluralism as a problematic fact, generalizing the model of political toleration which provided the solution to the religious conflicts of the sixteenth and seventeenth centuries, and progressing step by step to the ideal of neutrality not only as a guideline for public treatment of individuals, but also as the central feature of legitimate liberal institutions. Now let us see the place and the meaning of toleration within perfectionist liberalism, in order properly to compare the two emerging conceptions.

53 See Raz, "Facing Diversity: The Case for Epistemic Abstinence."
54 See Galston, *Liberal Purposes*, p. 10.
55 Raz, in *Morality of Freedom*, refers to rational humanism as the ethical core of liberalism.

TOLERATION AND PERFECTIONISM

According to perfectionists, liberal politics presupposes a certain kind of human character (autonomous, independent, self-reliant)[56] and it is sustained by a corresponding set of substantive virtues and values, among which are tolerance, pluralism, and diversity. In fact, the values of autonomy and independence require that the individual be actually presented with real choices concerning his or her life plan and style of living.[57] Thus, pluralism is a precondition for developing an autonomous personality and, hence, the toleration of diversity is a necessary constituent of a liberal society.

At this point, perfectionist liberalism has taken two diverging routes. The first, and earlier, circumscribes pluralism and toleration within the broad boundaries of the liberal good. The second, and more recent, starting from the crucial value of autonomy, leads to a pluralist perspective endorsing multiculturalism.[58] As we will see, these two routes need not be exclusive, though they look prima facie incompatible.

According to the former position, toleration and pluralism are secondary values, the absolute values being freedom, autonomy, and self-development. Pluralism and toleration of social differences are thus balanced against the protection of liberty and autonomy, which can be undermined by unconstrained toleration. Given that the principle of political toleration is already granted by the liberal constitution, the primary issue for this kind of perfectionism concerns where to trace the limits of the intolerable and how to justify them, despite the general value of toleration.[59] This concern is meant not only as a pragmatic defense of the liberal order against illiberal invasion, but also as an ethical defense of liberal integrity. Consider the example of a practice totally at odds with liberal values, such as clitoridectomy. Can liberalism tolerate clitoridectomy, which does not in fact undermine the stability of the liberal

---

[56] These traits of liberal personality are already presented by John Stuart Mill in *On Liberty*, ed. H. B. Acton (London: Dent Dutton, 1972), pp. 115–16.

[57] See Raz, "Autonomy, Toleration and the Harm Principle."

[58] In his *Morality of Freedom* Joseph Raz, who is probably one of the most outstanding spokespeople of the perfectionist position, seems to have endorsed a position on pluralism and autonomy as the key elements of liberal society, which leaves little room for accommodating alien cultures and puts severe constraints on their acceptability. He has been read this way by Jonathan Chaplin, "How Much Cultural and Religious Pluralism can Liberalism Tolerate," in J. Horton, ed., *Liberalism, Multiculturalism and Toleration*, pp. 32–49. In later writings Raz has given his position a twist so as to open it up to different cultures, a twist made possible by further reflections on the concept of well-being and on its link with cultural affiliation; see his *Ethics and the Public Domain* (Oxford: Clarendon Press, 1994).

[59] See D. D. Raphael, "The Intolerable," in *Justifying Toleration*, pp. 137–53.

order, but which runs against the ideals of personal and bodily integrity
and autonomous development of individuality that are so crucial for
liberal ethics? In other words, can toleration be granted to social differences, which can in no way be fitted into the rather open and hospitable
boundaries of the liberal good? In principle, for the liberal perfectionist
the answer is "no": toleration, in order to be a liberal virtue, cannot
be equated with acquiescence in practices or attitudes, which prevent
people from becoming independent and self-reliant beings. But does the
prohibition of certain social differences imply that the liberal state can
coerce people to be free?[60] In principle, the liberal perfectionist answer
is "yes," at least for those people who cannot be reasoned with, because
of their age or their cultural impediments.

This apparently harsh position is, in fact, patterned after Mill's argument in favor of a mandatory education for children: as they are mi-
nors, and given their limited intellectual development, children should
be forced by the state to attend school in order to become independent and competent citizens.[61] Compulsory education can be backed
by a utilitarian argument – that is, the right of society to self-defense
against a class of dependent, incapable, socially useless citizens; or it
can be founded on the moral responsibility of the state to protect new
generations from a foreseeable and definite harm such as the lack of
education. However justified, compulsory education has now been part
of the liberal program since at least the time of John Stuart Mill, and
is deeply identified with democracy; eventually the state's right to enforce compulsory education is transformed into the citizens' right to free
provision of public education.[62] Analogous to this familiar and by now
uncontroversial case, the perfectionist liberal sees no contradiction in

---

[60] This is the point made by Alan Ryan in his paper "Can We Coerce People to be Free?," mimeo,
Princeton University, 1992, where the author restates Mill's argument on the state's right to
impose a compulsory education on families as the basis for his own thesis about the compulsory
liberation of people who have not developed their rational capabilities.

[61] "Consider for example the case of education. Is it not almost a self-evident axiom that the State
should require and compel the education, up to a certain standard, of every human being who
is born its citizen? ... It still remains unrecognized, that to bring a child into existence without
a fair prospect of being able, not only to provide for its body, but instruction and training for its
mind, is a moral crime, both against the unfortunate offspring and against society; and that if
the parent does not fulfill his obligation, the State ought to see it fulfilled, at the charge, as far as
possible of the parent" (*On Liberty*, p. 160).

[62] Mill was strongly against this, considering public education to be an illegitimate interference by
the state in individuals' free choice, as well as an expression of authoritarianism and conformism.
See, *On Liberty*, pp. 161–3.

forcing people who have not yet developed the capacity for reasoning to become free, as long as this desirable result is attainable. Yet, in practice, this possibility is drastically reduced by the difficulty of implementing that option with any reasonable chance of success, and with a limited use of coercion. How can the Islamic fundamentalist be induced to become a free-thinker? As Locke argued, coercion is useless in matters of faith and moral beliefs.[63] In such cases, the resort to toleration is required for want of viable alternatives. In this instance, toleration may in any case be justified by another of Mill's arguments[64] (in fact already present in Milton's *Areopagitica*[65]) that mistakes and errors are often necessary on the way towards the truth.

Thus, for perfectionist liberalism, full political toleration should in principle be limited to those differences which can be accommodated within the fairly open boundaries of the liberal conception of the good, while the differences which appear incompatible with liberalism are in principle excluded in order to preserve the liberal order and its ethical integrity. For many incompatible social differences state coercion would in any case be useless and counterproductive.[66] In these cases, toleration should instead be adopted, but only as a second best, and only provided that (a) there is no risk to the liberal order as a whole and (b) no harm is done to people under age and no permanent mutilations produced, so that the state can continue to guarantee that all individuals retain the ability to relinquish their original culture, if they so wish.[67] Even though there is much discussion over what actually puts the liberal order at risk and over what constitutes harm, the theoretical limits of political toleration are thus clearly marked out.

[63] Locke, *Essay on Toleration*, 1667.
[64] Mill, *On Liberty*, pp. 80–5. The epistemological argument in favor of toleration is now restated by Popper, "Toleration and Intellectual Responsibility," in *On Toleration*.
[65] Milton, *Areopagitica*.
[66] Steven Wall in *Liberalism, Perfectionism and Restraint* explicitly claims that liberal toleration is to be reserved either for differences that fit into the liberal outlook or, by default, for alien differences for which coercion would be either ineffective or too costly. He considers the possible justification for toleration, and discards respect for others as too vague, while enlisting the "pluralist justification," which he takes from Raz. It runs as follows:
We might have good reason to tolerate conduct that is morally wrong, but which is an integral part of a larger way of life which is itself valuable. In such a case we tolerate the wrongful conduct because we wish to sustain the valuable way of life of which it is an integral part. The moral wrong we tell ourselves is the reverse side of what is valuable (p. 68).
See Raz, "Autonomy, Toleration and the Harm Principle." The second justification is what he calls the cost-based one, that is when the costs of repression outweigh the costs of toleration (p. 69).
[67] See Haskar, *Equality, Liberty and Perfectionism*, p. 290.

For this kind of perfectionism, therefore, political toleration has two meanings: a strong, generally positive one – recognition and acceptance – when applied to differences that fit within the boundaries of the liberal good; and a weak, negative one – putting up with and letting things go – when applied to differences that are deeply at odds with liberalism, differences which it is nevertheless useless or counterproductive to forbid or repress. In this way, three classes of social difference are implicitly distinguished.

There are, first of all, the social differences which can be accommodated within the moral outlook of the liberal order; for these, political toleration is in order, that is, recognition and acceptance of the people who are "different" as autonomous agents, and of the differences themselves as politically fully legitimate. These differences easily become part of the pluralist spectrum of possibilities, which is valued as a condition for the proper development of liberal society and the liberal personality. The civil coexistence of publicly accepted differences relies on the social practice of tolerance. In fact, under the perfectionist interpretation, tolerance is primarily the virtue of the liberal citizen, the proper dispositional attitude of individuals living in liberal society, who, being autonomous and self-reliant agents, respect others' autonomy, free-thinking and anti-conformism. As opposed to mere acquiescence, tolerance is a value if it is based on respect, and hence it should be limited to those differences which indirectly command respect – that is, to those that, no matter whether individually chosen or received from tradition, are in principle autonomously endorsed. If the differences that are compatible with the liberal order are those linked in a relevant way to choice and autonomy, the implication is that the differences which can be accommodated by liberalism, and which are fully entitled to toleration in the strong sense, appear to be reducible to properties of individuals, even if they are shared by groups. They concern individual opinions, values, beliefs, and lifestyles; in other words, they are the outcome of an individual's choice in relation to what is of value in life and how life should be lived.

Second, there are the social differences which are at odds with the liberal conception of the good but which do not threaten the liberal order as a whole and do not cause evident harm to anyone, apart from keeping the people who share that different conception of the good in a position of dependency on a traditional culture, thus preventing them from developing an autonomous individuality. Wearing the veil, as many devout Islamic women do, can be an example of this kind of difference, the veil being not only a religious symbol but also a cultural one, implying women's subordination and public invisibility. This makes it incompatible with the liberal ideals of autonomy, self-development, and women's equality, although it causes no physical harm and does not seem to threaten the liberal order as a whole. Concerning this second class of differences, which are ethically incompatible with liberalism, the liberal perfectionist does not think that toleration, in the strong sense of recognition and acceptance, is in order, since the differences are not the outcome of autonomous choice. Hence, their bearers, in a sense, are considered only potential moral partners, in that they could in principle develop their rational faculties if freed from their cultural impediments, but have not (yet) done so.[68] The liberal perfectionist of this sort would rather force those who are different in this way to become free, to enter the hospitable boundaries of liberalism, and to choose one of the conceptions of the good found there. Yet the option of effective coercion is rarely available, because coercion would prove ineffective and ethically too costly; consequently, these differences must be tolerated by default. In this case, toleration is not a moral value, but a modus vivendi, a pragmatic compromise, which can be accorded today and denied tomorrow, according to the circumstances and the judgment of the political authorities. In other words, toleration here takes on the negative sense, which Paine underlined, as a discretionary concession of political power, well marked off from rights. These differences, therefore, would not acquire proper legitimacy in the liberal order, but only a limited space outside the public domain. They would be tolerated in the private realm, but not accepted as public statements, as they trespass on the sphere of liberal politics.

Third, there are social differences which are not only ethically incompatible with the liberal order but (a) which also cause evident harm, that is harm in addition to the fact that they hold agents in a dependent position – such as clitoridectomy – or (b) which are pragmatically incompatible, in that they constitute a genuine threat to the liberal order as a whole – such as religious terrorist organizations. Differences of this type are intolerable, under any interpretation of liberalism, and should simply be excluded from and prohibited in liberal society either because they violate the harm principle, or on the grounds of self-defense.

Although the distinction between the differences in the second and third of these cases is clear in theory, it is usually very difficult in practice

---

[68] Ronald Dworkin attacks perfectionism on this very point, because it would introduce moral differences which, to his mind, would be incompatible with everybody's right to equality of respect. See *Taking Rights Seriously* (London: Duckworth, 1981).

to draw a line between them. Setting the limits within which the liberal order is safe is very controversial, as is the question of what constitutes harm and whether self-induced physical harm should be equated with harm to a third party, etc. For the moment, however, we can ignore these serious difficulties and focus on the general conception of toleration that I have worked out from the implications of the first perfectionist interpretation. Its basic underlying idea is the following: for a tolerant society to exist and maintain itself in existence political toleration in it should be limited, because in order to disagree fruitfully and civilly its members must share many beliefs, values, habits, ways of living, and so forth. Toleration is the product of liberal ethics and can be properly the object of a positive moral valuation only on the basis of the principles of respect for others, autonomy, and freedom of choice – principles which typically belong to the liberal conception of the good. Therefore, the defense of toleration and support for a tolerant society require the defense of liberalism, its ethical integrity, and its political stability. This, in its turn, implies clear constraints on the extension of political toleration. As a result, toleration turns out not to be such a universal value as is claimed by neutralists, and a tolerant liberal society reveals itself to be two-faced: open, understanding, and sympathetic on the inside; closed, hard, and selective on the outside. On the boundaries, suspended between full inclusion and exclusion, there is the gray area of differences that are tolerated by default. Finally, liberalism is shown to be a particular political ideal like others, without claiming any superior, universal appeal, beyond and above ethical pluralism.

This conception implicitly provides an explanation of why some social differences – those compatible with the liberal good – no longer raise genuine political questions of toleration: they are recognized as part of the diversity of human nature, both in private and in public; other differences, however, do still give rise to problems. Yet, by the same token, this conception of toleration makes it almost impossible to resolve hard cases of contemporary pluralism. Since the liberal view defines toleration as the acceptance of diversity, which is both the product and the condition for autonomous choice, difficult cases are simply excluded. Genuinely hard cases concern claims for public recognition of social differences linked with the collective identities of previously or currently oppressed, subordinated, or excluded minority groups. These social differences are not the outcome of individual free choice, being usually derived from ascriptive characteristics which define group membership more than individual personality. Such groups also usually do not encourage individual choice. As such, they are not proper objects to which the liberal virtue of toleration should be extended, and they do not contribute to that sort of pluralism which is valued and cherished by liberals, one which arises from the exercise of human imagination and non-conformism, and results in a pluralism of opinions, ideas, values, and lifestyles. The inherent differences of minority groups can at best be tolerated by default, provided that they do not cause harm and do not threaten the liberal order as a whole. But this form of weak toleration does not imply public recognition and acceptance, and does not mean that the members of such groups are granted equal respect and acknowledged as full moral partners. In fact, according to this model, members of minority groups, in order to be treated with equal respect and dignity, should conceal their difference and become as far as possible just individuals. In the liberal order, they must either become assimilated or live as second-class citizens, or, if dangerous, simply be expelled or excluded.[69] This is equivalent to saying that they can either adapt or perish and that it is their problem and not that of the liberal order. In this way, the major point of perfectionist liberalism, i.e. the question of the limited compatibility of liberalism with different cultures, appears to be a declaration of its inadequacy to deal politically with contemporary pluralism. At this point, even if this perfectionist interpretation *ex hypothesi* proved to be more consistent and coherent than the neutralist interpretation, liberalism as a political ideal would turn out to be not only out of tune with most urgent contemporary issues, but also problematic in itself. Taking seriously the ethical view on which the liberal order was based would imply making effective membership in the polity not an automatic universal right of all the inhabitants of a territory, but rather a conditional and discriminatory one: effective membership would depend upon moral conformity or even on conformity in matters that might be difficult for individual agents to change by their own powers, such as the lifestyle of a traditional community.

Recent developments in perfectionist thinking have, however, pointed out a different attitude towards social and cultural differences, which suggests that perfectionists are elaborating a distinctive liberal perspective on

---

[69] As I have said earlier, this conclusion is not endorsed by all liberal perfectionists. See Raz, "Multiculturalism. A Liberal Perspective." However, it represents a straightforward consequence of the perfectionist liberal position, and it corresponds to a widespread view about liberal tolerance, more or less directly stated in the current debate on liberal pluralism.

multicultural issues. The opening up to other cultures, however, does not imply a revision of the perfectionist conception of toleration, as we shall see. The perfectionist version of pro-multiculturalism is best represented by Joseph Raz,[70] and is shared by an increasing number of scholars, sometimes called the new autonomists. The theoretical framework is the same as above: liberalism is viewed as a political morality, aimed at fostering people's well-being. The latter is defined in terms of the ability to lead a meaningful active life, which requires liberty, autonomy, and pluralism as preconditions. Justice is derived from the duties that a concern for the well-being of each individual imposes on every other individual and on the government; these duties are the origin of individual rights. The conception of the good as well-being produced by meaningful and purposeful activity makes possible a different way of thinking about cultural pluralism. While the first kind of perfectionism, echoing Mill, conceives of autonomous choice as procedurally dependent on the critical examination of given preferences and options, and as substantively related to nonconformism, in Raz's interpretation (echoing Aristotle) the stress is on the meaningful and purposeful qualities of choice. This implies a reference to something more than purely subjective values and requires a background of something that is shared and that can be recognized as valuable, so that choices can be judged to be meaningful (rather than whimsical). In other words, some cultural identity must be presupposed as the background of choice, constituting both the necessary premise for envisaging goals, ends, and meanings, and the community within which one's endeavors could be recognized. Cultural identity is thus seen as a precondition for autonomous choice and for individual well-being; yet this view does not imply that cultures be internally monistic and monolithic. Within most cultures – in some, to be sure, more than in others – a plurality of values and ways of life often exists, and this usually causes tension and conflict. Nevertheless, human choices get their sense from the network of conventions, norms, values, and principles that constitute a given culture.

So far, there is no significant difference from the interpretation of perfectionism previously examined: the limits imposed on full toleration were intended to protect liberal culture and pluralism as the background of individual self-development. Raz and the new autonomists, however,

---

[70] Joseph Raz has presented his interpretation of liberalism as a form of political morality, taking issue with neutrality, and stating the priority of the good (autonomy, well-being, and self-development) in *The Morality of Freedom*. In later writings, he has adapted his perfectionist approach to the issue of cultural pluralism: see "Multiculturalism: A Liberal Perspective."

do not confine autonomy to liberal culture. By contrast, the role assigned to culture for autonomous choices and individual well-being means that everyone has a right to follow their own cultural practices and imposes on the state a duty to support the different existing customs. In this way, new autonomists endorse cultural rights and multicultural policies. They regard toleration as a first, tentative, and insufficient attempt to respond to the challenge of cultural and religious diversity. Their normative proposals then vary by degree.[71] Some, like Raz, argue for government support to allow alien cultures to persist and flourish, but conditional on a respect for the individual rights of the members of the cultural group. Others think that some internal restrictions on members' freedom are justified when the group's survival is at stake. Some maintain that cultural rights do not include a conservationist attitude towards cultures which are naturally fading away; while others think that since cultural rights consist in the individual's right to his or her own culture, it is the government's duty to support decaying communities. Despite these relevant differences, however, a common trait of the new autonomists is the adoption of the language of cultural rights and, consequently, the view that political toleration is the first provisional and pragmatical solution for a pluralist society, although one that is largely insufficient for contemporary democracies. By contrast, tolerance is valued as a crucial social virtue of multicultural societies, essential to smooth over the conflict and tensions which are the inevitable ingredients of pluralism. Tolerance here means the inclination to check one's dislike and disapproval of differences, feelings which are not canceled out by the theoretical appreciation of pluralism.[72] All things considered, the new autonomists hold a conception of toleration which is similar to that of the previously examined perfectionists. With reference to different cultures, toleration is only a compromise when coercion is ruled out. It is a compromise that does not imply equal treatment, let alone recognition, but simply the non-interference of governments; marginality may be the price tolerated groups may have to pay for this non-interference. In this respect, it perfectly matches the second meaning of toleration which is found in the writings of perfectionist liberals with reference to cultural differences. The proper normative response to cultural diversity is not toleration, but multiculturalism, i.e. a politics of cultural rights and active governmental support to minority cultures.

[71] A more detailed discussion of these various positions on cultural rights will be undertaken in chapter 7. See below.
[72] Raz, "Multiculturalism," p. 73.

TWO LIBERAL CONCEPTIONS OF TOLERATION: A COMPARISON

This sketchy reconstruction of the neutralist and perfectionist interpretations of liberalism and toleration makes it possible to compare and contrast the two corresponding conceptions of toleration. A first main point of divergence between them lies in the approach to the issue of toleration. For neutralist liberals, toleration is not simply one of the liberal values of an open society; it is the principle on which the legitimacy of liberal institutions is grounded. It is thus the bridge connecting the facts of pluralism with a just political structure. In contrast perfectionist liberalism holds toleration up as a social value for smoothing the tensions engendered by pluralism and paving the way to social peace, but also as limited in its scope and utterly incapable of coping with the claims put forward by various minority groups in contemporary pluralism. From the neutralist point of view, the essential feature of toleration is not self-restraint – refraining from exercising a power of interference with differences that are disliked – but rather the adoption of a neutral attitude vis-à-vis conflictual social differences, which have been recognized as irrelevant for political life.[73] Therefore, while, from the perfectionist perspective, dislike or disapproval of the difference in question are necessary conditions for the existence of toleration, in the neutralist interpretation, moral disapproval, even if it is at the origin of the conflict between certain social differences, is definitely to be politically disregarded. In the first conception, the reasons for tolerance are balanced against the reasons for disapproval; in the neutralist model, by contrast, the reasons for toleration are independent of the content of the difference, deriving instead from a general position which rejects repression and coercion in certain matters. Therefore, the only relevant circumstances in which political toleration comes to be an issue is conflict among groups or individuals that are socially different, conflict which, moreover, is non-negotiable, and not easily adjudicable by universally recognized procedures. Furthermore, if the generalization of the model of political toleration implies adopting the principle of public neutrality, then any public moral judgment about differences is excluded as a matter of principle. In fact, the whole point

---

[73] Perfectionists are keen to draw a distinction between toleration and neutrality, arguing that toleration merely implies the suspension of the power to interference. By contrast, neutrality demands the adoption of a non-judgmental attitude. See, for example, Wall, *Liberalism, Perfectionism and Restraint*, p. 66. While it is clear that toleration does not require equal treatment, it is also clear that neutrality has emerged as the generalization of toleration in the passage from the absolute to the liberal state, as remarked by Paine and Kant (see above, Introduction, fn. 1), and that in a liberal state political toleration is superfluous.

of the neutralist interpretation of liberalism is to prevent the state from taking sides over morally and metaphysically controversial views. This is intended, on the one hand, as a contribution to the peaceful and civil coexistence of the many beliefs and conceptions of the good that are present in a pluralist society and, on the other, such neutrality is important for reasons of fairness, as required by the principle of equal respect and the equal public treatment of all. In this sense, the notion that the state must stop short of any sense of dislike or disapproval towards social differences which do not directly threaten the liberal order belongs to the principles of justice, and constitutes the core of the claim liberalism makes to political legitimacy. Consequently, the state should adopt a neutral stance towards any set of conflicting different views, lifestyles, or cultures.

In this framework toleration follows from the principles of justice and, at the same time, is the condition for their effectiveness. Its justification presupposes the principles of justice, and is founded on a notion of fairness. Adopting toleration as a political principle is a condition for the possibility of generalizing the principles of justice which form the core of liberal legitimacy and applying them beyond the domain of those who belong to and already share the liberal tradition and culture. Toleration, from the neutralist perspective, is best understood through considering a two-step theoretical model: first, toleration is derived from a theory of justice, which roughly presupposes a liberal form of life; second, from there toleration is applied to the constitution of a broader version of liberal politics, which allows the extension of principles of justice to those who do not share the values of liberal culture and ethics.[74] Thus, toleration is required within liberal politics in order to ensure that people are treated fairly, but it is also necessary for regulating the constitutional reasoning that proceeds from the facts of pluralism to the common principles of justice. In the neutralist program, this second step is precisely what is required to make liberal society thoroughly pluralistic and genuinely open to alien cultures. Openness and potential inclusiveness are indeed the traits characterizing the neutralist versus the perfectionist interpretation; these traits are meant to constitute the appeal and the specificity of liberalism over other political ideals. The liberal commitment to them is precisely what, in the neutralist version, makes liberalism a universalist project where anyone and everybody of whatever origin,

---

[74] This appears evident in Rawls's theory. In *TJ*, toleration was required by the application of the two principles of justice; in Rawls's later work, focused on pluralism and liberal legitimacy, toleration is the premise in the reasoning to the overlapping consensus. See *PL*.

culture, or creed can find a just social arrangement which ensures that they will be treated with respect and in which their expectations and life plans can, in principle, be fulfilled. In contrast to the perfectionist perspective, toleration is thus a distinctive political quality of the liberal order, which is conceived as being ethically based on fairness; for the neutralist toleration is not simply the generalization of a typical moral virtue of the liberal personality. And the liberal society, emerging out of the neutralist interpretation, is committed to keeping its original promise of inclusiveness and universality, though, as we shall shortly see, within limits.

A further difference between the perfectionist and the neutralist perspective can be identified: whereas actual disapproval plays a central role in perfectionist views, and such disapproval circumscribes the subjects of toleration to chosen differences, excluding from its scope ascriptive characters such as race, sex, and ethnicity, the neutralist model does not imply such a restriction. Even though originally it developed as an answer to questions raised by religious differences, its theoretical structure can apply to any social difference. The general reason for toleration is, indeed, the unreasonableness and/or injustice of repression, which does not depend on whether the difference is approved of, autonomously chosen, or culturally received. In a sense, if repression of an opinion is wrong, intolerance of a physical trait is even less justified. This extensive application of toleration does not undermine the neutralist interpretation in the way in which it seems to threaten the more moralizing analysis characteristic of perfectionism.

Within the moral analysis of the concept of toleration, there is much debate over whether the proper conditions for tolerance should be only disapproval of differences or whether dislike should also be included.[75] The point of this discussion is that only in the case of disapproval is toleration held to be an intriguing moral puzzle worth close philosophical

[75] This issue is raised by Raphael, "The Intolerable," in *Justifying Toleration*, pp. 137–53, who maintains that the object of toleration should only be behavior or practices of which we disapprove morally; this is a condition for a distinctive definition of toleration as a moral virtue. In turn, this implies that the grounds for toleration be respect for persons, which, in his view, accounts for the apparent contradiction between toleration and disapproval: "Acts of which we disapprove, but which do not infringe rights may be tolerated despite our belief that they are wrong, and should be tolerated if those who do the acts have deliberately chosen to do them" (p. 147). In his argument, then, choice becomes a necessary condition for an act to be tolerated. Mary Warnock, on the other hand, believes that toleration may also concern subjects of mere dislike. See M. Warnock, "The Limits to Toleration," in *On Toleration*, pp. 123–39. Susan Mendus in *Toleration and the Limits of Liberalism*, pp. 8ff, underlines this problem, which she views as one of the various contradictory aspects of the liberal theory of toleration, her thesis being that only a socialist foundation for toleration can account for its moral character.

examination: it is thought that special reasons must be given to prove that it is a good thing to exercise "toleration" of forms of behavior which are the objects of reasoned disapproval. By contrast, non-interference with something that is disliked on the basis of personal idiosyncrasies or for reasons of prejudice is the obvious right thing to do and raises no puzzle for moral philosophy.[76] Yet restricting toleration to cases of disapproval limits it and construes it as applying only to chosen differences, thereby excluding the most divisive and problematic aspects of contemporary pluralism, such as issues arising from race, ethnicity, and gender. Thus the moral analysis of toleration (which is so important in the perfectionist conception) is trapped between losing its distinctive moral character and making toleration too restricted in scope to have any social relevance. But, as I have said, this problem does not trouble the neutralist conception of toleration, since, in this case, the perspective is thoroughly political, hence disagreement rather than disapproval is the relevant circumstance in which issues of toleration arise. So long as disapproval is disregarded, social asymmetries disappear as a relevance for political toleration. Disagreement is a necessarily symmetrical attitude, while disapproval may, or may not, be reciprocated. Disapproval in fact is often not symmetrical, insofar as the two parties enjoy different powers of interference with the conduct of which they disapprove. In other words, political toleration is shown by neutralists to be the fair (and not simply pragmatic) solution to the conflicts engendered by pluralism, quite independently of whether the differences to be tolerated are morally disapproved of or simply disliked, and whether they are chosen or not. The aim of the political principles of toleration and neutrality is the promotion of a peaceful and civil coexistence with prima facie incompatible diversity, where everyone is treated equally, disregarding all moral and all ascriptive differences.

In conclusion, the perfectionist and the neutralist interpretations of liberalism provide quite different accounts of toleration, and from different viewpoints, even though eventually what can or cannot be tolerated may, in practice, end up being more or less the same, regardless

---

[76] If the moral value of tolerance is based on respect, and respect on autonomy, then both respect and autonomy can reasonably refer only to moral choices. Besides, it is only when moral disapproval is at issue that the tolerator makes a special effort to overcome his or her feelings by appealing to the stronger reason of respect for others. If mere dislike of a certain form of behavior were to be a condition for tolerance, and thus the question was merely one of a difference in taste, not only would the moral effort required to tolerate what is disliked be less demanding, but its moral quality would be less compelling, as tolerance would then come close to indifference. See Mendus, "Introduction," in *Justifying Toleration*, pp. 1–20.

of which interpretation is used. While, for the perfectionist, full toleration is granted only to those who can ultimately be recognized as moral
partners, the neutralist reverses this argument since, in his or her interpretation, toleration should be granted to everyone because they are
moral equals, and hence must be treated as moral partners. The perfectionist's implicit distinction of three classes of differences, corresponding
to full toleration, tolerance by default, and intolerance, is here totally
rejected: social differences make no difference to the neutralist, once
they are placed in the private realm. The distinction that is relevant for
the neutralist model of toleration is not one among social differences but
that between the public/political sphere and the private domain (including social and domestic areas). Accordingly, the only justifiable limits to
toleration are those posed by the self-defense of the liberal order. This
justifies, for instance, measures against internal and international terrorism, and the protection of third parties. But no question of ethical
compatibility can legitimately be raised by the neutralist interpretation.

In this respect, the neutralist model widens the horizon of toleration,
insofar as it introduces consideration of equality and links toleration with
justice and fairness. The moral question to which toleration is supposed
to be the solution is not simply the defense of individuals' liberty and
autonomy in a situation of moral pluralism, but the protection of equal
liberty. What is at stake is not only the possibility of pursuing one's life
plan and conception of the good without impediment, but also non-
discrimination because of one's moral choice and lifestyle. Under this
interpretation, toleration does not aim to promote moral partnership
within the hospitable confines of the liberal good, as in the perfectionist
version; it aims to make citizens feel like moral partners in the social
enterprise, notwithstanding their differences and contrasts.

Yet this program aimed at openess, inclusiveness, and non-discrimination will be shown to be largely self-defeating, because of its
reductive interpretation of pluralism, the constitutional framework of the
argument and the public/private distinction around which the neutralist
model is built. I contend that these features induce a basic insensitivity
to social differences, which are consequently considered either as publicly irrelevant and as not pertaining to the public sphere or, at best, as
disadvantages to be compensated, in order to be justly dismissed in the
political domain.

2

The limits of liberal toleration

CRITICISMS OF LIBERAL NEUTRALITY

So far, the political conception of toleration framed in terms of the neutralist interpretation appears more encompassing than that provided by
perfectionism, while avoiding its moralistic flavor. Nevertheless, being
intrinsically linked to the notion of state neutrality, it is open to the many
attacks brought against this concept, first by communitarians, but also by
perfectionists and, more recently, by the supporters of multiculturalism.[1]
Though many of these criticisms are important and worth serious consideration, I will argue that they are by no means conclusive, and can be
convincingly answered by neutralists. What I hold to be the real problem with the neutralist model, on the other hand, is touched on only
tangentially by its critics.

The most common objections to liberal neutrality raised by its communitarian and perfectionist critics concern, first, its literal meaning
and, second, its justification. Such critics question the very possibility of
a plausible and coherent interpretation of neutrality.[2] Critics of neutrality ask what it actually means to be neutral:[3] does it, for example, imply
not favoring any party at all, or favoring all equally? And neutral about
what? Issues such as killing or rape or slavery are, for instance, excluded
by neutralists, who would favor, in these instances, state coercion. How
should polygamy or clitoridectomy be considered by neutralists? And

[1] For a presentation of the communitarian critique of liberalism, see, for example, Amy Gutmann,
"Communitarian Critics of Liberalism," *Philosophy and Public Affairs*, 14, 1985, pp. 308–22 and Will
Kymlicka, *Contemporary Political Philosophy* (Oxford: Clarendon Press, 1990). On the postmodernist
and multiculturalist critique, see Young, *Justice and the Politics of Difference*; Charles Taylor, "The
Politics of Recognition."
[2] Critical objections of this kind are pressed by Raz, *The Morality of Freedom*, pp. 110–23, and by
Bellamy, "Defining Liberalism: Neutralist, Ethical or Political?," pp. 23–43.
[3] This question is asked by Raz, *The Morality of Freedom*, by Mendus, *Toleration and the Limits of
Liberalism*, pp. 69–87 and 116 ff, by Peter Jones, "The Ideal of the Neutral State," in Goodin and
Reeve, eds., *Liberalism and Neutrality*, pp. 9–38 and by Galston, *Liberal Purposes*, pp. 93ff.

53

how can neutrality represent a value, instead of being a mere modus vivendi?

These objections can be answered in a number of ways. First, as to its meaning, there are in fact several interpretations of neutrality, some more convincing than others; yet there is also a common ideal underlying the various conceptions, namely anti-discrimination and anti-perfectionism – that is, the idea that the state has no business in making its citizens morally better, and hence has no right in making moral distinctions between them.[4] Critics of neutrality have pointed out that governments cannot avoid making some substantive stand which favors certain conceptions of the good over others. If, for example, policies supporting opera or the fine arts or archeological research are decided upon, the state is not acting neutrally towards all conceptions of the good.[5] However, such remarks overlook the fact that the point of neutrality is not so much one of moral indifference in politics, which is indeed unattainable, as one of a lack of discrimination between different citizens. In this way, it fails to appreciate the difference between a public policy that supports opera and the public choice for an "apartheid" social system. Though non-discrimination and non-perfectionism may not be fully realized, they nevertheless stand as regulative political ideals, making sense of the difference between social segregation and public support for opera.

Second, as to the subjects on which neutrality must be maintained, they are clearly limited to such social differences in individuals or groups which do not infringe rights. Thus, the professional killer cannot demand a neutral public consideration of his life plan if it involves killing others. And the answer to the question whether polygamy or clitoridectomy are entitled to toleration on the grounds that the state must be publicly neutral depends on a judgment about whether or not they are harmful practices. Third, as to the grounds of neutrality, the above argument from the point of view of fairness provides a strong, ethical and not merely prudential reason in its favor, and it is up to its critics to show why and how it is neither good nor convincing enough.

Another apparently more serious objection, however, has been advanced. This states that no version of liberal neutrality could be neutral concerning all conceptions of the good, since it would be tailored to include only those that already fit within the liberal ideal, while filtering

---

[4] This unifying idea is also implicitly acknowledged by Raz, *The Morality of Freedom*, who groups neutralist positions under the heading of "antiperfectionism." Raz, however, would not agree with the above definition of perfectionism which is shared by Rawls and Dworkin.

[5] For this argument see, for example, Caney, "Antiperfectionism and Rawlsian Liberalism."

out those produced by alien, non-liberal cultures.[6] The supposed universality of liberal theory would thus turn out to be only a disguised form of particularism, and the distinction between neutralism and perfectionism would amount to nothing, since the neutralist interpretation also implicitly presupposes a theory of the good which on close inspection would seem to be thicker than claimed.[7] For this reason, perfectionists believe that a better strategy is to argue directly for liberal values and purposes, without claiming to provide neutral support for liberal institutions.

However powerful, this objection is not, in my view, necessarily final. It is true that liberal neutrality can never be completely neutral. Neutrality is not an absolute but a relational notion, and by its very logic needs to be contextually defined.[8] Which differences are socially relevant, which are irreducible and what is at stake are matters to be decided by means of a historical and social interpretation of the case. Therefore, liberal neutrality is always partially shaped by particular circumstances. What is shared today may become a new issue of controversy tomorrow, requiring revision of the articulation of state neutrality.[9] In some European nation-states, neutrality emerged in relation to the divisive issue of religion and was articulated in the ideal of the secular state. Nationality and ethnicity were not considered issues to be neutral about. The United States, on the contrary, being an immigrant society, had

---

[6] This is the most common criticism of liberal neutrality; it is shared by communitarians and perfectionists. See Haskar, *Equality, Liberty and Perfectionism*; Adina Schwarz, "Moral Neutrality and Primary Goods," *Ethics*, 83, 1972–3, pp. 294–307; Neal, "A Liberal Theory of the Good?," pp. 567–81; Alexander and Schwarzschild, "Liberalism, Neutrality of Welfare vs. Equality of Resources"; Waldron, "Legislation and Moral Neutrality," in Goodin and Reeve, *Liberal Neutrality*; Michael Perry, "Neutral Politics?," *Review of Politics*, 54, 4, 1989, pp. 479–509; Riley, "Rights to Liberty in Purely Private Matters"; Young, *Justice and the Politics of Difference*.

[7] This is the argument of the perfectionists. See Haskar, *Equality, Liberty and Perfectionism*; Waldron, "Legislation and Moral Neutrality"; Alexander and Schwarzschild, "Liberalism, Neutrality of Welfare vs. Equality of Resources."

[8] "To be neutral is always to be neutral as between two or more actual or possible policies or parties . . . Questions of neutrality arise in reference to situations of actual or possible conflict between parties or politics; one cannot be neutral if there is, so to speak, nothing to be neutral between": Montefiore, "Introduction," to *Neutrality and Impartiality*, p. 4. In fact, Deborah Fitzmaurice argues for a "procedural conception" of neutrality, of Kantian inspiration, which aims at a form of neutrality, which is absolute insofar as it is "universally rationally justifiable," derived from reason alone independently of any conception of the good ("Liberal Neutrality, Traditional Minorities," pp. 52–3). However, such a Kantian conception of neutrality is nowhere adopted in politics, as she admits, given that some content is needed for political legitimacy and this shared content becomes the obvious candidate for delimiting a notion of neutrality.

[9] J. Waldron takes the contextual nature of neutrality as proof of the inconsistency of the concept. By contrast, I think that the acknowledgment of the non-absolute nature of neutrality does not undermine the possibility that this notion has a specific meaning: after all, there is a considerable difference between neutrality on a definite range of issues, and interfering or taking sides. Between all and nothing there is something.

to deal with ethnic differences and, consequently, developed a form of neutrality that applied to the ethnicity of its citizens.[10] In other words, the general principle of neutrality is always embodied in particular articulations. Supporters of liberal neutrality now generally acknowledge that their theories are less than strictly universal. In Rawls's *Political Liberalism*, only reasonable comprehensive views need to be encompassed in the overlapping consensus on the political principles of justice, while non-reasonable views may well remain outside that consensus. But even if neutrality is acknowledged as relatively limited, there is a significant difference between the neutralist and the perfectionist approaches.[11] In the neutralist interpretation, views outside the overlapping consensus are excluded from the liberal polity only de facto, and, one hopes, contingently. In the perfectionist interpretation, exclusion of incompatible views and cultures is instead principled, in order to preserve the moral integrity of liberalism.

Assuming now that the limits of liberal neutrality are not inconsistent with the concept of neutrality, there is a further communitarian objection to be considered. Is it desirable to live within a supposedly neutral state, which is a morally empty box and where all differences are treated with indifference and, as a result, lose their savor?[12] What this communitarian point highlights is that liberal neutrality would impoverish the life of a political community, emptying it of any substantive cultural values. This objection is also shared by the perfectionists, whose more sanguine interpretation of liberalism is meant as a response to this criticism. Yet the communitarian conception of social life under the neutral state is not correct. First, the political sphere covers only a limited area of the total life of society. In the wider sphere of society as a whole groups and associations can freely pursue their communal goals and aims, reinforcing bonds of solidarity and loyalty among their members;[13] second, the

---

[10] See Michael Walzer, *What It Means To Be an American* (Padua: Marsilio, 1992) and "New Tribalism," *Dissent*, 1992. That the United States is a culturally neutral society is contested by Will Kymlicka, who maintains that the US government, like others, actively supports and promotes its societal culture, for example, by using English as the common language of the country. See W. Kymlicka, "Liberal Nationalism," *European Forum on Citizenship* (Florence: EUI, 1996).

[11] In this respect, I find the following paragraph enlightening: "Unselfishness, impartiality and being unprejudiced are human virtues. They are not to be reduced to drivel by speaking of the impartial man being partial toward impartiality and the unprejudiced as being prejudiced in favor of lack of prejudice": B. J. Diggs, "The Common Good as Reason for Political Action," *Ethics*, 83, 1972–3, pp. 283–93.

[12] See, for example, Michael Sandel, *Liberalism and the Limits of Justice* (Cambridge: Cambridge University Press, 1992), pp. 133ff.

[13] This remark is made by Rawls, *TJ*, ch. 7, §67; then developed by Michael Walzer, *Spheres of Justice*, Basic Books, New York, 1983.

political sphere is not devoid of substantive commitments (nor can it be), although established political authorities should avoid taking substantive positions which would result in discrimination against some of its citizens.

The communitarian argument about the desirability of the neutral state tacitly raises another important issue, which needs to be further investigated. Under one influential interpretation, liberal neutrality construes the public sphere as disregarding any actual differences between the citizens, who are its members. These differences are instead protected by toleration in the private sphere. Given this, how could it ever be thought to be desirable for a member of a particular group to conceal his or her special difference – that is, the very source of his or her social identity – in order to gain access to citizenship? This is, moreover, a problem which does not concern all citizens equally: some differences do not, it seems, need to be concealed (whiteness, maleness, straightness, membership of the dominant church). Here one encounters a substantial weakness of the principle of liberal neutrality, at least under its most common interpretation, namely its fundamental insensitivity to differences. In fact, neutrality's basic goal is to free people from their differences in the public domain and to equalize all citizens in their political capacity independently of their human particularity. This goal is to be attained by denying public relevance to their special identity. Social differences are generally regarded by liberal neutrality as personal tastes and idiosyncrasies to be excluded from public consideration because (a) they constitute divisive and conflicting elements and (b) they do not pertain to matters of justice and social order.[14] And yet some special identities are actually admitted in the public sphere – only they are not perceived as special and different, but simply as human traits and features.

In the following pages, I shall critically analyze this conception of neutrality, showing how it works to exclude minorities from full citizenship. However, as I shall argue in the second part of this work, neutrality (or, maybe, the values underlying it) should not be dismissed altogether: what causes exclusion is only a particular though dominant conception of neutrality. I shall try to retain the constitutive ethical core of neutrality, that is anti-discrimination and anti-perfectionism, but to fashion it in such a way as to grant sensitivity to differences, and to allow for full inclusion of minority members. Whether this goal implies a reinterpretation

---

[14] See, for example, Dworkin, "Liberalism."

of neutrality or falls beyond the boundary of liberal theory, however, is
not a matter I intend to settle.

NEUTRALITY REEXAMINED

The perverse effects of liberal neutrality, which was originally meant
as a protection against discrimination, can be detected with reference
to two issues, namely the logic of the constitutional argument and the
representation of pluralism as implying the existence of many different
conceptions of the good.

Because of the nature of the constitutional argument for neutral political principles, the asymmetries between social differences are in principle
ignored. The consitutional argument assumes as a premise that there are
many different and conflicting positions held by the members of the society. Each position, seen from above, is taken to have the same standing
as each other position: each is just as different from the others as the
others are from it. In other words, the constitutional perspective cannot
but ignore that different burdens and privileges are attached to the various differences in real societies. In fact, the constitutional argument is
supposed, on the one hand, to justify the quest for equal liberty to pursue
a particular conception of the good as a trait of liberal justice and, on the
other, to offer reasons for supporting the liberal order as neutral, i.e. as
a non-discriminatory social arrangement, and as the best protection for
any conception of the good that one may entertain.[15] The first of these
points represents the "internal" argument, according to which toleration
is derived from the principles of liberal justice; the second constitutes the
"external" argument, designed to justify liberal legitimacy via toleration.
As a constitutional argument, it considers each party in the decision process impersonally, i.e. on an equal footing; accordingly, the conclusion of
the argument is the vindication of the principles of equal liberty and of
public neutrality, which are chosen as the best defense for those in minority positions. Since no one wants their own view, whether it is held by
the majority or by a minority, to be disadvantaged, and since this desire
is shared by everyone in the constitutional setting, the principle to select
should grant that no special privilege or advantage and equally no special cost or burden be attached to holding any view. The principles best

---

[15] De Marneffe, in "Liberalism, Liberty and Neutrality," draws a distinction between these two levels
("neutrality among conceptions of the good" and "neutrality of reasons") and states that only
the second characterizes neutralist liberalism. I think that both belong to neutralist liberalism,
the second being the generalization of the first, as shown in the previous chapter.

suited to protect all conceptions of the good and their holders equally are freedom of expression and of association, and neutrality in the public sphere.

Yet the question is, are these principles sufficient effectively to attack actual forms of discrimination that are linked to the different social weight and standing attached to the various conceptions of the good in real societies? Is not the burden of low status borne by some minority groups unfair, and hence politically relevant? And is public blindness to social differences enough to ensure fair treatment of asymmetrically situated, especially systematically disadvantaged, social groups?[16] I think that in the constitutional setting the adoption of a neutral stance is the most plausible and equitable way of neutralizing the rise of potential discrimination against the holders of what might become defined as different, minority views. The constitutional setting is indeed a hypothetical situation, where the social arena has not yet been divided up into sets of "normal" and "deviant" views and where, consequently, advantages have not yet been assigned to holders of the majoritarian conceptions of the good, nor disadvantages to the holders of minoritarian ones. But in the real world of contemporary democracy, where a division between a "normal" range of conceptions of the good, defined by the majority, and the "different" conceptions held by members of various minorities does exist, mere public disregard of differences is clearly insufficient and for two reasons. First, it is insufficient because in ongoing societies where privileges and costs have already been linked to moral and cultural differences and have been rooted in a history of discrimination and oppression, adopting a neutral attitude towards those differences, far from neutralizing the effects of previous discrimination, strengthens and reproduces them. Neutrality may be enough to ensure the freedom to pursue any minoritarian conception of the good as well as the equal treatment of citizens in the public realm, regardless of their ideas, moral positions, and lifestyle, but it is not enough to counter the advantages or disadvantages that have accumulated over a long period of discrimination, which now mark those who are different, let alone the inequalities of freedom that result from such a history. Second, public blindness is insufficient because the constitutional reasoning from which it results assumes a hypothetical situation of undifferentiated pluralism in which, in order to ensure justice, all asymmetries are ignored

---

[16] Montefiore, *Neutrality and Impartiality*, maintains that neutrality does not change previous asymmetries in the parties' positions. Referring to this argument, Raz holds that neutrality does not guarantee fairness (*Morality of Freedom*, pp. 113–14).

on principle, and in which therefore *a fortiori* the distinction between "normality" and "difference" is necessarily lost. From the constitutional standpoint, indeed, each view differs from all others; in that sense, each view is equal: equally different. However, the distinction between the normal range of traits and options and what differs from it is precisely what defines inclusion and exclusion in a society. This goes beyond a mere unequal distribution of costs and benefits in that it is what defines full and second-class membership. Inclusion here is not meant merely as the legal entitlement to citizenship rights but also as the effective ability to make use of them. Adopting a distinction drawn by Amartya Sen, inclusion is not just a matter of acquisition, but of capability and functioning. I shall come back to this point in the next chapter.[17] Meanwhile, it must be stressed that being entitled to citizenship rights, i.e. being formally included in the polity, does not necessarily imply having all the real powers of the citizen, i.e. the capacity to function as a full citizen. Legal rights and institutional blindness do not of themselves allow minorities to gain equal respect and dignity. And this failure is blurred by the constitutional argument which disguises the distinction between normality and difference. The constitutional perspective, while providing a normative principle for equal distribution – of liberty as of any other social good – cannot by its very nature deal with the problem of actual exclusion from society. From a constitutional standpoint, anyone is a potential member, if he or she is willing to be in that position.[18] But in fact, being a member of a minority or of a majority does make a significant difference which is not indicated simply by the acknowledgment of advantages or disadvantages affected to this or that position, and which the principle of public blindness is certainly not equipped to dispel.

To be sure, Rawls seems to acknowledge this problem when he states that the equal right to political participation is often undermined by the unequal value that political freedom has for citizens in a disadvantaged

---

[17] Sen, "Well-Being, Agency and Freedom"; A. Sen, "Rights and Capabilities," in T. Honderich, ed., *Morality and Objectivity* (London: Routledge and Kegan Paul, 1985) pp. 130–48; A. Sen, *Inequality Reexamined*, Oxford University Press, Oxford 1992.

[18] Among the theories of justice that have been proposed after Rawls's, the pluralist theory by Michael Walzer was the first to stress membership in the distributive unit as a special social good, namely as the precondition for being considered in the distribution. Walzer pointed out that membership is neither free nor freely distributed: see *Spheres of Justice*, chapter 2, "Membership," pp. 31–63. Moreover, formal membership in the polity need not necessarily grant the full status of citizen; that is a subject entitled to protection of rights, resources, and opportunities, as argued by Judith Shklar in *American Citizenship*, pp. 1–23, and Giovanna Zincone in *Da sudditi a cittadini*, pp. 187–232.

position. In his view, a just democracy cannot ignore this; his solution is distributive compensation for those who are at a disadvantage with respect to political influence. Yet I hold that the exclusion of minority groups from full citizenship cannot be fully reversed by a distributive mechanism which supplements institutional blindness by equalizing the distribution of resources and opportunities to different citizens. For one thing, in this way differences are understood only as disadvantages to be compensated, which is probably not the best strategy for addressing the issue of unequal respect and dignity that is raised by minorities in contemporary democracies. For another, the distinction between normality and difference is once again ignored by the Rawlsian solution. Being the bearer of a different identity, socially despised and politically disregarded, implies something more than having a less than equal share of basic goods, though this is often the case, as remarked above.[19]

To summarize: in the neutralist model, toleration is defended both as a political principle that grounds political legitimacy and as a trait of liberal justice, granting equal liberty to everybody in matters of conscience. In this latter respect, questions of toleration are equated with questions of justice – more precisely, with distributive questions about freedom of expression and privacy. Both the argument for toleration as required by liberal justice and that leading to liberal legitimacy are framed in constitutional terms; the constitutional argument implies that groups ignore their actual positions and any real existing discrimination against them[20] in order to reason impartially. This argument totally bypasses the inclusion/exclusion problem that mirrors the division of society into a majority and minorities. As a result, the selected principles, being neutral, should neither favor any of the existing conceptions of the good nor discriminate against anyone because of their beliefs. But, at the same time, they would not alter existing social asymmetries between those in the majority and members of minorities. In conclusion, I think that the identification of problems of toleration as a question of distributive justice with reference to equal liberty, together with the constitutional construction of the argument for a fair treatment of differences, blanks out relevant aspects of social discrimination from the neutralist model of

---

[19] I have argued elsewhere that an extension of principles of distribution cannot adequately solve the problem of exclusion. See Galeotti, "La differenza: politica, non metafisica."

[20] The requirement that one be ignorant of one's own position is a common feature of constitutional reasoning, whether it is represented as in Rawls's original position, or in terms of a rigorously impartial standpoint (a view from nowhere) as in Nagel's.

political toleration. This is particularly serious given that, here, toleration is justified on the grounds of justice.

However, it might be suggested that these difficulties are dependent upon the special conception of neutrality adopted by the theory; in this case a solution might be found by choosing a more appropriate version of neutrality. In fact, whether the concept of neutrality is understood in the intentional sense or in the causal sense matters significantly in this respect.[21] Intentional neutrality means that certain kinds of reasons should be excluded as admissible grounds for public action. In other words, state policies should not be based on claims such as that certain religious creeds or opinions are false or certain lifestyles unappealing. Basically, this amounts to an institutional blindness concerning certain differences and non-interference in certain areas. Intentional neutrality is thus vulnerable to the argument developed above. Causal neutrality, by contrast, focuses on the outcome of public actions and policies. It is supposed to guarantee equal standing to all parties in a society – that is, equal opportunities and resources for anyone to pursue their conception of the good. Consider, for example, religious education. While intentional neutrality implies that religious education is not a public goal – i.e. each family is free to bring up its children in its preferred religion, and churches are free, within the limits imposed by their financial resources, to organize their own forms of religious education in any way they see fit – causal neutrality supports a totally different public approach. It implies that the state should give financial support to all religious organizations (plus a voucher for children of free-thinkers) in a way that is inversely proportionally to their economic means, in order to achieve equality of all parties.[22] Therefore, causal neutrality, instead of ignoring

---

[21] The distinction between "intentional neutrality" and "causal neutrality" is traced by Weale in "Toleration, Individual Differences and Respect for Persons." A similar distinction is made by Raz in *The Morality of Freedom*, pp. 114–17. Actually, Raz singles out two possible forms of causal neutrality: the first concerns the prohibition of any public action that would alter the chances anyone has to attain their conception of the good; the second concerns the public duty to grant equal opportunity to everyone to satisfy their conception of the good. Yet Raz's distinction is either approximately equivalent to that between intentional and causal neutrality, or it shows that neutrality is an impossible ideal. In fact the chances to realize any conception of the good may change either as a transgression of intentional neutrality or as the unintended outcome of social policies in various areas. But clearly this latter case cannot be controlled by norms. Charles Larmore speaks of procedural neutrality and of outcome neutrality (*Patterns of Moral Complexity*, p. 44).

[22] Audi ("The Separation of Church and State and the Obligations of Citizenship") holds that the theory of the separation of church and state entails the principle of neutrality – that is, not favoring any religion or religious persons over secular people – but he is still unclear as

differences in public action, takes them into account in order to neutralize their differing social weight. In this respect, causal neutrality, the implementation of which rules out intentional neutrality from public policies, seems to overcome at least some of the difficulties engendered by the constitutional argument, insofar as it is aimed at reversing actual discrimination and not simply at excluding certain (discriminatory) reasons for public action. Causal neutrality takes account of and counters the asymmetry between different social groups and thus does not permit the blind reproduction of existing social inequalities and forms of discrimination against certain conceptions of the good.

Nevertheless, causal neutrality cannot represent a satisfactory solution for the treatment of differences by liberalism. In fact, liberal theorists have in general, and for good reasons, favored intentional neutrality, albeit with some corrections and adjustments in order to be more sensitive to social difference.[23] The problem with causal neutrality is not simply that it implies too much state interference in social life to be easily acceptable for any liberal;[24] it is also completely incompatible with the basic rationale of political liberalism. The compensation which the government is supposed to provide for minorities, according to causal neutrality, is not meant for individuals, but for communities and organizations. And it does not aim to lift from individuals the burdens they must bear because they are "different"; it attempts, rather, to give every culture, church, and community an equal opportunity to carry on and flourish. However, the pursuit of this goal would require the state to discriminate between groups in order to decide how much each is entitled to; moreover, it would raise the issue of whether the state should have the right to interfere either in a group's internal decisions and actions, or in intergroup relations. These are difficult and yet important problems in a pluralistic democracy, much discussed under the headings of multiculturalism and of group rights. But, in any case, the very goal of granting equal standing to each conception of the good lies outside the framework of liberal argumentation for neutrality and justice outlined above. Equal liberty for individuals with reference to their conception of the good is the goal of neutralist liberalism. Such a goal would imply, at

to whether neutrality implies favoring pluralism as well. According to Audi, the principles of equality between creeds and of public neutrality entail not only restrictions on public action, but also sometimes require positive interventions – for example, in order to modify the public holidays of a society (pp. 264–5).

[23] *TJ*, ch. 2, § 12; see also de Marneffe, "Liberalism, Liberty and Neutrality."

[24] See Weale, "Toleration, Individual Differences and Respect for Persons"; Larmore, *Patterns of Moral Complexity*; Nagel, *Equality and Partiality*, p. 166.

the very least, both toleration of divergent conceptions of the good, that is, non-interference with them, and intentional neutrality, so that no one is either favored or discriminated against as a result of public policy because of his or her conception of the good. Equal liberty can sometimes be interpreted broadly so as to include the requirement of freeing individuals from the disadvantages and burdens that are attached to their professed conception of the good. This further requirement would imply compensation for those holding a minority view, but in this case the recipient is the individual, not the community identified by that viewpoint. No extensive interpretation of equal (individual) liberty can entail equal collective opportunities for groups to exist and flourish. Hence, from the argument of neutral liberalism, there are no grounds for adopting a causal conception of neutrality. The latter may be an interesting principle for multiculturalism, but it cannot be derived from a constitutional argument for liberal neutrality.

In conclusion, intentional neutrality can at most be extended to take account of differences between individuals, but only as unjust disadvantages to be compensated by some distributive policy. Ultimately, the goal is a just social situation where social differences are accepted, but restricted to the private realm, where, it is assumed, they can be confined so as not to impinge on the public positions of the citizens. It is in the political community that the citizens can finally achieve equality as "naked" individuals, free from the burden imposed on them by the differences in their ideas and lifestyles. In other words, neutral liberalism can be sensitive to differences only as disadvantages to be compensated. In this way, it misses one crucial aspect of social differences: their significance as causes of exclusion; the extension of the distributive paradigm can in principle compensate for economic disadvantages, but not for exclusion in the sense specified above.

At this point we are back to the crucial weakness I have mentioned above: all things considered, the neutralist model of toleration in its dominant interpretation is basically insensitive to social differences, its ideal being the construction of a neutral public sphere where such differences do not count, where citizens are freed from the constraints and pressures that derive from their particular loyalties and commitments and can choose and act as agents of the general will.[25] It should be said that this political ideal is not inherently morally based or narrow-minded;

---

[25] See Audi, "The Separation of Church and State," and Rawls, *PL*, p. 219.

it has been extremely important in modern history in the process of emancipation from hierarchical and absolutist societies, and its universalism, particularly the requirement that rights be extended to all, makes it theoretically attractive and gives it a powerful ethical force. But the neutralist theoretical and moral framework is blind to the issue of substantive exclusion, much as it is blind to differences. We have seen how the constitutional argument disguises the question of membership in minority groups, and hence the problem of inclusion; we shall now see how the individualistic reduction of pluralism contributes to the misunderstanding of the kind of conflict that gives rise to issues of toleration, and hence also to an insufficient normative response to these issues.

PLURALISM AND TOLERATION

Neutralists suppose that pluralism is the presence of many different and potentially conflicting conceptions of the good, and that all relevant social differences are to be explained in terms of differences between such conceptions. On this reading, ethnic, linguistic, and cultural differences condense into world-views, engendering incompatible and irreducible moral positions, social practices, and ways of life. Being an Arab is thus conceptualized as endorsing a certain religion, belief, and morality. If the salient differences are those between world-views, they can be conceived of as chosen, at least in principle. Whether they are the outcome of a rational choice or are received from one's tradition, the individual can always rationally revise his or her world-view; and if world-views are, in the last analysis, choosable, then the relevant social differences pertain to individuals, whether or not they are shared by a group. Consequently, the problem of pluralism is understood as the conflict deriving from the irreducible disagreement about what is worthwhile in life and how life should be lived. For such a conflict, which liberals see as unavoidable and non-eliminable, the classic solution consists of toleration as non-interference – i.e. leaving everyone free to pursue their ideals and to practice their culture as long as no one else is harmed and the liberal order is safe – plus neutrality in public treatment. This notion of pluralism, and this understanding of relevant social differences, though philosophically intriguing and a source of endless discussion, is, however, incomplete and incapable of making sense of contemporary social conflicts. Behind "irreducible" world-views and "incompatible" conceptions of the good there are in fact groups in marginal and subordinate positions which demand to be recognized on an equal footing with majority groups and which fight for the public acceptance of their different identities.

In principle, there is no theoretical reason why cultural and group pluralism cannot be approached as pluralism of comprehensive views, so that identity conflicts can be reduced to the most philosophically relevant conflict, namely religious, moral, and metaphysical conflict. This is what happened in the early days of modern toleration. Although religious conflict following the Reformation actually took place between churches, sects, factions, and groups with military resources struggling to assert their beliefs and practice their rituals in public,[26] it was represented as a conflict between irreducibly different conscientious beliefs concerning the true religion. This representation constituted the grounds for the theory of toleration as political abstinence in matters of faith and conscience. At the start of the modern era the physical survival of religious minorities was at stake and toleration as abstention from repression and persecution was therefore the main concern of minorities under the circumstances. The reductionist conception of pluralism as a simple matter of divergent individual belief and choice was perfectly adequate because it provided sufficient justification for tolerance understood as non-interference with religious conscience, which then constituted the most one could reasonably hope for as a normative response to religious conflict. In contemporary democracy, however, freedom from persecution and political non-interference with religious creeds are taken for granted. Liberal neutrality promises more: equality in freedom of expression and association. Thus the present-day conflict does not concern (not primarily, at least) incompatible differences of value and culture (which are indeed taken care of by toleration as non-interference embodied in civil rights), but the unequal public standing of those professing minority views, who, therefore, demand toleration as a means of getting fair access to the public sphere.[27] On the whole, we can say that contemporary issues of toleration take liberal toleration for granted, but struggle for the fulfillment of its promises.

Sticking to the reductive interpretation of pluralism, neutralist liberalism cannot explain why issues of toleration still arise even in societies in which political interference in matters of faith, morals, and lifestyle is out of the question. The liberal normative solution is toleration as freedom of expression, which in fact is only the basis from which claims

[26] See J. A. Sigler, *Minority Rights. A Comparative Analysis* (Westport: Greenwood Press, 1983) and Michael Walzer, *On Toleration* (New Haven: Yale University Press, 1997).
[27] See Leader, "Three Faces of Toleration in a Democracy," pp. 47–8.

for public toleration as acceptance of differences are advanced. In other words, only if pluralism is reconceptualized as referring not merely to random variations between individuals, but to the fact that many groups, cultures, and identities are excluded or unequally included in democratic citizenship can one come to a proper understanding of the conflicts that give rise to issues of toleration in modern liberal societies; these conflicts go beyond mere individual disagreement about values, beliefs, and practices. The struggle over the public acceptance of differences can then be understood not simply as an issue of compatibility with the ideal and the practice of liberal neutrality, but rather as a contested attempt to overcome marginality and exclusion, and to achieve fair access. Since individuals are marginalized and excluded as a result of their membership in minority groups, the positive assertion of differences in the public space is seen as the first symbolic step towards full inclusion. If this is what is at stake in contemporary controversies about toleration, then the normative response cannot be toleration as non-interference, but toleration as the symbolic recognition of differences as legitimate options of pluralist democracy.[28]

To sum up the criticisms I have made of neutralist liberalism: the constitutional argument makes it impossible to recognize the issue of unequal membership which is the result of the division of society into those who are normal and those who are different. Because of the institutional blindness implicit in the neutralist liberal program, all differences become equally invisible from a political standpoint, or, if any carries a disadvantage, it can always be compensated for by some distributive policy. Exclusion, however, falls outside the framework of neutral liberalism, and is, I contend, precisely what lies at the heart of contemporary controversies about toleration, controversies which the neutralist conception cannot grasp, partly because of its reductive interpretation of pluralism. Understanding pluralism simply as a multiplicity of conceptions of the good disguises the nature of the conflicts that raise issues of toleration in the modern world, falsely presenting these as issues arising from the incompatibility between different practices and liberal principles and institutions. This makes these contemporary issues utterly incomprehensible. If, by contrast, pluralism is conceived of as referring to the existence of many different groups and cultures living asymmetrically side by side in the same society, then what is really at stake can be seen as a contested process of inclusion. In this case, toleration as non-interference cannot

---

[28] The argument for toleration as recognition, anticipated in the Introduction, will be properly worked out in chapters 3 and 7.

be the solution; toleration as recognition, on the other hand, would be the best available normative response. The shift lies in the reasons given for toleration. Consequently, when toleration is adopted under a neutralist interpretation, it is not done for the right reasons and so will not constitute an adequate normative response.

THE COUNTER-ARGUMENT OF THE NEUTRALIST LIBERAL

The critical argument above underlines the interpretative shortcomings of neutralist liberalism and its inadequacies as a normative solution to the problem of the social exclusion of minorities in contemporary liberal societies. The supporter of the neutralist conception of toleration might, however, attempt a response to my criticisms that would keep the theoretical framework of neutralism intact, while providing an explanation of why issues of toleration still arise in contemporary democracy and are so controversial.

The neutralist could, in fact, object to the above criticisms as follows: religious freedom and freedom of expression are already granted by the liberal state and toleration already protects individual choice in matters of faith. Indeed, no one wants Islamic students to give up their religion or homosexuals to be denied their rights. The controversial aspect of contemporary cases concerns the extension of toleration from its proper domain, the private realm, to the public one – e.g. to the public school, the symbol and cornerstone of the secular state, or to the army. The conflict then does not focus on the right to religious choice or to sexual orientation, which are beyond dispute, but on the incursion of special, particular identities into a public sphere which ought to remain neutral or common ground for all citizens. As we have seen, the neutralist model of toleration is dependent on the public/private distinction[29] and limits toleration to politically indifferent matters, i.e. to matters about which political authorities can afford to be neutral. Such issues are typically private, as by definition they do not (and should not) concern the political order; political toleration, as we have seen before, pertains to private

[29] The public/private distinction is highly controversial, but also essential to liberal thinking. A useful account of the dichotomy is found in "The Liberal Conception of the Public and the Private," in S. I. Benn and G. F. Gauss, eds., *Public and Private in Social Life* (London: Croom Helm, 1983), pp. 31–65. Kant's usage of the terms "public" and "private" is sufficiently eccentric to require comment: Kant uses "public" with reference to civil society, a realm in which public discourse is conducted which is aimed at the public good. By contrast, "private" refers to institutional roles and functions insofar as they are not universal. See I. Kant, *Answer to the Question: What is Enlightenment?*, pp. 54–60. For a comment on Kant's concept of the public, see Onora O'Neill, "The Public Use of Reason."

choices.[30] But should private choices be excluded from the public space? Here, reference to the double interpretation of institutional blindness is in order.

As I have already argued, institutional blindness, strictly speaking, implies only a disregard of differences when it comes to making public policy, although it has also been interpreted as requiring the complete neutralization of the public sphere and its transformation into a place where expressions of differences are banned and citizens can speak and act only qua citizens, stripped of their particular identities. According to the first "minimalist" interpretation of neutrality, the private nature of matters of toleration does not entail that they should be hidden from public sight and considered illegitimate in the public domain. The visibility of differences in the public domain is not at issue under this interpretation of neutrality, which is why under this reading the exclusion of gays from the army or the prohibition of the Islamic veil from schools turn out to be matters that are inconsistent with neutrality requirements, being instances of intolerance and bigotry. The prohibition of the veil, however, is consistent with the second neutralist interpretation, which stresses a reading of the public sphere as the common domain purified of differences and particularities (the exclusion of gays from the army is more problematic, though there are neutral arguments backing that too). Should we conclude, then, that the claims to public visibility which characterize most contemporary controversies about toleration must be ascribed to a contestable maximal interpretation of neutrality? Are these contemporary disagreements simply instances of the misapplication of the theory of toleration? I do not think so, because although the maximal interpretation of neutrality (particularly influential in continental Europe as the *laïcité* ideal) makes public toleration of differences particularly controversial, the minimal interpretation leads to issues of public toleration as well. Under the minimal interpretation, differences can be aired publicly, but only as long as they appear as the expression of private convictions and lifestyles. If, on the other hand, they are perceived as provocative demands for public recognition, then toleration becomes an open question even under the minimalist interpretation. A statement about religious or moral beliefs and practices *which is a tacit or explicit demand for positive public recognition* cannot, in fact, be ignored by the political order, above all because it violates the principle of neutrality. The minimalist interpretation of the neutralist model implies that different

[30] This position is explicitly held by Losano in "Contro la societá multietnica."

views about the good, as the private expression of an individual's deep convictions and beliefs, can be tolerated anywhere, but that certain kinds of public statement of difference constitute a demand for special consideration of the difference in question, thus representing a breach of the notion of institutional blindness and an illegitimate invasion of the public sphere by what is legitimate only as an object of private choice. This subtle distinction between expressions of private choices and public statements is the key to making sense of many contemporary disputes within the theoretical framework of neutralist liberalism. In this sense, there is no need either to reinterpret pluralism or to reconceptualize toleration: the point at issue in many of these disputes is the compatibility of social differences with liberal neutrality, and that compatibility depends on differences being private choices rather than public statements.

I would contend, however, that this distinction is also a source of problems for the neutralist model of toleration. In this model, what makes a difference intolerable is that it is affirmed as a public statement of a kind which implies an incursion on the neutrality of the state. Such acts of trespass, however, are usually no more than symbolic, given that the public statement is generally taken as part of a quest for public recognition. Hence it is not the incursion itself which makes the expression of the difference intolerable; it is the presentational definition of the difference as a matter for public recognition which identifies it as an act of trespass. This definition does not depend on anything intrinsic to the difference; it depends simply on the way it is perceived. There is no neutral criterion which enables one to say that the cross is a more private symbol than the Islamic veil or that straightness is more personal than homosexuality. Indeed, in order to make sense of this distinction, *one must refer to the definition of certain views, convictions, and lifestyles as being "standard" and the distinction of these from others that are considered "deviant"* – a distinction which is not, and cannot be, acknowledged by neutralist liberalism.

Although from the neutralist standpoint all world-views, whether religious or secular, are equally different, in contemporary democracy not all creeds and views are in fact labeled as "different": *pace* public neutrality, some differences are more different than others. For example, in the western world the Christian faith is not considered "different," but, on the contrary, quite "normal"; and, being normal, it enjoys full religious freedom in private and public visibility as a matter of course. Creeds that are considered different, while granted toleration in the private arena, are denied this in public. This explains why in France, for example, going to school wearing a cross, or crossing oneself in court, are seen as "normal" habits and gestures, expressing no more than a private preference. By contrast, if a Muslim believer, in the very same situation, were to lay a carpet towards Mecca and start praying, it would be considered strange and extreme simply because such behavior does not accord with the norm, and would probably cause embarrassment. Thus, the distinction between behavior which expresses private choice and that which is a public statement refers back to the disparity between the public respect accorded to majority and minority characteristics, habits, and practices. Such inequality, ignored by the constitutional argument, cannot be justified in terms of neutralist liberalism. In conclusion, intolerable differences turn out to be those that are unfamiliar to the cultural norms of society, a result which makes neutralist liberalism closer to perfectionist liberalism than expected.

At this point, the supporter of a maximal interpretation of neutrality might respond as follows: the presence in the public domain of majority traits, characteristics, behavior, and practices is a de facto incursion of special identities. And even though such an incursion may be general practice, it is nonetheless illegitimate according to the principles of the secular state, and, indeed, is the very source of the feeling of exclusion and discrimination experienced by minority members. But the remedy cannot be the generalization of an illegitimate and unjust practice. Justice and fairness can better be served by making neutrality thoroughly universal. If no one is admitted into the public sphere with a special collective identity – if all have to wear a mask and conceal their membership of any group – everyone will be on an equal footing and no newcomer will experience discrimination. In other words, if the public marginalization of differences were generally and impartially practiced, issues of toleration would be preempted and there would be no reason to advance claims for public recognition of differences. Differently stated, the public presence of "normal" particular identities is held to be a case of the contingent practical failure of neutralist liberalism, but this is no reason to reject the theory. However, we are confronting a real issue here: is it possible to conceive of a public sphere where all the characteristics, practices, and attitudes that make up a person's identity are effectively banned, and where individuals participate only as members of humankind? Furthermore, is not neutrality, by its very logic, only a relative notion, so that it is possible only in given and specified alternatives, never among all possibilities?

Not only has institutional blindness never been fully and completely achieved, but, I suspect, it never can be, either conceptually or logically. This remark will not be subscribed to by supporters of minimal neutrality, who would argue that the public visibility of differences is not an issue, nor does it infringe neutrality, since neutrality concerns the grounds for public reasons, unless demands are advanced for special consideration, such as public recognition of a difference. In this way, we are back to the previous argument, according to which the criterion for the distinction between legitimate public visibility and illegitimate public statement is traced back to the divide between "normality" and "difference," a divide which cannot find justification within the neutralist framework.

Let us now go back to the distinction between private choices and public statements. Since what makes behavior striking and provocative lies in its being different from what is normal and familiar, the claim that to behave differently is to make a public statement is correct from an objective viewpoint. Moreover, when the agent becomes aware of the special visibility of his or her act and persists in it, he or she is doing something more than quietly expressing a private preference. Indeed, the act becomes provocative and a way of affirming in public a right to an identity that has otherwise been acceptable only provided it is withdrawn from public view. And it is only by resisting the more or less explicit attempts of others to check and repress such behavior that the person who is different may eventually be publicly accepted in the same way as the Christian who wears a cross. As in the Hegelian master–slave model, recognition is achieved by resisting and fighting against the other's denial.[31] If, on the other hand, the difference is underplayed and made quasi-invisible, its bearer is publicly accepted only as a "naked individual" despite his or her difference, and not on an equal footing with those who exhibit the accepted faith, opinions, or behavior of society. In other words, the provocative visibility of a difference depends directly on its exclusion from the normal range of views and practices of a society. This visible display of difference, however, is precisely what makes it a public statement, both objectively and subjectively. The notion of a difference as a public statement as opposed to a private choice turns out to be dependent upon the distinction between normality and difference, that is, between inclusion and exclusion. This distinction, however, is not part

---

[31] G. W. F. Hegel, *The Phenomenology of Spirit* [1807] (Oxford: Clarendon Press, 1970).

of the neutralist language; there is no appropriate normative response to it within the neutralist framework.

The neutralist can make a final point along approximately these lines: the previous criticisms, mainly those concerning the interpretive framework, do not alter one basic fact, namely that the politics of the public recognition of difference implies a breach of the ideal of neutrality, since, under any interpretation, it requires that special consideration be given to certain differences. Such public consideration, after all, is not given to "normal" identities and characters. In this respect, public toleration of differences goes beyond the boundary of liberalism and cannot be accommodated in liberal politics. I contend, however, that matters are more complex, and that this conclusive stand against the public recognition of differences is questionable in terms of the very principles and values which are crucial to the neutralist.

On the one hand, the demand for public recognition aims at inclusion: of different identities within society's normal range and of their bearers on an equal footing with the majority. In this respect, the public recognition which can be secured by public toleration is in line with the ideal of neutrality. On the other hand, public recognition, even though only symbolic, requires a positive consideration of the difference in question, and this goes beyond a merely neutral stance. By positive consideration, I do not mean a positive evaluation of the difference, but, rather, a special attention intended as a sign of its public acceptance. The exclusion of certain differences and their bearers from the public space is, in fact, the problem from which a demand for their public recognition starts. Exclusion, in the form of marginality, oppression, or invisibility, implies that some obstacle makes it hard for the bearers of different identities to be "normally" present and "quietly" visible in the public space. The obstacles – whether legal impediments, customary practices, or the minority's own timidity – need to be actively removed, a task for which state neutrality is insufficient. That all are free to express their ideas and to practice their way of life is not enough to counter the circumstances which have made public invisibility the norm for the bearers of certain differences. The non-neutral, but positive attitude needed is, in any case, justified by the neutral principle of the rectification of injustice, in this case the injustice of exclusion. Moreover, the public positive attitude which characterizes symbolic recognition can be (neutrally) extended to all differences, and is, hence, impartial. Given that recognition is intended here as the declaration that different identities and practices are just as legitimate and valuable as those that constitute the social norms, recognition can be extended to all claimants (provided that the difference in question does not violate anyone's rights); it is not a scarce resource. But I shall come back later to the meaning of recognition. At present, I only want to stress that the kind of recognition required when public toleration is in question is not simply the blind political stance towards differences typically prescribed by neutralist liberalism; it is justified by the principle of neutrality itself (no difference should be grounds for public exclusion) and can be neutrally extended to all differences (with the proviso that no harm is produced).

In conclusion, neutralist liberalism has treated issues of toleration as questions of justice – more precisely, as questions of the equal liberty and equal treatment of all citizens.[32] But the kind of injustice which gives rise to contemporary issues of toleration cannot be grasped from a neutralist standpoint; the reason for this is given by the constitutional argument and its conception of pluralism. Yet contemporary cases of toleration imply claims for fair access by those who have "different" identities to the public realm, i.e. for equal consideration and respect for members of minorities. The normative problem to be faced at this point is that, while equal liberty and equal treatment have been understood as including anyone, regardless of their creed, culture, ethnicity, and sex, equality of respect is now demanded for individuals qua bearers of collective identities and differences. Although such demands are based on arguments from social justice, they appear to go beyond the boundary of liberal justice. In other words, in order properly to grasp and deal with contemporary issues of toleration it is necessary to go beyond neutralist liberalism, at least in its dominant version, while retaining its anti-discriminatory ideal, and its prior commitment to justice.

A step beyond liberal theory also seems to be required to understand the evolution of the role of toleration in political theory. Classical toleration has been understood as the response to the question of how anyone who sincerely believes their ideas and values to be true and right can peacefully coexist with people who are in error and who fail to have the correct values. Contemporary liberal toleration, taking up the same problem, has largely rephrased and extended it to political and civil coexistence under conditions of pluralism and in the face of disagreement.

---

[32] I have explored the connection between toleration and justice in A. E. Galeotti, "*Tolérance et justice sociale*," in J. Affichard and J. B. de Foucauld, eds., *Pluralisme et équité* (Paris: Esprit, 1995), pp. 103–19 and also in "Questioni di giustizia e questioni di tolleranza," *Filosofia e questioni pubbliche*, 1, 1995, pp. 64–78.

The answer to the question which classical liberalism poses is to be found in the fundamental equality of human beings, which is the precondition to acknowledging the equal liberty of others and to tolerating the outcomes of their free choice. We tolerate the sin, so to speak, because we accept the sinner. The interpretation of contemporary cases which I have briefly sketched reverses the role of toleration: public toleration of differences is thought of as the premise on the basis of which those who are different can achieve equality of respect. The conflicts engendered by pluralism form the context within which toleration becomes necessary, but these conflicts should not be viewed from above – from a constitutional standpoint – and hence as matters of compatibility.[33] Rather, they should be considered from the point of view of the excluded, as part of the struggle to be recognized as full members of the polity, not despite but because of their differences.

CONCLUSIONS

Summarizing the argument developed so far, the neutralist model of toleration has linked the concept with justice and introduced considerations of fairness, thus avoiding the moralistic tone of the perfectionist model. However, the constitutional structure of the argument makes neutralism insensitive to the problem of social differences, and blind to the related issue of inclusion of members of minorities or oppressed groups. Moreover, the individualistic reduction of pluralism, construing it as if it referred only to individuals' moral and religious views, does not adequately represent the kind of pluralist conflict which is the origin of the contemporary demand for toleration. As a result, the neutralist model suffers from a special paradox which the perfectionist model avoids. On the one hand, the neutralist model proposes liberalism as the political ideal for an open, inclusive, and free society, whose appeal is its tendency to universality and whose basic tenets can in principle be recognized and accepted by people from alien cultures, given the neutrality of liberal political legitimacy. Thus openness and inclusiveness are a prominent part of the liberal outlook and represent crucial commitments to liberal justice. On the other hand, this move towards openness, which actually underlies the generalization of the ideals of toleration and neutrality and

---

[33] The issue of compatibility is not done away with altogether in the conception of toleration as recognition, but is not considered the primary criterion for adjudicating contemporary claims for public toleration of differences. See also chapters 3 and 4.

provides support for their application to the constitutional argument, is combined with a fundamental insensitivity to social differences as marks of collective identity and to the issue of the inclusion, via public recognition, of those who are different in the liberal public arena. The quest for inclusion of "different" collective identities is seen by the neutralist liberal as a breach of public neutrality (either because it entails an intrusion of particular memberships and loyalties into the allegedly neutral sphere of liberal politics, or because it implies a demand for special consideration as opposed to institutional blindness).

As a result, the original liberal promise of openness towards the inclusion of anyone whatever their origin, culture, language, religion, or race, is transformed into a resistance to the acceptance of alien or oppressed groups into full citizenship. The reason given for this unexpected resistance is the alleged threat to the neutral public sphere represented by groups which do not accept the principle of neutral citizenship. In other words, it is an argument for the self-defense of the liberal order. Yet I contend that this argument can be granted only if the liberal state has first made a move toward the admission of all marginalized groups into full citizenship, a move which is required by its promise of openness. Moreover, the fundamental commitment to justice, which, in the neutralist perspective, constitutes the ground for the neutralist conception of toleration, fails in this respect. The neutral public sphere, which, liberalism claims, needs to be strenuously defended against invasion, is in fact already inhabited by particular and partial identities – those of the majority – so the rigorous exclusion of different identities seems straightforwardly unfair. In the face of such inequality it is not enough to respond that perfect equality is difficult to achieve in practice, since there are good reasons, conceptual and logical, to suspect that neutrality can never be absolute.

The result is that toleration, as proposed by the neutralist model, turns out to require extending as far as perfectionism, though the theoretical process that allows one to get to that final point is significantly different from any process standardly recognized by neutralism. Briefly, all differences in the conception of the good, as long as they do not directly undermine the liberal order, are entitled to toleration, and their holders to equal liberty and to equal public treatment, i.e. to public blindness to their differences. This means, in effect, that the majority, i.e. those whose conceptions of the good are consistent with the majoritarian collective identity, are not only accorded toleration of their private creeds and lifestyles, but are also accepted as full citizens and have no need to conceal their collective identity in the public sphere, since that is what constitutes the very "normality" of liberal citizenship; institutional blindness should prevent certain opportunities from being formally open only to them. Minority groups, by contrast, while equally entitled to toleration of their private views and ways of life, cannot be admitted into citizenship to the extent to which they vigorously assert their deviant identities, since the condition of their inclusion is the concealment of their different and particular identity. At the same time, institutional blindness grants them, as it does any other citizen, access to rights and public office independently of their deviant views. The result is an overall distribution of toleration which is very similar to that proposed by the perfectionist model, which reserved full toleration only for views fitting into the hospitable, but not unlimited liberal conception of the good. But it is very likely that the various views that fit into the liberal good are those expressed by groups which are already established within the liberal polity. So, in effect, the recipients of full toleration are those already included. Similarly, in the neutralist model, the established groups are those which are entitled not only to have their views privately tolerated and neutrally treated, but also to have their collective identity "normally" included within liberal politics. Thus in both models, full toleration, in the sense of public recognition and respect, benefits the same people, namely those already included.

The perfectionist model also reserves toleration by default for those differences which are ethically incompatible with the liberal good, but which do not either undermine the liberal order or harm anyone, and for which the cost of repression would be too high. These differences, clearly connected with groups which do not belong to the liberal culture, are actually admitted but only in the private sphere and only as a modus vivendi. The bearers of these differences can therefore be recognized as equal citizens only apart from or despite their differences. The same outcome results from using the neutralist model, though the argument and the moral tone are different: members of non-established groups can freely participate in and reproduce their culture and worship their gods in the private sphere, but can gain access to citizenship only as naked individuals. Finally, both models deny toleration to some differences and their bearers on the basis either of the harm principle or of a self-defense argument.

Some critics of liberalism argue that the two interpretations, under close analytical inspection, amount to the same thing, namely a perfectionist version, which is then contested with arguments drawn from the same neutralist framework.[34] Their position is, in short, that inasmuch as the neutralist approach presupposes a theory of the good, so liberal neutrality is, in fact, only a disguised form of partiality. In other words, neutralist liberalism is criticized as being inconsistent with its own premises. I do not agree with this line of reasoning. On the one hand, as already stressed, neutrality is never, by its very logic, an absolute concept; being neutral about a definite number of alternatives is different, theoretically and morally, from being partial to some. On the other hand, there are many other distinctive theoretical and normative differences between neutralism and perfectionism. My point is a different one: I have argued that there are some theoretical weaknesses which prevent the neutralist model from properly grasping what is at stake in questions of toleration. Hence the normative solution ends up by being very similar to what is put forward by perfectionist liberalism. In perfectionism the solution is sustained by consistent normative premises, while in the case of neutralist liberalism it is inconsistent with normative commitment to justice, openness, and inclusiveness. The conception of toleration I am arguing for proceeds from those commitments and attempts to fill in the gaps and to remedy the inconsistencies in the neutralist model. Whether the result would then be an extensive reinterpretation of liberal theory or a definite breaking down of liberal boundaries escapes my judgment and, in a sense, does not really concern me. The reader is free to make up his or her own mind, from his or her standpoint.

APPENDIX: MORAL CONFLICT

All liberal theories take moral conflict to be one of the essential conditions that make toleration an issue. I maintain, however, that if moral conflicts were the only questions at issue, then toleration would concern no more than (a) individual differences over private choices, i.e. cases to which a solution has already been found within the system of rights which is already built into liberal democratic constitutions; (b) politically trivial instances, confined to the realm of daily interaction; (c) residual cases, typically exemplified by the recurrent discussion over the enforcement of morals[35] – that is, cases which have not yet been resolved, but which

---

[34] This point of view is, for example, argued by Richard Bellamy in "Defining Liberalism."

[35] See the debate between Patrick Devlin, *The Enforcement of Morals* (Oxford: Oxford University Press, 1959) and Herbert Hart, *Law, Liberty and Morality* (Oxford: Oxford University Press, 1962). More recently, the thesis of the enforcement of morals has been argued by Michael Sandel in "Moral

might be considered similar to those in (a). These latter cases, relevant as they may be in some cultural contexts, in my view do not present genuine theoretical challenges to the liberal theory of toleration in that, in principle, they can be satisfactorily resolved within the solid framework of liberal theory.

By contrast, genuine contemporary cases where toleration is at issue, those which provoke wide public controversies and which require political settlement, do not fit into any of these three classes, since, first, their solution is not, by definition, obvious and routinized; second, their relevance is political and clearly exceeds the realm of everyday interaction; and, third, they prove resistant to being treated simply as an extension of arguments for freedom of expression and privacy. That is in fact how they are usually dealt with by liberal theory, but we have just seen how, given their nature, they escape the standard liberal grid. In sum, moral conflicts are not always the initiators of situations in which toleration comes to be an issue. Why then is this the focus of liberal theory? In order to provide an answer, and before putting the question aside, I think it better to understand what is meant by moral conflict, why it is important, if at all, and whether it is of any political consequence.

Moral conflict is primarily a philosophical problem, but it does occasionally have political implications. It includes both first-order conflict between different obligations and among moral principles and values, and second-order conflict among moral codes or systems of moral values.[36] In both cases, it constitutes a genuine issue only if moral pluralism is true;[37] that is to say, only if the conflict of values cannot be accommodated by reference to some overarching principle or unifying procedure, so that the different views are eventually resolved into a unifying order and all moral questions can receive definite answers.[38] If, on

Argument and Liberal Toleration. Abortion and Homosexuality," *California Law Review*, 77, 1989, pp. 521–38. A more nuanced position in favor of partial enforcement of morals is expressed by Gerald Dworkin in "Equal Respect and the Enforcement of Morality," *Social Philosophy and Policy*, 7, 2, 1990, pp. 180–93, which is the response to Ronald Dworkin's radical liberalism ("Do We Have A Right to Pornography?").

[36] On the distinction between first- and second-order conflict, see Susan Wolf, "Two Levels of Pluralism," *Ethics*, 102, 1992, pp. 785–98. Steven Lukes has pointed out four main sources for moral conflict: (1) conflict between moral obligations; (2) conflict between ends, purposes, goals and, in general, values; (3) conflict between conceptions of the good; (4) conflict between moral theories, such as deontology and teleology. The latter, though it is the source of serious philosophical disputes, has little bearing on politics. See Steven Lukes, *Moral Conflict and Politics* (Oxford: Clarendon Press, 1991), pp. 5–9.

[37] This position is argued by Lukes, *Moral Conflict and Politics*, pp. 3–20.

[38] See Lawrence C. Becker, "Places for Pluralism," *Ethics*, 102, 1992 (pp. 707–19), p. 708. Becker emphasizes that what distinguishes moral pluralism from moral plurality is indeterminacy.

the other hand, the plurality of values and moral codes is understood as irreducible, incommensurable, and unadjudicable,[39] for the lack of a unifying principle, a common metric, and a shared criterion for adjudication, respectively, then moral pluralism follows, and moral conflict appears to be impossible to solve by appeal to moral theory. In other words, if moral pluralism is true, moral theory exhibits an intrinsic indeterminacy in facing some moral dilemmas. This fact, however, does not strictly entail either relativism or subjectivism, though it may lead to them.[40] Rather, what moral pluralism primarily entails is a more complex view of the moral world and the acknowledgment of genuine moral dilemmas and, consequently, of moral losses.[41] Though reasons can, and ought to, constrain moral choice, they cannot always univocally determine a decision, either because two moral principles or two obligations pull in opposite directions, or because the boundaries of application of a moral principle are contestable, or because different moral codes suggest different solutions. This last is an evident case of interpersonal conflict, while the first can equally well be a case of intrapersonal conflict.

Contemporary ethical theories, which, by and large, have abandoned the dream of creating uniform moral systems founded objectively on reason, nature, history, or God, have thus to confront the plurality of values and conceptions of the good. Though this does not directly entail the acknowledgment of moral pluralism, many contemporary moral theories have taken moral pluralism seriously. Consequently, they must

---

39 The issue of incommensurability was first stressed by Isaiah Berlin in "Two Concepts of Liberty," in *Four Essays of Liberty* (Oxford: Oxford University Press, 1969), and then taken up by Rawls, *A Theory of Justice*, and Raz, *The Morality of Freedom* and *Ethics and the Public Domain*. Many criticisms have been made of this notion, especially by utilitarians, but a somewhat new strand of criticism has recently been advanced, which argues for the incompatibility between strong incommensurability and liberalism. See John Crowder, "Pluralism and Liberalism," *Political Studies*, 42, 1994, pp. 293–305 and John Gray, "Where Pluralists and Liberals Part Company," *International Journal of Political Studies*, 6, 1999, pp. 17–36.

40 According to Steven Lukes, "ethical relativism is another way of depriving moral conflict of any sense, for the point of relativism is to explain it away by proposing a structure in which apparently conflicting claims are each acceptable in their own place" (*Moral Conflict and Politics*, p. 4), and, likewise, subjectivism aims at the same result, rendering the notion of conflicting claims meaningless. But it is not clear which alternative meta-ethical position Lukes endorses. In this respect, Susan Wolf has a more definite view: she rejects subjectivism and subscribes to a limited form of relativism, based on the notion of "range of acceptable moral codes" derived from rational constraints on the acceptability of moral codes. See Wolf, "Two Levels of Pluralism." This notion comes close to the concept of reasonable pluralism advanced by Rawls in *PL*.

41 This theme has been classically treated by Max Weber, under the well-known notion of "polytheism of values" (see Max Weber, *Science as a Vocation*, and *Politics as a Vocation* in *Selections in Translation*, ed. W. G. Runciman [Cambridge: Cambridge University Press, 1978]). Later, it was brought to the attention of moral philosophy by Berlin, *Four Essays on Liberty*, as an implication of the incommensurability between values.

cope with intractable moral conflict; this is why some have taken a special interest in tolerance. Tolerance is, indeed, one of the typical ways of coping with intractable moral conflict, yet, from the point of view of moral theory, the problem is whether tolerance, in addition to its non-moral merits, can be regarded as a proper moral value.[42] Recently, it has been suggested that accommodation might be a more suitable way of coping with moral conflict than tolerance.[43]

Having settled that moral conflict is a significant moral issue, does this imply that it is also a political issue? And, more precisely, do the political implications of moral conflict engender genuine questions of political toleration? Insofar as moral conflict is not merely an intraper-sonal problem, it definitely does have political implications. But do such implications specifically raise questions of toleration? Only partially, I think, since political toleration can be adopted only when uniformity is unnecessary; personal freedom can then be politically granted to all parties. In that case, however, moral conflict, as a rule, is already solved. The principle of toleration, built into a system of constitutionally pro-tected rights, has historically dealt with it reasonably well, starting with religious convictions and later expanding to include moral beliefs, val-ues, lifestyles, and so on. In this respect, as we have seen, toleration has already yielded a solution to potentially difficult cases involving moral conflict. Moral conflict could therefore be a personal problem, for exam-ple, for someone living in a small conservative community, and practicing a comparatively heterodox morality, but this is hardly a political issue.

However, moral conflict is not confined to such "easy" cases for which toleration, in the form of individual rights, is the obvious and routine solution. It is also relevant to economic decisions about income distri-bution and welfare, in international affairs, in choices of war and peace, and, most prominently, in a wide variety of bioethical contexts, starting with the abortion issue. In such cases, and many others, moral conflict is the source of serious political problems. Yet the underlying conflict is not amenable to solution by simple appeal to political toleration; it needs to be settled by a decision that is binding for all. It may be argued that questions of toleration also require a political decision specifying whether certain practices or behavior can or cannot be tolerated. But

---

[42] See chapter 1.
[43] See Gutmann and Thompson, "Moral Conflict and Political Consensus"; and David B. Wong, "Coping with Moral Conflict and Ambiguity," *Ethics*, 102, 1992, pp. 763–84. A quite different, but most interesting approach to alternative ways of coping with moral conflict can be found in Alan Gibbard, *Wise Choice, Apt Feelings* (Cambridge, Mass.: Harvard University Press, 1990).

when moral conflict becomes a genuine political issue, as in the examples mentioned above, part of the problem is that political authorities cannot resort to toleration for settling the issue, leaving people free to choose for themselves. Uniformity is required, and some measure or policy has to be adopted, and enforced, even on those who morally disagree with it. This is clear in economic policy, where libertarians, like everyone else, must pay taxes for the provision of public goods, including those about which they disagree. This is also evident in foreign policy, where a decision involving military intervention is binding on the whole country (though, in this case, some accommodation for pacifists has been devised, allowing them to apply formally for the status of conscientious objector – measures that do not mean that all those who oppose military intervention are free to boycott the national decision).

It is, however, less clear whether the abortion issue is a question of toleration. Many liberals contend that abortion and other bioethical issues are instances of unadjudicable moral conflict engendering genuine questions of political toleration.[44] But I would argue that this is not correct, and that there are significant differences between abortion and problems of censorship, for example, which mean that the former cannot be fitted into the same framework as the latter. Indeed, a political pro-choice decision cannot be compared with one in favor of freedom of expression for the following reasons. Let us first take the case of censorship. Suppose that on the one side there is the prude who wants *Lady Chatterley's Lover* to be banned,[45] and on the other the liberal who holds that it should not be. Here we have a classic case of contrasting moral opinions concerning what is ultimately an individual private preference. Without even entering into discussion about the specific case, we can conclude that these are exactly the circumstances for which liberal toleration has been repeatedly argued to be the appropriate solution.

In fact, the prohibition of this particular book would be consistent only with a very strong paternalistic state, endorsing a thick conception of the good, which could scarcely be defined as liberal. Liberal perfectionism implies a Millian conception of the good, where the values of

[44] This is the position maintained by Nagel in "Moral Conflict and Political Legitimacy," where he sees the abortion issue as a typical case of deep moral disagreement which must be faced by the highest level of impartiality, in conditions of public neutrality. Not surprisingly, this view is rejected both by the critics of liberal neutrality and by anti-abortion activists.

[45] I refer to Lady Chatterley because this book was used as an example by Amartya Sen in order to discuss what has become known as the Lady Chatterley paradox, that is, the problem of the logical impossibility of consistent satisfaction of external preferences. See Amartya Sen, "Liberty and Social Choice," *Journal of Philosophy*, 80, 1, 1983, pp. 5–28.

self-development and autonomous individuality are at the forefront, and freedom of the press is acknowledged as the main resource for promoting the liberal good. Therefore, for a liberal perfectionist, whether the content of the book is regarded as morally good or bad, useful or harmful, it is a matter of private choice and preference that the liberal state ought to protect. The kind of harm which reading *Lady Chatterley's Lover* is supposed to produce in some people is certainly not physical. At this point, any alleged harm cannot be greater than the general harm that society as a whole would suffer if freedom of expression is silenced. A neutralist can argue even more straightforwardly for the toleration of such a book by claiming that the state ought to be neutral regarding individual moral views, whatever their content, and ought not to take sides on what is morally good for people. In conclusion, censorship cannot in this case be justified by any publicly recognizable reason.

So why cannot similar arguments apply to the abortion issue? Where does the crucial difference lie? The fact is that the pro-life position contends that abortion involves the killing of an innocent (though not yet independent) human life.[46] Given this contention, the abortion issue cannot be described as a case of morally irreducible differences concerning ultimately private choices – i.e. the typical argument adopted for mainstream toleration cases – because the killing involved in the anti-abortion claim makes it a public issue. While the liberal state grants its citizens the right to hold any moral view they wish, it does not allow them to kill other human beings as a result of a given moral position. The protection of life is the most basic civil right and, consequently, its prohibition is a fundamental imperative – and not only in liberal society – and, furthermore, it constitutes the strongest limit to toleration. On this very general point there is general agreement throughout the liberal tradition, between perfectionists and neutralists. Following from this, a pro-choice public position cannot simply be defended on the grounds of liberal neutrality, since the state cannot easily be neutral about a supposed killing, nor can such a position be held in the name of individual experiment, because this value cannot have priority over that of the protection of human life. In other words, since one position presents abortion as a form of killing, it goes beyond the usual definition of circumstances for toleration. Hence,

---

[46] On the abortion issue there is a very wide literature. Just as examples, I recall some widely known essays on both sides: Judith Jarvis Thompson, "A Defense of Abortion," *Philosophy and Public Affairs*, 1, 1971, pp. 47–66; Michael Tooley, "Abortion and Infanticide," *Philosophy and Public Affairs*, 2, 1972, pp. 37–65; Richard Hare, "Abortion and the Golden Rule," *Philosophy and Public Affairs*, 4, 1975, pp. 201–22; R. Dworkin, *Life's Dominion: An Argument about Abortion, Euthanasia and Individual Freedom* (New York: Knopf, 1993).

arguing for abortion on the grounds that the state should not interfere in conflicts between ultimate values, but should leave people free to make up their own minds and act accordingly, is a very weak defense. A case for permitting abortion cannot rest exclusively on principles of political toleration; abortion cannot be justified simply by the principle of toleration, just as toleration cannot be used to justify murder or rape. Therefore a pro-choice position cannot dispense with assessing the nature of the case and taking sides – at the minimum it must commit itself to the claim that the question of whether abortion involves taking a human life is so controversial and disputable that it is too weak to give the pro-life position the force and support it would need to override the pro-choice arguments. Finally, to permit abortion is not simply to tolerate it, but also to enforce it on those who disagree with it: on the father of the foetus, on the parents of the under-age girl, on the public hospitals where it is performed (at least in countries where there is a national health system, though usually a right to conscientious objection is recognized for doctors and nurses). In sum, for abortion to be legalized, the state must decide that the pro-life argument is not finally proved, otherwise abortion should be prohibited. On the other hand, the state cannot decide to "tolerate" abortion on the mere grounds of neutrality, because that would imply too blunt a dismissal of the pro-life claim. The same line of argument holds for other bioethical issues, such as euthanasia, control of reproductive technologies, research on embryos, etc. All these controversial issues need to be legally settled in a way that is binding for everyone in the political community. By contrast, in cases of moral differences where toleration is the obviously standard solution, the state need not become involved in individual beliefs and values: these are simply defined as pertaining to the realm of the individual's preference and choice.

In conclusion, cases of moral conflict which have significant political implications and constitute genuine issues are not cases for toleration, but require the implementation of political measures which will be enforced even on those who disagree with them morally. Moral conflict which is amenable to resolution through toleration, on the other hand, constitutes, by and large, a problem which has already been solved in liberal democracy. Therefore, assuming that moral conflict is the major problem behind genuine questions of toleration is definitely misleading not only for understanding what is properly at stake in genuine cases of toleration, but also for grasping the nature of politically relevant cases of moral conflict.

3

Toleration reconsidered

CONDITIONS FOR TOLERATION

Contemporary non-trivial cases that raise issues of toleration typically involve situations in which members of a new minority exhibit their differences in some public–political space – differences that are regarded by the cultural majority as unfamiliar and strange, often outrageously excessive, and potentially threatening to the standards of proper behavior and civility of that society. The public visibility of these differences produces a general feeling of uneasiness among the majority, some of whom may also hold political office. Such uneasiness usually occurs when the differences show themselves to be incompatible with liberal principles, demonstrating a lack of shared moral values, or when they appear to pose a potential danger to the liberal order as a whole. Based on these arguments, the need to limit public toleration of cultural differences is a view which comes to be strongly and consistently held among sectors of the majority and the political class, cutting across the traditional left–right cleavage and joining conservatives with liberals and traditional leftists, both groups concerned about what they see as the breakdown of universalism.[1] On the opposite side of the coin, representatives of minorities advocate the public acceptance of their differences as the symbolic recognition of the legitimacy of their public presence.

I have argued that to see these issues as the product of a clash between religious, moral, and cultural differences, as liberal theory does, is to adopt not merely a limited, but also a misleading view. Although it might appear the simplest way to approach the matter, it actually makes it difficult to grasp what is really at stake, and is no help in reaching a fair solution that is acceptable to all parties involved. I do not deny that

---

[1] This process is well described by Geoff Dench in *Minorities in the Open Society: Prisoners of Ambivalence* (London: Routledge and Kegan Paul, 1986). For an example of liberals' worries about minorities' assertion of their cultural identity, see Arthur Schlesinger Jr., *The Disuniting of America* (New York: Norton, 1991).

cultural differences may sometimes pose problems of ethical and legal incompatibility (the typical example being cliterodectomy), nor that fundamentalism is widespread among Islamic immigrants and may nurture terrorism (as has happened in France); yet I hold that, as a rule, neither incompatibility nor political self-defense are sufficient justification for stopping public toleration of differences, with some clear exceptions (such as the two just mentioned). In what sense, for example, is the public presence of gays ethically incompatible with liberal principles? And why are Islamic symbols immediately associated with fundamentalism, hence with intolerance and terrorism, while there is no such association between Christian symbols and the activities of the Ku Klux Klan or pro-life terrorism? In fact, the argument for limiting toleration which rests on the interpretation of the issue as a case of religious, moral, or ideological incompatibility will not stand up to close inspection.

The source of genuine issues of toleration is pluralism, understood as the coexistence within the same society of a plurality of groups and cultures with unequal social standing.[2] Such pluralism, which, I have argued, is irreducible to ethical and religious diversity, leads to a variety of potential and actual conflicts: conflicts of interest over issues of distribution, which do not directly concern questions of toleration; ideological conflicts; and, especially, identity conflicts.[3] I hold that non-trivial contemporary questions of toleration are basically made up of conflicts concerning the assertion and the recognition of (usually ascriptive) collective identities linked to the excluded, marginalized or invisible groups inhabiting contemporary democracies. Ideological and moral disagreement is also present, and reinforces the identity conflict, allowing us to single out and identify the issue as pertinent to toleration, according to the traditional definition of the problem, but it is neither the primary nor the salient issue.

If the salient conflict generally concerns ascriptive collective identities, this makes groups the relevant analytical unit for properly understanding the circumstances in which issues about toleration arise. This is the case notwithstanding the strong liberal preference for individuals as the main or even exclusive analytical category.[4] If no groups were significantly

---

[2] The distinction between various types of pluralism is clarified by Anne Phillips, *Democracy and Difference* (Cambridge: Polity Press, 1993).

[3] This typology of conflicts is outlined by Pizzorno, *Le radici della politica assoluta*, pp. 195–200.

[4] For liberal thinking, leaving groups aside is seen as an advantage, since it allows a neater theoretical analysis which can more easily fit into the individualistic framework of liberalism and into the

involved in questions of toleration,[5] the recourse to the argument of the state's self-defense would be inexplicable. The threat to the liberal order, to its persistence and flourishing, cannot possibly come from an individual's action. Individuals' deviant behavior does not raise problems of political toleration: why should the state take any interest in the dandy's behavior, which can easily be accepted as a curiosity, or marginalized, or even repressed without much fuss or public attention? But, if the state has no interest in checking the sort of individual behavior which, generally speaking, can be accommodated in the social context, albeit often at high personal cost, then why should it take any interest in the headscarves worn by some girls – to return to the already mentioned *affaire du foulard*? The liberal purist can answer that in the case of Muslim girls a whole conception of the good is concerned – indeed, to be precise, an unfamilar religious faith, which is irreducible to the most basic liberal values and principles – while in the case of the dandy a mere difference in taste is involved. But this reasoning does not hold: for the dandy, taste is a fundamental value, denoting a lifestyle and a world-view, so that, in effect, there is no significant difference between the dandy and the three Muslim girls. At this point, however, it can be said that the dandy's conception of the good, even if ultimately it clashes with religious and conformist moralities, is, nevertheless, politically innocuous, while the religion held by the Muslim girls is fundamentally anti-liberal and thus potentially dangerous. But here is exactly my point: the supposed threat represented by the Islamic creed can be perceived as such only because Islam is not a conception of the good held by a few isolated or casually related individuals. A belief is dangerous only so long as it can direct action, but the action of a single or of a few unconnected individuals does not threaten the social and political order. In order for a belief to become and to be perceived as dangerous, there must be some group willing to act on it. So, neither the headscarf per se nor the *chador* as a symbol of an illiberal religion are reasons why this case became such a potentially volatile issue; rather, it stemmed from the Muslim community which stood behind the girls' actions, a community which, rightly or wrongly, is perceived as posing a threat to western liberal democracy. By the same token, if *ex hypothesi* dandyism were to become

---

universal language of rights (see my "Individualismo metodologico e liberalismo," *Biblioteca della libertà*, 96, 1987, pp. 27–47). In general, the category of individual is more open to the process of abstraction and universalization than that of the group, whose very definition is controversial.

[5] Bernard Crick acknowledges the crucial analytical relevance of groups in questions of toleration, but he does not elaborate on this point. See "Toleration and Tolerance in Theory and Practice."

the unifying creed of a large and organized social group, the perception of it as socially innocuous could rapidly change. For a group to be seen to pose a threat, its supposedly illiberal culture certainly plays a role, but is not in itself enough. In such cases the non-liberal nature of a group is most likely the reason why it is perceived to be "different" rather than a direct cause of social conflict. A community whose culture, language, and religion are easily assimilated into the dominant tradition simply ceases to be a distinct unit within the wider society. Therefore it is part of the definition of a distinct social group that it is not readily assimilated. The salient fact behind the *foulard* case, and that which marks it out from the extravagant clothing of the dandy, is the widespread presence of Muslim groups throughout western societies. If we are to understand why certain differences are the source of genuine questions of political toleration, the group dimension should be regarded as fundamental.

If the collective dimension is crucial, we still have to analyze which differences count, under what circumstances, and how.[6] First, not all group differences give rise to questions of toleration: there are differences of interest which can engender harsh conflicts, but which do not result in problems of toleration. Indeed, it is commonly held that conflicts of interest can and must be adjudicated. How this should be done is a hotly contested matter, but adjudication is in principle available, given that conflicts of interest are always negotiable and open to discussion, making it possible to compensate for losses. By contrast, questions of toleration cannot be settled simply by paying off one of the parties, or by any easy compensatory measure. The proposed solution must be accepted, insofar as it is publicly justifiable, as fair, just, or reasonable. Distributive justice, rather than toleration, can be applied to cases concerning different and contrasting interests – though often the issues involved are inextricably intertwined, and, in my reading, toleration is grounded on reasons that derive from social (but not distributive) justice. Accordingly, interest groups do not fit into the category of groups for which toleration is an appropriate model.

So what differences between which groups constitute the circumstances in which toleration is called for? In general, toleration is needed when certain groups are "different" in ways which are disliked by the majority in a society. First, the groups in question have to be genuinely disliked – a difference which is seen as a pleasant change, far from creating

---

[6] See my "La questione della tolleranza," *Working Papers* (Politeia, Milan: Bibliotechne, 1990), pp. 15ff.

a case for toleration, is likely to be readily accepted and well received. Second, they have to be disliked by the majority, by people and groups whose characteristics, customs, and ways of life are traditionally settled and dominant in that society; it is irrelevant whether or not this feeling is reciprocated by the minority group in question. As already noted, the very concept of toleration entails asymmetrical power relations between the potential tolerator and the potential tolerated.[7] If toleration is defined as the suspension to exercise the power to hinder or interfere with any given behavior or practice, then toleration is appropriate only when a group or groups in a position of relative power vis-à-vis some "different" group also dislikes the members of that deviant group. Otherwise, acquiescence, not toleration, best describes the situation. This also explains why the dislike of a minority for the behavior of the majority has never given rise to any question of toleration.[8] It is the cultural, ethnic, linguistic, and religious majority of a given society which is in fact in command of the standards of that society, and which defines the status quo.

Any aspects of the powerless group, which I will call the "minority" in a broad sense,[9] might be defined by the majority as different and become a collective mark of identity: they may be physical or cultural traits, exclusive to the group or not, and they may or may not be acknowledged by the members of the group in question as their own. What is relevant is not the actual content of the difference, but the fact that, whether or not its nature is ascriptive (e.g. race and ethnicity) or elective (e.g. culture and morality), it is construed as if it were ascriptive, i.e. as a fixed characteristic of the group, which readily identifies and marks it off from other people. Therefore, even if an individual member is able to reject these attributes, it is difficult to break free from them entirely, since he or she remains socially identified with them.[10] In this respect, incidentally, I hold that the reduction of social differences to differences in the conception of the good, i.e. to an elective element, is deeply misleading: indeed for

---

[7] See chapter 1.

[8] Think, for example, of the picture of the Hassidic communities in Poland provided by Isaac B. Singer's novels: there was a clear feeling of dislike of Gentiles' habits and practices, along with an obvious mistrust and fear of their hostility. However, such negative feelings could not be acted upon nor taken outside the community.

[9] The concept of "minority" stands for a social group which is comparatively small in size and in a disadvantaged social position within the larger society. Thus, we do not use the term for the ruling elite, although it is sometimes used to describe women, even though they make up half the population. Disadvantage and oppression seem to represent the crucial qualifications for a group to be defined as a minority. I will use the term in a broad sense, to cover all social groups which are defined as "different" from "normal" people. For a more precise definition, see Sigler, *Minority Rights*, p. 5. Here, also, a clear distinction between minority and interest groups is drawn.

[10] In this respect, see Young, *Justice and the Politics of Difference*, p. 59.

members of minority groups, elective aspects of their collective identity tend to work as ascriptive.[11]

Understanding the circumstances in which the need for toleration arises as those in which there is a contest between majorities and minorities allows us to take into account the crucial aspects of power asymmetries implied in the concept of toleration, aspects overlooked by the neutralist model and, moreover, it offers a vantage point from which we can provide a distinctive explanation of dislike and hostility towards social differences. In fact, apart from psychological or idiosyncratic motives and moral or ideological disagreement, more structural reasons for dislike must be pointed out. These are linked to the respective social standing, power, and capabilities of majorities and minorities. In this respect the crucial aspect of power that is enjoyed by the social groups which constitute the society's majority is the power to define the characteristics, physical traits, habits, practices, and beliefs of other groups as deviant compared to their own, which they assume, implicitly, to be normal. Minority groups may share a symmetrical perception, but they are in a social position from which it is impossible to assert their characteristics as normal outside their own group and throughout society at large. Defining something as "different" does not directly imply any negative connotation: "different" and "normal" can simply be descriptive qualifications, ways of relating and marking distinct objects for cognitive and practical purposes. Since the "different" is by definition what diverges from "the normal" the "different" shares the semantic ambiguity of "normal," which vascillates between a descriptive and a normative use.[12] Once social groups are seen to act in ways that depart from

---

[11] In a recent paper, Iris Young has modified her position on social differences, drawing a clear distinction between differences and group identity. While social differences are presented as perspectival views corresponding to inequalities, hierarchical relations, domination, and exclusion among groups, in her opinion there is no such thing as group identity because the existence of such an identity would imply an essentialist notion of differences. I do not think that group identity corresponds to the essential, generally ascriptive, characteristics of the group which all members share and acknowledge as their identity, as she seems to imply. I think that group identity, socially constructed on differential traits of groups, is generally imposed on the powerless group from outside, and that the members of the group cannot detach themselves from this definition at will; individual members are recognized, identified, and marked by it, quite independently of whether or not they acknowledge such an identity as their own. See Iris M. Young, "Differences as a Resource for Democratic Communication," forthcoming in her *Democracy and Deliberation* (Cambridge, Mass.: MIT Press).

[12] In analyzing phenomena of "difference," I prefer to use expressions involving reference to "exclusion" rather than the notion of cultural domination, which is more common in the literature on minorities, differences, and groups (see particularly Frazer, "From Redistribution to Recognition"). I prefer, in fact, to emphasize the obstacles to fair access in the larger society, than the imposition of the majority's culture. The point is that if the culture of the majority could be

recognized social standards, a feeling of dislike or distaste can become attached to them, and it becomes easier to justify a description of them as abnormal. Even if they are not directly disliked, they still mark their bearers out as "others," leading to a sense of "them versus us," and to a belief that they are "alien" to the rules, standards, and values of society.[13] In sum, the distinction between what is normal and what is different, which only the majority can draw in a socially effective way, although not in itself the source of dislike of minority groups, does prevent differences from being assimilated into the social norm and, furthermore, enables the majority to articulate a sense of dislike, thus reinforcing and sustaining the differences and, as a result, excluding members of minority groups from full membership of society.

Dislike, leading to an intolerant and hostile attitude, is often traced to the intrinsically conflictual nature of differences, which are thought of as being incompatible on various grounds: logical, moral, or ideological. These can all certainly be motives for disliking other groups; yet, as such, they are as available to majority as to minority groups. Moreover, such reciprocal feelings of dislike do not prevent the development of forms of social accommodation. These are usually costly and less than satisfactory for the minority, but they do nevertheless establish a modus vivendi which stops short of toleration. There is, however, one ground for dislike which is open only to majorities and which is usually overlooked in discussions of toleration, but which, to my mind, plays a major role in the build-up of hostility between different social groups, even amongst enlightened sectors of the majority. The source of such dislike lies in the perception of the "different" social group as unduly upsetting traditional and customary ways of life and thinking. What backs this feeling up are not so much the emotional and sentimental links with one's roots and tradition (though such feelings may be present too), but the resistance to changing one's habits, conventions, and ways of thinking. This resistance is often articulated as an unwillingness to modify what has always been there, since it has already been tried and shown to be good. The fact that certain rules, conventions, customs, etc. have been there for a long time does not make them better or superior in any sense, but it does gives them a salience: for the majority, they represent solutions that have already

effectively and successfully imposed, the minority would soon cease to be distinguishable from the majority, as has happened with many linguistic groups in history.

[13] Iris Young calls this process "cultural imperialism" (see *Justice and the Politics of Difference*, pp. 58–61), but this notion can easily be associated with some conspiracy theory, which I would rather avoid, since the process is clearly unintentional.

been found to problems of social coordination, and constitute the network that sustains stable and reliable expectations, and successful devices
for coping with the uncertainty of an interdependent social world and
with the limits of knowledge and rationality.[14] In this respect, for agents
within a community, resorting to conventions and traditional rules is the
obvious way of coping successfully with most social intercourse, though
it is not necessarily based on rational thought or calculation. But that is
exactly what makes tradition an optimal resource for any rational agent:
one can rely on it without thinking. By contrast, confronting cultural
differences implies questioning traditional solutions which have so far
kept things running reasonably smoothly, saving time and intellectual
energy; confrontation may make it necessary to revise expectations and
open up new issues. For example, questioning whether Sunday should
be a holiday or whether Christmas is the best time for a winter break
comes to be seen by the majority as an unnecessary complication of or-
dinary social life and a waste of energy, diverting attention from other
more important issues. The fact is, obviously, that traditional solutions to
problems of social coordination are usually exclusive to majority groups
and tend to keep minorities at the margin of social life. Seen in this light,
questioning tradition may be perfectly justified from the viewpoint of
social justice. And, for reasons of fairness, it is up to those who are disadvantaged by traditions and conventions to decide whether and when to
question them. Still, if we consider the specific salience of conventions,[15]
traditional rules, and customs in achieving social coordination, we find
a less idiosyncratic or ideological explanation of the majority's dislike of
social differences than we might expect. It also helps to clarify an intrinsic

---

[14] The crucial role of conventions and spontaneous rules as guidelines for social coordination is the
main theme of Friedrich Hayek's social philosophy. See F. A. Hayek, *Individualism and Economic
Order* (London and Chicago: Routledge and Chicago University Press, 1948); F. A. Hayek, *The
Counter-Revolution of Science* (Glencoe, Ill.: The Free Press, 1952); F. A. Hayek, *Law, Legislation and
Liberty* (London: Routledge, 1982). For a critical appraisal of Hayek's conceptions of spontaneous
rules and tradition, see A. E. Galeotti, "Individualism, Social Rules, and Tradition," *Political
Theory*, 15, 1987, pp. 163–81. For a reconstruction of the spontaneous origin of rules and order in
his theory, see A. E. Galeotti, "L'insorgenza delle regole e dell'ordine nella teoria sociale di F. A.
Hayek," *Working Papers* (Politeia, Milan: Bibliotechne, 1987).

[15] The concept of salience in connection with the coordination problem and with the emergence of
stable expectations and conventions was introduced by Thomas Schelling, *The Strategy of Conflict*
(Cambridge, Mass.: Harvard University Press, 1960), and then spelled out by David Lewis,
Convention (Cambridge, Mass.: Harvard University Press, 1969). In an interdependent context,
when the outcome of my action largely depends on others' actions, and there is limited knowledge
of others' intentions, social coordination is eventually brought about by means of the common
reference to the most obvious, visible, and prominent characteristic, which represents the salient
element of the situation. Once conventions, rules, and tradition are defined, they become specially
salient for helping social coordination.

difficulty in the solution of questions of toleration, namely the difficulty for society as a whole of finding a new network of conventions that suits anyone from any group.

Yet, for a dislike of differences to become manifest and socially significant, another condition must apply: the minority group must be perceived by the majority as an actual threat to the traditional social and political order. In other words, although there are various possible reasons, including moral and ideological ones, for the majority to dislike the minority, resentment is likely to become widespread even in highly enlightened sections of the majority when it is thought that the minority might possibly upset traditions and undermine the stability of the social and political order. And this happens either because the numerical ratio between the size of the majority and minority group changes to the advantage of the minority group,[16] or because the power balance is modified in favor of the latter.[17] Under these circumstances, when the minority, rightly or wrongly, comes to be perceived as powerful enough to pose a real threat to customary social life, even the less prejudiced section of the majority may experience resentment against being unsettled in its own traditional way of life. By contrast, when the minority group is small or powerless, the feeling of dislike for its differences may be scattered among the members of the majority, but because of its perceived social irrelevance the group is usually left alone. Episodes of intolerance and abuse may happen without being resisted; they may simply be endured by the frightened and powerless minority members. Under these circumstances, toleration is not an issue. In order to become so, it is not enough that the group becomes larger and stronger; it must also begin to resist intolerance and abuse, and put forward claims for a different public treatment.[18]

In conclusion, the argument I have developed so far reconceptualizes the circumstances of genuine cases of toleration as follows: the issue of toleration develops (a) around a contest between majorities and minorities, coexisting in a given society; (b) over traits, behavior, beliefs, and practices of minority groups, labeled as different and disliked by the majority; (c) when the minority group is perceived as posing a threat to the traditional order and the customary life of that society; and (d) when

---

[16] The group dimension is crucial for the group to be perceived as a threat. See Gerald Fitt, "Toleration in Northen Ireland," in Edwards and Mendus, *On Toleration*, and, at a more theoretical level, see Raymond Boudon, *Effects pervers et ordre social* (Paris: Presses Universitaires de France, 1977).

[17] See Dench, *Minorities in the Open Society*.

[18] See Crick, "Toleration and Tolerance in Theory and Practice."

it is willing to resist intolerance, and to claim public toleration for its
differences.

The presence in society of threatening minority groups whose differences
are not liked by the majority can be dealt with without resort to toleration, but with straightforward repression. It is only when repression is
excluded, on pragmatic or ethical grounds or both, that toleration can be
envisaged as a possible solution in a hostile stand-off between majority
and minority. This was the case during the religious wars which followed
the Reformation: toleration was proposed as a way out of a disruptive
and seemingly endless war when it became evident that no side was
strong enough to win definitively. It was the military force of some of the
religious groups involved which led to the idea of a non-military settlement and which opened the way to toleration as the solution. In other
words, in order for repression to be ruled out on pragmatic grounds, the
minority group must not only be willing, but also strong enough to resist
it. The problem for the Muslims in Bosnia has been that they were few
and militarily weak. This made repression a viable option for the Serbs,
and the Muslims' call for a multiethnic Bosnia, appealing to the principle
of toleration, became totally irrelevant.

Even if the possibility of repression is de facto available, it may be
excluded on ethical grounds. This is normally the case in a liberal democratic state, where any recourse to coercion needs to be publicly justified,
and where the commitment to toleration is inscribed in the constitution.
In fact, it is only when repression is excluded on ethical as well as pragmatic grounds that toleration can become a widely shared value, rather
than an ad hoc policy, always open to revision if it becomes inconvenient.
And for toleration to become the preferred alternative, two conceptual
conditions are required. The first is that the "others" be considered equal
in some respect with the majority. Viewing others as human beings on
an equal footing, all as God's children or rational beings, rather than
as aliens, barbarians, or *Untermenschen*, leads to their being considered
at least as potential moral partners, and hence to regarding their oppression as morally wrong.[19] Yet once the "others" are acknowledged as
potentially equal, one possibility is then to force them to become "really"
equal, for example, by making them endorse the "right" religion, culture, and morals. In this sense, persecution can be seen as the first step
towards toleration. In the sixteenth and seventeenth centuries the aim of

---

[19] See Gibbard, "Communities of Judgment," in *Wise Choices, Apt Feelings*, pp. 235–45.

all sides involved in the religious wars was to save Christians from their own mistakes and to put them back on the right track. However, the same kind of concern was not shown towards the non-Christians, the Muslims and the Jews, who were usually left more or less alone, though they were discriminated against and at times targeted for expulsion or physical suppression.[20] The relative tolerance that the non-Christians enjoyed during the Middle Ages was, in my interpretation, worse, from a moral viewpoint, than the persecution of Protestants: it was in fact grounded not on respect, but on a lack of recognition of or concern for the equal worth of non-Christian groups.

So although some notion of equality across groups is a necessary condition for toleration to emerge as the properly ethical solution of a conflict, it is not sufficient for ruling out repression as definitely wrong. A second conceptual condition is required, namely it must be the case that repression is considered to be politically unacceptable and morally wrong, unless used by the political authority for preventing or punishing violence and harm to third parties or the general public.[21] In fact, in the sixteenth century the first arguments in favor of toleration originated from the rejection of persecution as a reasonable and moral way of dealing with theological deviance and mistakes.

To summarize: the need for toleration arises in situations characterized by contests, broadly speaking, between majorities and minorities concerning the latters' differences which are disliked by majorities and which cause those who are different to be offended, abused, or marginalized – in a word, excluded. The stand-off emerges when the minority group, perceived as threatening, but also prepared and willing to resist intolerance, starts asserting its collective identity in public. Then, if straightforward repression is ruled out, for either pragmatic or ethical reasons, toleration might follow. When toleration already exists in the private sphere, as is the case in liberal democracies, then it can also be claimed in the public domain.

TOLERATION IN PUBLIC: WHAT IS AT STAKE?

So far we have seen how social differences are construed by the majority, how dislike comes to be directed at those who are different, and under

[20] John Locke in fact pointed out the paradoxical fact that religious persecution was aimed at Christian groups, while Jews and Muslims were relatively tolerated. *A Letter Concerning Toleration*, p. 233.
[21] Note that repression is not rejected on the grounds of a skeptical position about the truth, but because it is ineffective in inducing the true faith.

what conditions a need for toleration arises. In contemporary democracy, the latter already exists, as non-interference in the private sphere, so today's issues of toleration mostly concern the public arena. In order to assess whether the quest for public toleration is justified and sensible, we have to understand the reasons behind it.

I argue that the minorities' aim is to change their position as social pariahs by fighting against the public exclusion of their identity, which prevents them from being full members in the polity. But how can toleration help? Some reflections on the conception of inclusion are in order here.

The first interpretation of inclusion corresponds to the standard liberal view – namely, the extension of equal rights and opportunities to individuals who, for various reasons, have so far been deprived of them. But this is not the kind of inclusion that is especially relevant for contemporary claims of toleration, because, to start with, it is generally already granted (with the exception of immigrants for whom, in any case, legal procedures for formal inclusion already exist).

There is, however, a more encompassing conception of inclusion, one which takes into account and emphasizes the aspects of dignity, respect, and worth which allegedly accompany citizenship – i.e. those very elements which confer the "status" of citizenship, of full and active membership of the polity. Although historically and logically it may seem that the idea of universal citizenship should oppose any notion of status[22] and eschew the particularism that is implied by the concept of differential membership,[23] the fact that citizenship constitutes a status is not only a widespread subjective perception, but can also be explained in theoretical terms. Amartya Sen made the distinction between acquisitions (goods, resources, and opportunities) and capabilities,[24] by means of which an agent can actually make use of his or her acquisitions, and hence function more or less efficiently. Adopting this distinction, citizenship can be conceived as the acquisition of a legal entitlement to certain rights, and as the capability to make use of those rights as resources and opportunities, making it possible to function more or less effectively as a citizen. The problem, however, lies in the fact that possessing the necessary rights – i.e. being formally included in citizenship – does not automatically entail the ability to enjoy fully the status of citizen, or to function as a full member in the polity. Legal inclusion coupled with a public disdain for those who are different, and with persistant social

[22] See Shklar, *American Citizenship*.   [23] See Zincone, *Da Sudditi a cittadini*.
[24] Sen, "Rights and Capabilities."

discrimination, have so far failed to ensure equal respect and equal dignity to members of formerly excluded groups.

Legal inclusion in fact implies the admission into citizenship of individuals, whatever their origin, membership, or ethnic, cultural, or sexual identity. But the disregard of differences (i.e. public blindness), conceived as an anti-discriminatory provision, exhibits perverse effects for members of minority groups, because their membership and collective identity cannot be dismissed at will. Their identity cannot be equated with that deriving from interest groups or voluntary associations whose members come together for specific purposes but who bear no specific identification with the group beyond that temporary and contingent common effort and, in general, beyond their choice. By contrast, minority groups do not come together ad hoc and their members have not joined voluntarily. As mentioned already, given the social construction of differences as ascriptive marks of the minority group, the individual member is, so to speak, forced into his or her collective identity, and has very little room for personal identification. To be included in the polity as an individual, independently of any group identity, implies that inclusion is not granted to individuals as members of minority groups. But, on the one hand, such membership is not contingent, nor is it simply a matter of choice; it is a given social identity, rarely innocent, often encapsulating an individual against his/her will. On the other hand, the intolerance, discrimination, and invisibility[25] experienced by the members of minority groups are not simply individual misfortunes, but are intrinsically attached to their membership and collective identity. The public disregard of such identity, then, while granting equal dignity and rights as abstract individuals, does not fight their exclusion in the proper way. The latter derives from their "different" collective identity which condemns them to minority status. Bracketing that identity in public treatments does not lift the attached stigma nor erase the minority status, but, implicitly, sustains the public non-acceptability of that identity. Individual legal inclusion, under these circumstances, means admission of the single individual despite his or her collective identity, a fragile admission which is always undermined by the majority's negative perception of the group from which the individual cannot really be detached at will. The public bracketing of social differences and collective identities, far from canceling the burden of socially despised membership, actually reinforces the feeling of humiliation and

---

[25] Invisibility seems a paradoxical condition for people marked by differences as "others" (see Young, *Justice and the Politics of Difference*, p. 59), but invisibility is linked to the lack of consideration of different people as full and proper citizens.

shame by keeping the different identities publicly invisible and socially marginal.

In recent decades, liberal politics, under pressure from more assertive minorities, has attempted to accommodate differences and to offset their burden by devising special policies, such as the highly controversial affirmative action programs. But, despite such attempts, the rationale behind this change in the liberal attitude is basically that of freeing individuals from the disadvantages and burdens associated with a different identity, and providing them with equal opportunities, independently of group membership. In other words, social differences have received public consideration only insofar as they can be viewed as disadvantages, to be compensated for as a redress for past discrimination. Dealing with the problem in this way, however, suggests a condescending or even patronizing attitude towards minority groups, rather than real respect and consideration.[26] Moreover, as we have mentioned above, the problem for the member of a minority group is not simply a lack of opportunities, but the inability to make efficient use of those opportunities they have. And the latter is intrinsically linked to the negative social perception and the public exclusion of them as "different." Being marked by such an identity, socially despised and publicly invisible, usually leads to an incapacity to function as a "normal" social agent and as a full citizen.

In sum, the strategy of individual inclusion, which is what liberal democracy actually offers to minority members, even when it is supplemented by affirmative action policies, implicitly requires the minority member to forge and to exhibit a social identity which is independent of those characteristics, traits, and behavior which are usually associated with his or her group and which generally have a negative connotation. But the fact is that such disentanglement is not easily done, given the constant social identification of minority members with their group; moreover, it can never be successfully achieved. No one can feel at ease and retain self-esteem and self-respect if he or she is socially accepted despite being a woman, a black, an Arab, a gay, since such acceptance would amount to denial of significant components or elements of one's (personal) identity. The social pressure to disguise oneself and to act as a white, a macho, or an "Anglo" (a WASP) in order to achieve a condescending and fragile acceptance is humiliating and an impediment to

---

[26] As has been pointed out by the many critics of affirmative action policies (who, however, have no good reason to be in favor of public blindness).

the development of a healthy, autonomous, and self-reliant personality (such as the liberal citizen ideally should have).

The public recognition of differences is meant to reverse these unacceptable consequences: if formal individual inclusion does not eventually produce a comprehensive inclusion of group members, and if what makes individual inclusion an impossible dream for most minorities is the dislike and suspicion attached to their particular identity, leading to public invisibility, then the public recognition of this identity, purified of its negative connotations, appears to constitute the premise for minority members to feel accepted and respected for what they actually are. Adam Smith pointed out that one of the most relevant conditions of personal well-being, beside the possession of material goods, is the lack of shame in one's appearance in public (a condition which, in his opinion, in eighteenth-century Britain corresponded to the possession of a pair of leather shoes).[27] This condition, recently revisited by Amartya Sen and proposed as crucial for any decent life,[28] cannot be met if one's collective identity is despised and stigmatized, and is denied public legitimacy.

Given that the social stigma attached to certain differences is sustained and reinforced by their exclusion from the public arena, toleration of them is claimed as a form of and a first step toward a public recognition of different identities. This can indeed lead to inclusion, if it is understood as a symbolic public gesture implying the public acceptance of social differences.

TOLERATION AS RECOGNITION

Questions of toleration erupt when minority members refuse to keep their differences quietly within the private sphere, where they are confined and accepted, but decide instead to display them. Asserting one's differences in public in a provocative way, breaking institutional practices and customary habits, is viewed as a form of trespass on public neutrality – even under the minimal interpretation of toleration which excludes consideration of difference as the grounds for differential public treatment. The actual point of contention may range from whether blacks can use public transport and services alongside whites, to whether women and homosexuals can join the army, or whether Islamic students

---

[27] Adam Smith, *An Inquiry into the Nature and Causes of the Wealth of Nations* [1776], 2 vols. (London: Everyman's Library, 1954), vol. II, p. 352.
[28] Sen, "Well-Being, Agency and Freedom," p. 199.

can wear headscarves at school. In all such instances, there is a first, literal sense of toleration, which is in line with the traditional conception, and there is a further symbolic meaning, which is much more important than the first. As in the more traditional versions, granting toleration in such cases means literally increasing the liberty of group members and opening up public spaces which are currently closed to them, at least in their capacity as members of different groups. In this respect, the conception of toleration I am arguing for is in line with liberal doctrine, and that is why this book is an argument around and for toleration, focused on a revision and expansion of the traditional conception.

Concerning the literal aspect of toleration, however, a difference between typical liberal toleration and the present version must be pointed out. In contemporary instances, toleration typically concerns the public sphere. In a sense, this is obvious, given that in the private arena toleration already exists and is well entrenched in individual rights. Yet it raises problems for liberal theory. Toleration in public is perceived by liberal theory either as troublesome or as perfectly normal, depending on which reading of public neutrality is favored. Supporters of the ideal of *laïcité* (maximal interpretation of neutrality) view public toleration as an infringement of neutrality, and argue for a public space devoid of any difference and particular loyalty. They therefore oppose public cultivation of any collective identity, and thus consistently propose a total implementation of the principle of neutrality in all respects, thereby excluding the majority's identities as well.[29] Supporters of the minimal interpretation of neutrality (exclusion of differences as the grounds for public treatment) do not see public visibility of differences as an issue, but nor do they acknowledge the quest for recognition which underlies claims for public toleration. Consequently, they are in favor of public toleration, but only in its liberal sense, dismissing what is really at stake. If demands for public recognition are acknowledged, then public toleration becomes questionable even for the minimal neutralist, since they are taken as demands for special consideration and support, thereby involving a breach of neutrality.

Public toleration of differences is, however, pursued for its symbolic meaning: the official public acceptance of a different behavior or lifestyle, if properly grounded, signifies recognition of that difference. If the government declares that homosexuals can be admitted into the army, or

---

[29] Losano ("Contro la società multietnica") views toleration and secularism as opposite irreducible ideals, and opts for secularism, against any enlargement of toleration in the public sphere.

that Islamic symbols can be admitted in public schools, what is gained by the direct beneficiaries of such decisions is more than the literal freedom involved. The public visibility of differences that has resulted symbolically represents the legitimization of their presence in public. In its turn, the legitimization of their presence in public signifies their inclusion in the public sphere on the same footing as those whose practices and behavior are "normal." This inclusion then implies the acceptance of the corresponding identity and, hence, the acceptance of those who are marked by such identities. As a result, they not only acquire the possibility of appearing in public, and being and behaving as they are, without having to hide their differences (at least as long as their behavior does not harm anyone or violate any right), but they are also made to feel that they are entitled to that identity, since it is backed by a public decision. Their appearance in public may thus cease to be an occasion for feeling ashamed. In other words, by admitting different behavior into the public domain, toleration symbolically affirms the legitimacy of that behavior and of the corresponding identity in the public domain. As a consequence, the public presence of minority identities is publicly declared acceptable, not just the public presence of the individual members *as individuals*, but with their full-blown identities, customs, and ways of life, in the same way that majority identities have always been recognized. The explanatory hypothesis which gives support to a policy of toleration as a symbolic recognition of differences is that the humiliation and timidity experienced by minority members can be reversed by legitimizing the public presence of differences. The argument for the symbolic meaning of toleration as recognition is based on the hypothesis of a causal chain linking the legitimization of different identities, as the symbolic result of their public toleration, with the feeling of public respect of one's identity and, consequently, the opportunity to build up self-esteem and self-respect, feeling confident in themselves as members of the polity and of society at large.

However, the public recognition of differences can occur only if toleration is backed up by apposite reasoning, allowing its symbolic meaning to unfold. If public toleration is endorsed on the grounds of the maxim "anyone can do whatever he or she wants as long as no one else is harmed," it does no more than grant someone the freedom to do something. In other words, toleration must go further if it is to enable the comprehensive inclusion of minorities: its symbolic meaning as a public gesture, which recognizes and legitimizes the presence of certain differences, and hence of collective identities, must be clear. And, for this to happen, the reasons given for any decision involving toleration become crucial; they are what will give this form of toleration symbolic meaning as recognition of difference.

That is why construing questions of toleration in terms of moral conflict is an inadequate way to try to understand genuine cases in which toleration is at issue in the contemporary world. In fact, even if those who hold this view eventually settle on toleration as the eventual solution, the reasons they will give will usually concern the compatibility of the contested behavior or practice with liberal values and other people's rights. Thus, the argument for toleration on the one hand is primarily directed at tolerators (both the political authority and citizens), taking no account of the viewpoint of those who are potentially to be tolerated, and, on the other, it simply expresses a negative judgment ("there are no sufficient reasons to exclude this behavior from toleration"). That makes it extremely difficult to interpret such a decision as a symbolic form of recognition. In this case, toleration will generally not settle the issue (as happened with the case of the Islamic veil) and will be judged insufficient by its recipients.[30] This is because it meets only the literal claim to toleration, while totally ignoring the real issue at stake. The achievement of public toleration is therefore not worthwhile for minority members. Indeed, what is gained by toleration in non-trivial cases is either intrinsically of little consequence or could be achieved at lesser cost in more roundabout ways. So if one sticks to the literal meaning, such uncompromising efforts to attain toleration appear inexplicable.

Yet what kinds of reason would be appropriate to the symbolic meaning of toleration? In general, in order for toleration to be satisfactory to both parties, it is crucial that the problem of exclusion be recognized as a central concern of both parties. The right reason would be one that did not reduce the issue to a clash of values and cultures, but recognized that behind that clash there is an asymmetry between the dominant cultural standards and the different practices, attitudes, and lifestyles of

---

[30] It may actually happen occasionally that even if backed by reductive reasons, liberal toleration nevertheless works as a step towards comprehensive inclusion. This happens as a side-effect of the public visibility of a difference. If the public presence of a difference can become stabilized over time, just by being there, it will gradually become familiar and will eventually be included in the range of the normal. This process may not only take a very long time to occur, but also, in order to develop in the right direction, it might need to be the case that it is not contested by either side, majority or minority. Since the immediate results of such a gradual process will be unsatisfactory for the tolerated, who will need to wait in order to receive recognition, it is likely to be contested.

minorities. It would also acknowledge that such asymmetry engenders a special injustice which results in less respect and dignity for minorities. The reasons in favor of toleration aim to counter such inequality, by recognizing differences and including them fully in the public arena – assuming that (but not because) the harm principle is not infringed and such inclusion is compatible with the liberal order. Thus the harm principle and the compatibility requirement become genuine conditions for toleration, not as the crucial issues, but as side constraints to be met. If the real situation is properly understood, and if what is at stake is adequately acknowledged, then toleration is endorsed for reasons of justice, or, more precisely, in order to repair the injustice of the unequal respect paid to those who are different. The policy of public blindness is not equipped to reverse this unequal respect, but indirectly it reinforces it. In this case, the normative quality of the argument is strictly connected with the interpretive framework within which the issue is located and grasped.

We still need to understand what form of recognition can (symbolically) be implemented by public toleration, if backed by the right reasons. This comes down to the proper meaning of "recognition of differences." It is something which worries liberals because it suggests a stretching of the liberal framework and also because it is the source of many misinterpretations and misunderstandings. There is a widespread belief that public recognition of differences and collective identities will disrupt social justice in that it will bring about group struggles which will not only be detrimental to the lower classes, but will also eventually destroy social cohesion and democratic coexistence in general. But these worries are mostly a result of the confusion about the possible meanings of the recognition of differences.

First of all, recognition can be interpreted as acknowledging, and even endorsing, the intrinsic value of the difference in question.[31] I think that this strong notion of recognition is utterly inappropriate in this context. For one thing, I do not see how it can apply to liberal democratic institutions. How can a liberal democracy affirm the value of all the different, and often incompatible, religions, cultures, and forms of life? Strong recognition cannot be granted to all differences a priori without assessing the worth of the difference in question. Presumably, not all will pass the test, and the endorsement of all differences per se is not possible because of their incompatibility. Finally, in this scenario the ideal of anti-perfectionism and neutrality would definitely be dismissed.

[31] This is the notion of recognition used by Charles Taylor in "The Politics of Recognition."

However, recognition can be interpreted, in a weaker sense, as the acknowledgment that any culture, any form of life, any way of being has some value in some respect as a form of human endeavor. For example, liberal institutions may find themselves at odds with the political implications of Islamic orthodoxy, but may, nevertheless, admire Arabic art and literature.[32] Though grounded on the probably true belief that any civilization and any institution possesses something good, at least aesthetically, this weaker recognition of diversity seems inadequate for producing inclusion for two distinct reasons. The first is that it does not do justice to the quest of the excluded group. To claim that Islam has no political or religious value, but that Islamic art is wonderful is not to give a ringing endorsement of the inclusion of Islamic groups. The second is that this weaker form of recognition, like the stronger one, is aimed at the public assertion of the value of differences per se. And, in line with liberal orthodoxy, I think that it is not up to liberal democratic institutions to affirm any value, beside strictly political ones. From this viewpoint, a public recognition of differences should be instrumental in achieving the full inclusion of members of minority groups into democratic society.

Differences should be publicly recognized not because they are important or significant per se, though they may well be, but because they are important for their bearers and because expressions of public contempt for them, on the grounds that they depart from the social "norm," are a source of injustice. Differences and identities which essentially have no political relevance, but only existential significance, become concerns for liberal justice. Because of the social stigma attached to them, those who are different are not treated with the same public consideration and respect as the majority. Following this reasoning, public recognition comes down to the official acceptance of diversity within the normal range of viable options in society. In fact, the content of the difference in question need not be assessed and judged once it is ascertained that the harm principle and the rights of others are not violated. As in cases of traditional toleration, what counts as harm is inevitably controversial, but this pertains to the intrinsic indeterminacy of the theory. What is important and must be stressed is that, in this sense, public recognition, with the aim of legitimating the public presence of diversity, is content-independent and, hence, can be fitted into the ideal of neutrality (which does not necessarily coincide with difference blindness). It neither says nor implies that the difference in question is intrinsically valuable, beautiful, or important for

---

[32] This point has been suggested to me by Joseph Raz.

the human good, but it does imply that there are many different codes of dress, lifestyles, religious rituals, and so on among the viable options in society at large. In other words, it is a symbolic, and yet very real, way of extending the pluralism which is already part of democratic society, its final aim being the comprehensive inclusion of minority groups.

It must be stressed that although symbolic recognition can, in the last analysis, be reconciled with a revised notion of neutrality, it requires a more active and positive attitude toward differences, which goes beyond the usual interpretations of neutrality. Symbolic recognition implements the liberal ideals of justice, equal inclusion, and equal respect of all citizens, but it does so in a different way from standard liberal politics. Its aim is not to cancel all differences by compensating for the disadvantages attached to them, but to make all citizens positively at ease with their full-blown identities in public as well as in private. In a word, public recognition ultimately aims to distribute the benefits of inclusion enjoyed by the majority to all citizens, whatever their ethnic, national, cultural, or gender membership.

This form of symbolic inclusion does not mean that people marked by a different identity will ipso facto be socially accepted; nor that the social stigma associated with that identity will suddenly disappear. And it will definitely not remove all the material disadvantages which accompany membership of minority groups. The recognition achieved by public toleration will symbolically signify the end of the public exclusion of certain social differences and certain identities, and assert their admission into the public sphere alongside the identities and character of established social groups. In so doing, symbolic recognition indirectly redraws the map of the standards of action and belief a society accepts.

It should also be stressed that, being symbolical, this kind of public recognition does not entail any pluralist encapsulation or ghettoization of group members[33] – quite the opposite, if the causal chain outlined above holds. Such recognition should help to free minority members from the burden – which they do not choose – which is attached to their identity. Without losing that identity, public recognition should free minority members from the restricted space of personal identification where they are kept by oppression and discrimination. Once the Islamic veil is admitted in school, or the gay into the army, it is up to individuals

---

[33] The concept of pluralist incapsulation is put forward by Donald Moon (*Constructing Community. Moral Pluralism and Tragic Conflict* [Princeton: Princeton University Press, 1993], p. 182) as the alternative to democratic individuality in dealing with social pluralism.

to decide whether or not to wear it and whether or not to declare their sexual preference; they need not feel committed to asserting their difference simply because loyalty to their oppressed group seems inescapable. In effect, it is up to the individual to choose the terms of his or her membership – to take the opportunity to be the writer of his or her parent's will, as Michael Walzer once nicely put it.[34] One should feel at ease with one's collective identity, choosing to stress or to dismiss any particular aspect of it, to exhibit or to keep private a cultural practice, to live one's life in the community, or to be an anonymous individual in the wider society.[35] In short, members of minority groups should relate to their social identity just as members of the majority have always done.

If this notion of recognition can be reconciled with a revised notion of neutrality, it can also be reconciled with impartiality. In fact, it does not entail favoring some particular group, and therefore giving up the principle of universal justice. I hold that symbolic recognition is not exclusive, i.e. it is not a scarce commodity, posing problems of distribution. Once the harm test is passed, I do not see why symbolic recognition should have any limit. This does, however, raise a problem, which explains why the matter is so contentious and why recognition (though symbolic) is sometimes so strenuously opposed. In passing, this explanation also provides a response to those who think that "symbolic" means "unreal," and that it changes nothing in real life. In fact, the inclusion of differences in the public sphere, on an equal footing with majoritarian characteristics and practices, implies that societal standards need to be redrawn (and not just symbolically). What has until now been considered "normal," proper, and "obvious" has to be extended so as to take into account others' practices. If, for example, in Italy the electoral date has always been fixed according to political convenience, but implicitly taking account of the obligations of Catholic citizens, the symbolic public recognition of other religions on an equal footing implies that the choice of the date should also take into account the obligations of Jews, Muslims, etc.[36]

[34] See A. E. Galeotti, "Intervista a Michael Walzer," *Notizie di Politeia*, 1988.

[35] In this way the worries expressed by Steven Lukes with reference to the fact that the politics of recognition would not be neutral among group members with a strong identification, those with a weak identification and those positively rejecting their membership, are misplaced, because the logic of the argument for recognition is the enpowerment of minority members as individuals in terms of self-esteem and self-respect so as to allow them a real choice about their membership according to their inclinations. See Lukes, "Toleration and Recognition."

[36] Here I am referring to a case which occurred in Italy in 1994, when the date of the general election was fixed on the day of Passover. After a protest by the Jewish community, and much public discussion, it was finally decided to extend the ballot for an extra day so as to allow orthodox Jews to vote.

Such a change is generally perceived by members of the majority as a worsening of their position and social standing, as in cases of redistributive policies. The fact is that the even distribution of symbolic recognition across all social groups destroys the "positional good" or advantage held by the majority – i.e. its exclusive command of societal standards.[37] Thus, even though symbolic recognition is not a scarce good, its generalization engenders the same social effects as those induced by redistributive policies. However, from a normative point of view, the worsening of the majority's position does not constitute a reason against symbolic recognition of differences, since the majority's privileges in terms of social standing and consideration have no justification in terms of the liberal conception of justice. Citizenship should be a thoroughly universal condition, not an exclusive status, dividing full members from second-class or marginal participants. Yet, if the majority's social standing is basically a positional good, that is, if it is especially valued as an exclusive position, then its generalization by means of symbolic recognition will benefit the newly included much less, while worsening the situation of established groups. Again, this pragmatic argument does not justify the opposition to a public toleration of differences or full inclusion of minority groups. Even though full membership in the polity will be less advantageous as a universal condition, losing its positional value, it is nevertheless required by the commitment to equality, and is a precondition for individual well-being. Exclusion is, in any case, unjust and a barrier to the well-being of individuals; it is therefore unacceptable.

The redefinition of the standards a society applies to the beliefs and actions of its members may lead, in time, to a number of non-symbolic transformations in public life, usually involving some costs. Once the Islamic headscarf is admitted into public schools and Islamic identity receives public legitimization, there are no reasonable grounds for refusing to provide special meals for Muslims in the school cafeteria. But such arrangements will have financial and organizational costs, so the apparently modest symbolic recognition may come to be viewed as an unpredictable slippery slope which threatens the status quo.[38] But, again, I hold that no matter how problematic these developments may appear, they do not constitute a sufficient reason for stopping toleration; they

---

[37] On the concept of positional goods, which needs to be added to the traditional distinction between private and public goods, see Fred Hirsh, *Social Limits to Growth* (London: Routledge and Kegan Paul, 1977).

[38] This process opens up the way to questioning conventions, and I have already argued that the resistance to changing conventions can be explained by reference to rational choice theory. See above.

raise questions which are no different from the usual problems involved
in establishing public policies – that is, questions of priority, budget limitation, cost–benefit analysis, and so on. I do not see how the decision
whether to build a nursing home or a swimming pool is in any relevant sense different from, or easier than, the decision to revise shopping
hours so as to accommodate Jewish and Muslim as well as Christian
holidays. Also, it should be stressed that public toleration as symbolic
recognition of differences does not commit the government to meeting
all further claims advanced by minority representatives; in a sense, the
opposite is true. While public toleration cannot be denied to any identity
(once the harm test is passed), after this first step towards inclusion has
been made, then all other claims should be subject to negotiation and
reciprocal accommodation. Decisions need to take into account com-
peting claims, costs, and benefits, as well as political convenience. In
other words, the public decision on such claims no longer belongs to the
non-negotiable area of toleration, but is subject to the familiar modes of
political bargaining.

Summarizing the argument so far, I have, first, identified exclusion
from full citizenship as the basic reason for public toleration as symbolic
recognition of differences. I then specified that symbolic recognition is
not intended in its strong sense, i.e. as acknowledging or endorsing the intrinsic value of differences, but more modestly, as their public acceptance
within the range of viable and normal alternatives making up society's
mainstream. Thus this form of recognition, while implying a positive
public attitude which contrasts with the requirement of a neutral public
stance, is content-independent, and in this way can be reconciled with a
revised conception of neutrality. Moreover, symbolic recognition is also
compatible with impartiality, since it does not favor one group at the
expense of others, but can be universally extended to all claimants, if
the harm test is passed. Up to this point, the argument seems to deflate
the issue, and to underline its basic compatibility with liberal constraints.
But we then go on to show why symbolic recognition of differences is
not a trivial step (explaining why it is so contested). In fact, it implies a
transformation in the standards a society uses to define what is "normal."
This transformation, in turn, implies costs for the majority, because of
the need to accommodate the newly admitted identities. These costs
may include not only a loss of status for the majority, but possibly actual
monetary expenses. These, however, cannot be legitimately avoided if
they are necessary to ensure that minorities are socially included. Finally,
we point out that public toleration will also lead to some non-symbolic

claims, which will be matters for political negotiation between the government and the various groups involved (in ways not different from present political negotiations with interest and pressure groups).

ACCEPTANCE AND STABILIZATION

In contemporary democracies, genuine questions arise when toleration is claimed for the public acceptance of social differences linked to excluded groups, and also when the limits of acceptable toleration are invoked in order to ban behavior and practices that are allegedly offensive to the bearers of newly admitted collective identities.[39]

The analysis has so far focused on claims for toleration aimed at achieving the symbolical public legitimization of social differences. I will now consider claims that are made for limiting toleration. I argue that contemporary arguments against tolerating certain behavior and practices should not, in general, be interpreted as residual attempts to censor social life and to impose certain moral ideals (attempts that are occasionally still made by conservatives and bigots), nor should they be considered simply as countering arguments for toleration. That is, such claims do not express a resistance to the public acceptance of differences. They generally represent the development of previous claims for toleration and in this respect they fall within the same interpretive framework outlined above.

Claims for toleration in this sense are a first and obvious way in which minorities can argue for their inclusion in contemporary pluralist democracy. Confronted with the majority's intolerance and with the liberal practice of public blindness to social diversity, minorities first demand public acceptance and legitimization in the public sphere. But public toleration of their differences by no means results in the full inclusion of oppressed, marginalized, and invisible identities. It simply represents a first, necessary step in the process. Arguments against the toleration of practices and behavior, which are alleged to be offensive to the newly admitted and still weak identities, constitute a further step. As noted above, only claims for public toleration of differences are non-negotiable, while further claims such as non-toleration of practices which are offensive to minorities are more complicated to meet and can indeed be matters for negotiation. Before asking whether these claims should be satisfied, here I reconstruct the argument in their support, trying to show how it can be fitted into the theoretical framework of toleration as recognition.

---

[39] This is clearly stated by Leader in "Three Faces of Toleration."

The logic of claims for a limit to offensive speech and behavior is easily grasped. In order to be an equal member in a new club, admission is not sufficient. The newcomer's presence needs to be stabilized over time, until the memory of his or her previous exclusion is forgotten. Prejudices and stereotypes do not disappear overnight, and their persistence, often linked with more or less disguised discrimination, undermines the newcomer's still weak public position, reproducing conditions for second-class citizenship. Desegregation, for example, has been a crucial step towards extending equal citizenship to black people, but, by itself, the legitimization of the black presence in the public sphere has not resulted in inclusion. Against the risk of marginalization brought about by persistent prejudices and stereotyping, the newly admitted groups claim special political protection against practices seen as offensive to their image and, consequently, likely to undermine the stability of their public presence. Such special protection is demanded as a redress for past exclusion and discrimination, and implies drawing limits to public toleration (as non-interference) of certain kinds of racist and sexist language, or attitudes promoting racial hatred, and practices such as pornography, seen as offensive to the public image of women.

The public discussion around these controversial issues, such as the ban on pornography or on hate speech in the USA, and the outlawing of Nazi skinhead groups in European countries, is usually understood as a contest between the harm principle and the justifiability of limiting free speech.[40] Thus, typically, around these controversial cases there is a stand-off between a liberal position and those who demand that free speech should have limits. The liberal purist argues that free speech is an absolute priority which cannot be limited by appeal to any alleged (non-physical) harm, since the general (also non-physical) harm suffered in society if any voice is silenced would be far greater and more significant. Those who demand a ban on pornography, hate-speech and Nazi groups, on the other hand, claim that the harm produced by these practices on members of groups which have been discriminated against, excluded, and oppressed for a long time in the past, is very often physical, since these practices engender forms of intimidation, harassment, and assault.[41]

---

[40] The controversy is particularly heated in the USA because of the First Amendment, and its jurisprudence, prohibiting any content limitation of speech. See chapter 5.

[41] This thesis is strongly and vividly argued by MacKinnon, *Only Words*; for a presentation of the theoretical issue between free speech and the harm principle, see Fredrick Schauer, "The Phenomenology of Speech and Harm," *Ethics*, 103, 1993, pp. 635–53.

Even when there is no evidence of physical harm, they claim that the psychological harm is serious enough to justify the limitation of free speech.

I contend that neither approach to the issue exclusively captures what is really at stake, since both limit discussion to the literal aspect of non-toleration, totally overlooking its symbolic implication. The point is that neither censorship nor the enforcement of morals is the goal of contemporary forms of opposition to hate speech or racist marches. The limitation of freedom that results from curtailing toleration in these instances has a further symbolic meaning: it aims at taking a public stand against racism, sexism, and homophobia. Certain speech codes and attitudes are thereby implicitly acknowledged as offensive to bearers of the newly admitted identities and likely to undermine their process of inclusion. Regardless of whether or not it is in fact successful in purging public speech of racist insults, the ban on hate speech is valued for its symbolic meaning, as a public gesture against complacency and complicity in racist verbal attacks, as a signal and a public stand against racial hatred. By the same token, it also provides symbolic support to the dignity of the public image of previously excluded groups.

The fact that the symbolic meaning of curtailing toleration in such cases is more important than the literal limitation of freedom does not imply that the latter should not be taken into account in assessing such claims. The problem is that free speech and the harm principle have so far been the only focus of the discussion. As a consequence, any decision, whether for or against toleration, tends to be taken for the wrong reasons and does not take into consideration what is really at stake. This, moreover, prevents political agencies from devising viable alternatives.

I will examine this problem properly in chapter 5 when I will take up the question of racism. In general the argument for limits to toleration is not easily conceded, though it cannot be simply dismissed. Its acceptability depends very much on particular circumstances and given contexts. At present I intend just to underline that claims against toleration are best understood as a development of claims for toleration, and that they should not be exclusively reduced to a discussion of free speech and the harm principle. Attempts to limit offensive practices can be defended by a complex argument which highlights the symbolic meaning of such attempts; these are more crucial in this context than the literal meaning of preventing offensive behavior against weak members of society. In this respect, claims for public toleration and claims for non-toleration of certain practices can be grouped together as non-trivial contemporary instances of situations in which toleration is seriously at issue; both kinds of claims can be understood by means of the same interpretive framework, although the arguments in favor of non-toleration may be more complex and problematic.

CONCLUSIONS

Toleration has traditionally had to do with the range of behavior, ways of life, and morals which, though not generally liked, are nevertheless considered acceptable in society and without danger to the social and political order. Within contemporary society, this question is intrinsically linked to the characteristics of groups whose modes of life and culture appear not to fit the established social norms. I have argued that in the context of contemporary pluralism to view toleration in terms of the conflict of non-orthodox individual choices is reductive and inadequate. I have therefore proposed that we should see the issue not as a problem of what can or cannot be made compatible with the liberal order, but as a problem concerning the exclusion of members of minority groups. The kind of exclusion I am referring to here is not that associated with being deprived of legal entitlements or of resources and opportunities. Rather it specifically concerns a lack of social consideration and public respect which prevents the bearers of certain identities, because of their differences, from developing self-esteem and self-respect. Members of minority groups whose identity is socially stigmatized and who are publicly invisible therefore lack two crucial conditions for being fully functioning social agents and citizens.

Questions of toleration thus involve a contest between minorities and majorities within the same pluralistic democracy about the public acceptance and protection of the minorities' identities. Toleration of differences has so far been granted mainly in the private sphere. In the public sphere, by contrast, special identities are generally banned either because of a certain interpretation of neutral citizenship (*laïcité*) or because of a certain understanding of what it would mean to recognize differences (trespassing on neutrality). The public ban on differences and special identities is nevertheless unfair because it strikes only minority groups. Majoritarian identities have always inhabited the public sphere, simply disguised as the norm. The exclusion of different identities is contested by minorities because public invisibility has the effect of reproducing and reinforcing discrimination against their members, with the result that they are considered unfit to be full citizens. Therefore public toleration of differences is pursued by minorities not so much for its real effect of enlarging the freedom to express religious beliefs and lifestyles, but for the symbolic implications of legitimization of the public presence of identities. Public toleration is in fact considered as the first symbolic step taken by liberal institutions to include members of minority groups, by reversing the chain which links public invisibility, persistent social prejudice, and discrimination with humiliation, self-hatred, and a lack of self-esteem and self-respect. The declaration of public acceptability of social differences implies their recognition among the viable alternatives of that society, hence redefining social norms.

Viewing toleration in terms of inclusion instead of in terms of compatibility does not solve the problem of accommodating differences within the liberal order. But I think it better that this problem be faced in the end, although the solution to it involves a possible pragmatic exception to the argument for general public toleration of all differences. There are two important advantages of reasoning in terms of exclusion rather than compatibility: on the one hand, the normative force backing public toleration is more powerful if the reasoning is based on considerations of justice rather than on compatibility; on the other, the compatibility argument does not provide the right reasons for revealing the symbolic meaning of toleration. Hence, if my argument is correct, toleration would miss its intended goal.

Questions of toleration can also arise over claims for the exclusion of certain behavior and practices which are allegedly offensive to the public image and dignity of only recently included groups. I have suggested that this second kind of question be interpreted as a development of the first, even though it appears to run in the opposite direction. What is claimed here is public protection against offenses which undermine the stabilization of the public presence of different identities and their bearers.

Whether the argument for toleration as recognition holds, and whether some limits to toleration can be justified are both controversial matters, as is the question of whether the symbolic recognition and protection of differences achieve their intended goal. This will be the topic of the final chapter, but, first, I should like to stress the significance of looking at toleration from the standpoint of those whose mode of life will potentially be tolerated. In my proposal, toleration appears as an aspect of social justice, thus developing the line of justification pointed out by John Rawls. At the same time, the scope of social justice turns out to have widened too, concerning not only people's endowments and entitlements, but also the way they are viewed and considered by others and by political institutions. That the search for honor, glory, and distinction constitutes a crucial issue for civil coexistence, peace, and justice was acknowledged and emphasized by classical political thinkers such as Hobbes and Rousseau. Democratic theory believed it had solved this issue through equal citizenship and by means of the abolition of ranks, so theories of justice have mainly concentrated on the extension of rights and on the distribution of material goods such as income, education, and health. And yet citizenship is not simply a set of legal entitlements; it includes a more substantive status which is effectively held only by those who meet certain standards of propriety, civility, and sociability. Those who do not meet these standards (newcomers or internal minorities) are not regarded as full citizens and are thus excluded from the "status" of citizenship, which itself implies a lack of social consideration and respect. Public invisibility of different characteristics, traits, and identities is the sign of, and at the same time reinforces, such exclusion. By means of toleration, therefore, the aim is to achieve public respect and consideration equal to that enjoyed by any full citizen, and hence to make minority members feel included: both necessary conditions for being effectively part of society.

4

The Islamic veil in French schools

In the next three chapters I will look at some exemplary cases concerning toleration, employing the theoretical framework outlined above. I have picked out three examples which I take to represent different steps in the comprehensive argument for toleration as recognition.

The argument for toleration as recognition has arisen from the distinction between trivial and genuine questions, the former concerning cases that find an easy solution in the liberal tradition, while the latter do not. What I intend to discuss first in this chapter is a classic example of a genuine question of toleration, namely, *l'affaire du foulard* – i.e. the contested acceptance of the Islamic headscarf in French state schools. This involves a genuine case of toleration insofar as, first, it engendered a long-standing public controversy within and outside France; second, it necessitated the intervention of the state; and, third, normal liberal views of toleration were unable to provide a satisfactory settlement: under standard interpretations, this case appeared either inexplicable or insoluble. I am going to reconstruct the various arguments in favor of and against toleration in this case drawn from liberal theory, and show their shortcomings. I shall argue that the problem lies in the interpretive framework rather than in the normative structure of liberal toleration. I shall then outline a different understanding of this kind of conflict – what is at stake and what the claims amount to – which will point to toleration as recognition for the solution of this controversy.

The public acceptance and visibility of a difference linked to a minoritarian identity represents the first step of toleration as recognition. Once the presence of social differences is affirmed as publicly legitimate, then practices and forms of speech that are offensive to the dignity of members of newly included groups can be called into question. As we saw in chapter 3, the quest for public protection against offensive behavior and humiliation stems from the very same reasons as the quest for toleration as recognition of difference. Though to accept these claims would imply curtailing the toleration of such offensive behavior, the claims themselves are to be seen as a direct development from those for public toleration of differences; the only difference is that they are not so easily granted. The complex interplay between toleration as recognition – which is aimed at full inclusion – and intolerance of social practices – which are aimed at marginalization – is reconstructed in chapter 5 dealing with the issue of racism. Is racism, that is the quintessential expression of intolerance, to be tolerated? How can limits of hate speech and racist expressions – grounded on non-discrimination and equal respect – be reconciled with the fundamental liberal principle of free speech? I will discuss these questions referring to different debates developed in different political and legal contexts, i.e. Italy, the United States, and Germany.

Finally I will consider the case of same-sex marriage. The demand for legal recognition of same-sex marriage represents a natural development of the demand for toleration as recognition; it is a demand that social norms be revised so as to accommodate a newly accepted group. The homosexual identity has been publicly accepted throughout democratic countries, though the process is by no means completed, and the public visibility of gays is still resisted in many ways; the controversy over the World Gay Pride March in Rome in July 2000 is just an example of powerful social agents, such as the Catholic church, still opposing toleration as recognition for gays, favoring instead negative toleration outside the public sphere. But, once the public presence of same-sex orientation has been legitimized as a viable way of life of our society, then societal standards and public conventions need to be redrawn accordingly. In chapter 6 I will discuss the issue of same-sex marriage as an implication of gays' and lesbians' acquired visibility and inclusion into full citizenship, not despite, but given their sexual orientation.

Toleration as recognition shares its final aim with liberal toleration – that is, the peaceful and respectful coexistence of different people and groups – but devises a different strategy to achieve it. Liberal toleration tries to free people from the burden of their differences by means of ignoring them. So individuals are all made equal citizens: no one is of special importance, no one receives any particular precedence or favor, and no one is publicly excluded because of his or her religion, way of life, manners, or culture. This strategy, however, although it has removed some public discrimination by granting civil and political rights to all, is insufficient to fight other forms of exclusion linked to the invisibility and the

subordination which characterize marginal and minority groups. Toleration as recognition, instead of amounting simply to non-interference
with differences in non-public spheres, states the public acceptance of
differences linked to marginal or excluded groups. In so doing, it constitutes a first condition for full membership in a democratic citizenship.

L'AFFAIRE DU FOULARD AND LIBERAL TOLERATION

The so-called '*affaire du foulard*' involves a long story, which began in
October 1989 at Creil in France when three French girls of Muslim faith
went to school with their heads covered by the traditional Muslim scarf.
The controversy erupted at once; the school authorities ordered the girls
to uncover their heads, claiming that they had to dress like all the other
students; the girls, supported by their families and by the Islamic community, refused to comply and, as a consequence, were expelled from
school. The case then became public and was widely debated throughout
the country and also abroad. Similar episodes began to occur in other
state schools. At that stage, in order to provide clear guidelines for the
whole school system, the socialist Minister of Education Lionel Jospin
asked the opinion of the Conseil d'état, which, in November 1989, made
a formal statement on the matter, ruling that French students had the
right to express their religious beliefs in public schools, as long as they
respected the liberty of others and on the condition that such expression did not hinder normal teaching or order within the school. Thus,
although the girls were readmitted, wearing the Islamic veil, the legal
decision in favor of tolerance looked more like a de facto compromise
than a principled choice. That this was so has since been confirmed with
the (restrictive) reinterpretation of the Conseil d'état's ruling, as provided
by the new conservative Minister of Education, François Bayrou, in an
official directive addressed to all public school principals in September
1994. Without expressly mentioning the Islamic veil, the minister pointed
out that only discreet and modest religious symbols should be tolerated
in school. Ostentatious and provocative ones were forbidden, since they
might be seen as an attempt to proselytize or to discriminate between
students. The obvious result of the directive has been the prohibition of
the Islamic veil which, given its visibility, can easily be considered ostentatious and provocative, while the more familiar Christian cross and
the modest Jewish kippah, being discreet symbols, are tolerated. However, this did not stop the controversy over the veil – coupled with a
general tolerance of the *hijab* in most schools – from raging in France,

a controversy that spread to other Europeans countries with growing Muslim minorities and similar problems.

This case is difficult not because, as some liberal or leftist intellectuals have claimed, the Islamic veil is a sign of religious fundamentalism and, moreover, of women's subordination, which can lead to intolerance and obscurantism; nor because of western prejudice or French chauvinist views of different cultures, as some radical postmodernist writers like to think. All these elements have been present throughout the debate, but none has been crucial. The real problem is that while toleration has generally been more favored than prohibition, this has not been for the right reasons. In fact, the issue has largely been considered, explicitly or implicitly, within the traditional framework of liberal toleration. On the one hand, the reasons given for toleration sound ineffective in explaining why the episode has become a political issue. If toleration is a fundamental principle of a liberal democracy such as France, permitting personal diversity in religion, morality, and lifestyle, with the proviso of not harming any third person, then the wearing of headscarves looks like an obvious case for toleration. But why, then, has this created an issue of toleration in the first place? On the other hand, the arguments against toleration, although they provide an explanation for such a long-standing controversy, either referring back to the fundamentalist threat to democracy or to the issue of women's protection from a patriarchal culture, do not stand up to close scrutiny. In either case, the actual nature of the problem is not properly analyzed and understood, and as a result no solution can be satisfactory. I shall argue in favor of toleration, but for different reasons, leading us to the conclusion that the overall meaning of toleration needs to be reconceptualized. But let us reconstruct these alternatives step by step.

In the light of the most common conception of toleration, which I would call the naive liberal view, the headscarf case appears inexplicable, at least if we assume that the French school authorities are not guilty of harboring racist or chauvinist attitudes. The naive liberal view conceives of toleration as the principle according to which everyone should be free to follow his or her ideals and style of life as long as no harm is done to anyone else. Headscarves do no harm to any third party, and the choice to wear one for whatever reason rests in the proper domain of personal freedom. This simplistic approach to the case suggests that toleration is the obvious solution, but, in doing so, it disguises the *raison d'être* of the controversy. Toleration turns out to be endorsed for the wrong reasons – that is, it dismisses the religious and cultural implications of wearing the veil and equates it with any piece of extravagant or unorthodox clothing. Seen in this light, toleration cannot be a convincing solution for the supporters of prohibition, or even for the three girls, their families, and community, since it is based on a misrepresentation of the facts. In effect, the symbolic meaning of public recognition of differences is missing from the decision to opt for toleration, and therefore the girls' claim is not met. The school officials know very well that the Islamic headscarf is not just a funny hat. And the girls themselves do not want to be accepted as clowns, but as Muslim students – that is, as students with a specific religious and cultural identity. The Islamic veil is in fact a symbol of a growing minority, which worries western democracies, partly because of prejudice and bias and partly for good reasons. It is precisely for its symbolic meaning that the veil is worn and contested: were it simply a funny hat, it would not raise such a political outcry. A funny hat might be accepted or prohibited, according to the discretion of the teachers and principal concerned. In that case, though, the event would certainly remain within the school walls, becoming at most a matter for local comment and gossip.

Liberal theories of toleration, however, are more sophisticated than the naive view seems to allow. In liberalism, both in the perfectionist and the neutralist version, toleration is valued within limits, beyond which it becomes dangerous, harmful, and self-destructive; but these limits are always difficult to define in practice, and are, as a result, always contested. The veil controversy, then, can be made sense of, within the liberal framework, as a contest over the justifiable limits of toleration. In this case, the veil need not be reduced to a funny hat, but is properly considered as a religious and cultural symbol. Understanding that there could be limits to the toleration of headscarves in the public sphere can definitely account for why a headscarf has become such a heated political issue. Yet whether such limits are convincing is another matter.

According to the perfectionist model, the value of toleration is grounded on a respect for the autonomy of others: toleration is a respectful attitude adopted toward any autonomous choice, no matter how disliked. By the same token, then, non-autonomous choices, supposing such a distinction can easily be made, are not automatically entitled to toleration. In this case the grounds for toleration are doubly shaky. First, the Islamic veil is, rightly or wrongly, considered a symbol of women's invisibility and subordination. Hence, under this reading, making the choice to wear the veil appears similar to giving up one's freedom. Thus, even if it is a free choice, it is one which impairs the very possibility of the girls' future free choices.[1] One might argue that the girls' decision to wear the veil demonstrates a lack of autonomy, by claiming that religious choice, at their age, cannot count as autonomous, since it must be the outcome of family pressure. If we were dealing with a non-autonomous choice, whose content might prevent the agent's future independence and freedom, then the state would find grounds to intervene in order to protect the weak party – in this case, an under-age female – against the dominance of the family. For this would restrict the very possibility of her becoming an autonomous citizen.[2] Hence, the *raison d'être* of the controversy is made clear: it concerns whether questionable behavior exhibited by people under age is entitled to toleration, or whether it necessitates the intervention of the state in order to prevent harming the life chances of an individual.

This was basically the position expressed by Elisabeth Badinter, a feminist writer and the wife of President Mitterrand's Minister of Justice.[3] She maintained that the veil should not be tolerated, for the following reasons: the veil is a cultural symbol, rather like punk style, which is a symbol of youth culture. But while the latter represents a rebellion against the conventions and conformity of parents, the former suggests submission to family culture. Hence, the punk style reveals autonomy and independence, whereas wearing the veil represents no more than blind obedience, and, moreover, obedience which works against any hope of liberation. For these reasons, according to Badinter, the veil should be forbidden, and punk style should be permitted. This argument, however, cannot be accepted. It presupposes a state's right, first, to make judgments and, second, either to tolerate or to interfere with symbolic dress codes which in the liberal state are not, by definition, matters for political intervention. We cannot, from any liberal standpoint, provide public reasons to justify why one type of dress code is tolerable while another is not, given that toleration is the general rule for cultural, religious, or

---

[1] As is well known, in *On Liberty* John Stuart Mill discusses this point in relation to the freedom to enslave oneself, but denies that such a choice can count as one to be respected, just because it impairs the agent's future liberty.

[2] It is well known that paternalism is a *vexata quaestio* for liberals; the possibility of justifying paternalistic state intervention has recently been defended by Danny Scoccia, "Paternalism and Respect for Autonomy," *Ethics*, 100, 1990, pp. 318–34. In general, the right of families to transmit to their children their values, beliefs, and practices is interestingly discussed by Michael Walzer in "What Rights for Cultural Communities?," mimeo, Turin, 1998.

[3] Badinter's position is keenly reconstructed by Norma Moruzzi, "A Problem with Headscarves. Reply to Galeotti," *Political Theory*, 22, 1994, pp. 653–72.

non-conformist dress codes; we must, rather, provide specific reasons for making an exception in cases in which we wish to limit toleration in a particular instance.

In general, the paternalistic line of reasoning against the *foulard* at school is deeply questionable. By definition, people under age are subject to the choices of their family in matters concerning social life, culture, and education. The liberal democratic state, as a rule, interferes only when there is clear evidence of harm done to the person or to society in general. It is far from evident that wearing a *hijab* would be more harmful than, for example, allowing a ten-year-old boy to enter a Catholic seminar. After all, there is evidence to show that many boys and girls, men and women, have been able to withdraw both from Catholic seminars and to stop wearing a *hijab*, of their own volition. At this point the argument concerning the subordination of women, which is supposedly implied in the issue of the Islamic veil, sounds decidedly lame. Autonomy and liberation, like religious convictions, should not be forced, both for reasons of principle, and also because coercion is ineffective. Finally, an argument for paternalistic intervention in the case of the *foulard* opens the way to a wider range of state interference than we would be prepared to accept. In conclusion, an argument for banning the Islamic veil from schools based on reasons concerning the girls' future autonomy vis-à-vis the cultural imposition of the family is not justified for a number of reasons. First, it is a question of fairness, because the same paternalistic intervention does not apply to other comparable family decisions in the majority's religious and cultural education. Second, it is inappropriate, because there is no reason to believe that such an intervention, by its intrinsic nature, will achieve the intended goal of liberating the girls from an oppressive culture. Lastly, there are pragmatic reasons, because it would widen the range of government intervention beyond any acceptable threshold in a liberal democracy.

ISLAMIC SYMBOLS AND THE STATE/CHURCH SEPARATION

According to the neutralist interpretation of liberalism, there is, however, another crucial argument for limiting toleration of the veil at school. The neutralist version of toleration, as we have already seen, is strictly dependent on the public/private divide. Briefly, the neutralist argument for toleration runs as follows: on the one hand, there is the primitive fact of differences, understood as reducible to differences between particular individuals; on the other, there is the moral principle of individual sovereignty over one's preferences and choices – a principle that can be presented either in negative form, as in the prohibition of interference by others, or in the positive sense of personal autonomy. The liberal holds that political obligation arises from the consent of those who are to be subject to it. Given, then, the difficulty of reaching general agreement on many issues and questions, the liberal solution limits the political to a restricted and well-defined sphere,[4] which is the subject of legitimate political decision and intervention. It separates the political from other social spheres, defined as private (or non-political), recognized as politically neutral and therefore pertaining exclusively to individual choices (always with the proviso of reciprocal respect of boundaries). These private social spheres constitute the proper subject of political toleration. In sum, the individualistic presupposition of the liberal model construes what is to be tolerated as strictly private, vis-à-vis a public sphere where, on the contrary, the same rules apply to all.[5] Therefore toleration pertains to questions that are defined as having no relevant public consequences, which is why political agencies can afford to be neutral about them.[6] By contrast, the political sphere is guided by the principle of neutrality, prescribing institutional blindness to diversity in matters of religion, morality, culture, and lifestyle.

At first glance it would seem that the principle of liberal neutrality requires toleration of the Islamic veil as a matter of course, since it prescribes non-interference by the state in individual choices regarding the conception of the good (and wearing the headscarf clearly belongs to such a sphere). This reasoning, however, overlooks the public/private dimension that regulates the working of the neutrality principle, under the strong interpretation of the secular state (*laïcité*).[7] State neutrality indeed implies that, while political authorities and officials should practice toleration with reference to the many different conceptions of the good within the 'private' realm of civil society, in the public sphere they should be neutral, blind, and indifferent to diversity, in order to treat everybody equally. This may mean that public officials should disregard differences

---

4 The argument for limiting the political domain can be found in Rawls, "The Domain of the Political and Overlapping Consensus."
5 This argument is classically worked out in Locke, *A Letter Concerning Toleration*.
6 This point is clearly stated in all classical theories of toleration: Milton, *Aereopagitica*; Locke, *A Letter Concerning Toleration*; Voltaire, *Traité sur la tolerance. A l'occasion de la mort de Jean Calais* [1763], in *Mélanges* (Paris: Gallimard, 1961), pp. 563–650. In a somewhat different style, this point is underlined by Kristie M. McClure, "Difference, Diversity and the Limits of Toleration," *Political Theory*, 18, 1990, pp. 361–91, in her analysis of Locke's political discourse. See p. 378.
7 On the distinction between weak and strong neutrality, see chapter 2.

as the proper grounds for action (weak neutrality) or that differences should be kept out of the public sphere (strong neutrality).

According to the idea of *laïcité*, in the public sphere everyone participates in his or her capacity as a member of the polity, and, as such, is just a citizen like everybody else. The equality of citizens qua citizens constitutes the basis for universal public policy and the liberal guarantee against discrimination. Therefore, although citizens are free to pursue their own ideals and to practice their own culture and religion within the private sphere, in the public arena of the secular state they should put aside their special and particular memberships and be "just citizens," on an equal basis with all. The boundaries of the public arena are those of political obligation and are intended to preserve the loyalty of citizens against pressures from any other particular demand.[8] In continental Europe, the private/public distinction is particularly deep, being embedded in a legal tradition that was built around this opposition and which reaches back to Roman law. In France, moreover, the neutrality of the public sphere is historically articulated in the ideal of the secular state, where the *citoyen*'s choices and actions should be instances of the general will, as opposed to the particularistic, interest-oriented decisions of the bourgeois. The historical tradition behind this conception is clear: the Enlightenment, Rousseau, the Jacobin state with the republican tradition revisited. No matter how unrealistic and faulty such a conception of neutrality proved to be in its application, it is relevant for making sense of the framework in which the case was understood and dealt with by French public authorities. The public sphere here includes the public education system: the school is an instrument of the secular state for the public education of future citizens, where all religious symbols are banned and public spirit should be taught. In this picture, the initial prohibition against wearing the headscarf in school was the reaffirmation of the boundaries of the secularized public sphere against any religious interference.[9] It should be stressed that the banning of the veil is not perceived as intolerance within this framework, but, rather, as the legitimate limit to liberal tolerance in order to preserve the neutrality of the public school and the equality of the students as would-be citizens, beside and

---

[8] This problem is very vividly present in Greenawalt's *Religious Convictions and Political Choice*.

[9] Such a position is strongly endorsed by Losano, "Contro la società multietnica," who contrasts the ideal of the secular state with the ideal of toleration, concluding that toleration is out of place in the public domain of the secular state. What is odd in his position, widely shared in Europe by leftist liberals, is that the state, especially in Italy, has never been completely separated from the Catholic religion.

beyond any particular memberships. The aim of ensuring equality for all students is not simply an instance of stubborn unwillingness to recognize diversity so long as it is not discriminatory; teachers should disregard any difference which has no effect on merit, but should be helped in this by a minimization of visible differences.

The argument against wearing the Islamic headscarf at school based on the defense of the secular state has been the most pervasive one used throughout the debate, and it is also the most insidious, because it has cut across left–right political affiliations. The problem with this argument is that what counts as trespassing is contestable. After all, the girls were not asking to study Islamic religion at public school (where no other student is provided with religious education); they were simply wearing a symbol of their faith. Nor was this symbol a matter of "indifference," according to a classical distinction,[10] but one that pertains to the integrity and the identity of the female believer. In this respect, admitting the scarf as an instance of conscientious objection could have been an honorable solution within the framework of the secular state.

At this stage another question arises: is it actually true that in French state schools all religious symbols are banned? Is it not the case that certain religious symbols enjoy a privileged status? Apparently, wearing a chain and cross has never created a similar problem. It is not a matter of formal acceptance or prohibition, but a matter of course. Before the headscarf case broke out, no one was even aware of whether religious symbols were present in school or not. This might suggest that, as the critics of liberalism have remarked, neutrality is not so neutral after all, and the secular state not so thoroughly secularized. But before concluding that French officials, while formally applying the liberal model of toleration, were actually discriminating against the Muslim students, a difference between the cross and the Islamic veil in the context of French culture should be pointed out. In general, wearing a chain with a cross is not very visible. Its quasi-invisibility stops it from being a public statement

---

[10] The doctrine on "indifferentia" was part of the original fabric of the ideal of toleration. It has to do with tracing the demarcation between the state and the church; while it was affirmed that political power was independent from spiritual invasion in worldly matters, toleration was originally limited to the protection of creeds and faith, and not extended to religious ceremonies and rituals. Those were proclaimed to be a matter of "indifference" to faith and salvation, and therefore subject to political authority. This position was endorsed by Locke in his first writings on toleration (*Essay on Toleration*), and later rejected in the *Letter*.

It is interesting to note that a similar argument is presented by Muslims who want to absorb some aspects of western tradition; they make a distinction in the Koran between principles concerning faith and matters of discipline that are indifferent to the faith; the latter can be given up with no consequence for the believer. See *New York Times*, January 1992.

of religious faith, trespassing over the boundary of the public sphere. In this respect, had the girls simply wore a chain with a crescent, would that still have created problems? I am not sure that it would. On the other hand, the girls were not wearing a *chador*, but simply a headscarf, and, while the difference in visibility between the cross and the *chador* is great, it is much reduced in the case of the headscarf.[11] But two issues are relevant to the visibility question. First, whereas from an abstract objective viewpoint, a cross and a headscarf might be argued to have the same visibility, in France, where a secular political culture has overtaken the original Catholic tradition, a chain and cross has lost its visibility, much in the same way as a man with gray pants does not particularly stand out. A woman who covers her head with a scarf indoors is, on the other hand, as visible as the first woman to wear a miniskirt in the 1960s. Thus, it is the fact that the French are accustomed to the cross and not to the Islamic headscarf that makes the first unnoticed and the second very visible. Second, and more important, even if a headscarf is less emphatic than a *chador* as a religious symbol, the students who insisted on wearing it also refused to attend physical educational and biology lessons for religious reasons – and this in a school system where there are no optional classes and all students take the same courses. All in all, their behavior was not only much more noticeable than coming to school wearing a chain and crescent, but explicitly put forward a demand to the school authorities, who had to make a positive decision about whether the girls could abstain from certain classes. There is no doubt that what the girls were aiming for was not simply acquiescence or indifference towards their different religious and cultural identity, but actual recognition.

In this respect, the distinction traced first by the Conseil d'état and then, more explicitly, by the subsequent Minister of Education was not completely arbitrary. It is true that in France the cross is a discreet religious symbol, while the Islamic veil is loud and ostentatious (whereas in Saudi Arabia it is probably the opposite); it is because of this that the veil makes a public statement. What is unjustified is the further implication that the veil is intended to proselytize other students. This possibly signals a flavor of prejudice, and the unwarranted tendency to portray all Muslims as fundamentalists, preparing themselves to take over democratic institutions. But I will come back later to the fundamentalist threat. Leaving aside this aspect for the moment, the contextual distinction between "discreet" and "ostentatious" religious symbols is not totally

---

[11] On the differences between the various Islamic ways of covering women's heads, see Moruzzi, "A Problem with Headscarves."

unjustified, independently of the actual motives of French authorities. Yet I hold that the prohibition of the veil cannot simply be derived from such a distinction: it is one thing to argue that the Islamic veil is a public statement, as I believe is the case, but quite another to suggest that public statements of certain differences should be banned from state schools.

The argument for excluding public statements concerning differences in religion, morality, and lifestyle is supposed to be implicit in the very idea of the secular state, and the neutral public sphere, where diversity is allowed only as an expression of personal choice and character. Only those differences which, being strictly personal, are irrelevant, or "indifferent" to public and political matters, are admitted, since they are not likely to raise a political issue or to undermine orderly public life. But this argument, which has never received a proper and clear formulation, is liable to two criticisms. First, how can public officials and authorities draw the line between public statements and private values, given that they are also supposed to be neutral and blind to differences? Such a distinction can legitimately be made by neutral officials only if it is grounded on independent evidence of consequences for law and order and the security of others. Neutrality seems to preclude an evaluation of the content of differences. In this respect, whether the cross is more or less visible than the headscarf should not even be noticed by difference-blind officials. Visibility or invisibility, ostentation or discretion can be relevant in the private sphere, but, strictly speaking, should not matter in the public political arena. The result is that the prohibition of the headscarf in school for the sake of neutrality would derive from an argument which infringes the very principle of neutrality. Second, not all behavior which can be classified as a public statement receives the same treatment. Consider punk style, which is quite common among French students and is accepted in school, albeit maybe unwillingly, with no apparent problems. Some may answer that punk style is, after all, just a fashion, while the veil is a more lasting religious symbol. In this case, the relevant difference would be between religion and fashion or lifestyle: given the state–church separation, the first is entitled to toleration only as a private matter, whereas the second is accepted even though it is meant as a public statement. In any case, it is not up to public officials to decide what is fashion and what is religion. Yet, a fashion may be endorsed as a religion, and, moreover, state neutrality has expanded to issues far beyond those of religion. If, by contrast, discreet differences are to be distinguished from ostentatious ones by reference to an objective criterion, then the only one available is whether differences can be ascribed to majority or to minority groups. Diversity within a majority is in fact not perceived as "difference," but as the display of the normal range of characteristics and options exhibited by the citizens. In this sense, such differences, being normal, are a fortiori discreet. The differences displayed by minorities are, on the contrary, seen as different from the societal "norm," and, thus, implicitly loud, visible, and shocking. In no way can such differences be disguised as discreet expressions of religion and culture. In any case, the distinction between discreet symbols and public statements, however considered, cannot be made sense of within the usual framework of neutrality.

In sum, the argument from the point of view of the secular state, while accounting for the *raison d'être* of the controversy, making sense of the underlying conflict between the liberal secular state and groups demanding the right to public display of ostentatious religious symbols, does not provide convincing reasons for prohibition. Adopting this point of view would imply that differences belonging to minority groups, being implicitly loud and emphatic, should have no access to the public sphere, although normal majoritarian traits and options are entitled to free circulation, given that they are perceived as discreet. Contrary to the intention of the political authorities and the majority, an objective discrimination can be detected in the public exclusion of the Islamic veil.

At this point, there is, however, a final liberal argument supporting prohibition of the veil: one which refers to the right of self-defense of the liberal institution against the invasion of particular and potentially illiberal identities, loyalties, and memberships. The risk may be, first, that group loyalties take over in public decisions and that conflicts between different groups and cultures become political. Second, the liberal order may be exposed to illiberal attacks from fundamentalist groups. Against such possibilities, it could be argued, the principle of maintaining a neutral public sphere, to which everybody belongs purely and only as a citizen, should not be modified, even symbolically. Two arguments are in fact interwoven here: one relating to the risk that particular memberships and loyalties might threaten the universality and independence of the citizen's role, and the other concerning the fundamentalist challenge to the liberal order.

The first argument can be countered, by pointing out that the liberal public arena has always been open to a particular collective identity, namely the white Christian male. The public/private divide does not require him to change his dress, appearance, behavior, or habits concerning religion and everyday life. What it does ask is only that his obligations and their prioritization should differ in the two domains. More precisely, the public domain does not require that personal beliefs, convictions, or attachments be dismissed, but that the selection of arguments and reasons be relevant, adequate, and open to public discussion and criticism.[12] Whether these requirements can be or are met in liberal practice is another matter, but human imperfection in this regard, widely recognized and discussed in political discourse, has never been seen as a threat to the principle of the public duty of citizenship. In the case of the white Christian male, this identity is not considered to have impaired dramatically the dutiful performance of his role as a citizen. Moreover, his public obligations have been recognized as compatible with personal convictions and beliefs, which can be defended by public reasons, so no division between the private and the public self is produced. Hence, the exclusion of different identities from the public sphere is unjustified, or could be justified only for special reasons. If the obligations of citizenship come down to the use of relevant and appropriate arguments, then only public discussion and a free press can check the proper use of the public sphere, and not just its fictional representation as a homogeneous physical space.

However, a special justification for banning any signs of Islamic identity can still be invoked, because of the supposed fundamentalist invasion of liberal politics. Liberal theory and politics have always acknowledged that toleration cannot be extended to the intolerant, if the tolerant society is to be preserved. Following from this generally shared principle, already stated by John Locke, it might be possible to invoke a special and strong justification for excluding the Islamic veil (as a symbol of fundamentalism) from public toleration. But the question is more complicated than this: while the self-defense principle is clear and sound, its application is always a matter of controversy.

First, what does a threat to the liberal order and institutions entail? Is it the undermining of the ethical integrity of liberal democracy and the loyal consent of citizens, or an actual threat of violence, terrorism, and social disorder? Though there is a possible link between detachment from liberal institutions, withdrawal of consent, and an actual threat to the

---

[12] See O'Neill, "The Public Use of Reason," and Gutmann and Thompson, "Moral Conflict and Political Consensus," who propose something similar to my conception of public reasons. The legitimacy of making a public choice on the basis of personal convictions, provided that those convictions can be backed by public reasons, is widely discussed by Greenawalt, *Religious Convictions and Political Choice*. Criticisms of Greenawalt's position are made by Perry, "Neutral Politics?"

persistence of liberal society, the two risks should be kept separate for present purposes. In fact, it is one thing to fix limits to toleration in order to preserve the actual "physical" order of liberal society, and quite another to attempt to preserve ethical integrity and loyal consent to liberal institutions. Liberal theory has so far tackled the fundamentalist challenge only from the latter point of view (and in a sense obviously so, since liberal theory can only take up a general theoretical problem; it cannot provide any useful answers to a particular crisis or contextual emergency). As we saw in chapter 2, supporters of the perfectionist version of liberal theory are worried that the exposure and openness of liberal society to non-liberal cultures may undermine its ethical core. They are therefore suspicious of tolerance toward differences which contradict such crucial liberal principles as autonomy, self-reliance, and free-thinking. Yet such suspicions, as liberal perfectionists have explicitly recognized, cannot be directly translated into a prohibition of those practices, even if there do appear to be reasons against toleration of them. Moreover, some perfectionists have pointed out that autonomy, the crucial value of the liberal theory of the good, is a function of a healthy cultural identity – so they wish to open up liberal society to different cultures, and to argue for the right to diversity.

Neutralist liberals do not share this concern: discussion of what constitutes adequate social conditions for fulfilling liberal values is not part of the political agenda. But the fundamentalist challenge has been taken seriously by neutralist liberal theory, which asks whether the political legitimacy of the liberal order can be recognized even by someone who holds a non-liberal world-view.[13] In other words, neutralist liberals are concerned about whether loyal consent to liberal institutions can exist, given that citizens do not share a common conception of the good, whether thick or thin. The answer is highly controversial, and fundamentalism has become, in both theory and practice, the limit for contemporary neo-liberalism. However, the constitutional question of the justifiability and acceptability of liberal institutions for the fundamentalist, despite its general theoretical interest, is not relevant to deciding cases such as that of the headscarf, which western culture associates with fundamentalist symbolism. Toleration for the *hijab* does not follow from showing that even the fundamentalist has good reasons to endorse

---

[13] The problem of the political legitimacy of liberal institutions is a crucial issue in recent liberal literature; see, for example, Rawls, "The Idea of an Overlapping Consensus"; Nagel, *Equality and Partiality*; Larmore, *Patterns of Moral Complexity*; Douglass, Mara, and Richardson, eds., *Liberalism and the Good*.

liberal institutions. When toleration is at issue, the question is whether liberal democracy is justified in curtailing the application of the general principle in a particular instance. So even though there may be sound arguments showing that citizens from illiberal cultures have, in principle, good reasons to be loyal citizens, in practice those good reasons may not actually be operative. Thus we are back with the original question: what can plausibly be considered a real threat to the liberal order? An illiberal creed endorsed by a group, but not apparently translated into action? A religion shared by many groups and sects, whose interpretations range from the more secular, to the orthodox, or the fundamentalist? There is no difficulty in justifying a ban on fanatical groups which are willing and ready to undertake acts of terrorism. But what about a group which holds revolutionary or anti-institutional views, but which is not willing to take action until it has achieved a much wider level of participation, satisfying itself for the moment in producing revolutionary propaganda? Should the leaflets and pamphlets of such a group be censored, given that they are aimed at gaining followers willing to join it in overthrowing the existing order? And should any such association be legally banned? These questions are very hard to answer in the abstract and are obviously very controversial. During the wave of terrorism which erupted in Italy from the mid-1970s to the early 1980s, neither revolutionary publications nor extra-parliamentary groups with revolutionary and anti-establishment ideologies were prohibited. And although the situation constituted a real emergency, anti-terrorist laws were widely debated and resisted by liberal public opinion. This is just one example which demonstrates that the application of the principle of self-defense is highly indetermined and readily contested. It follows that the argument in favor of banning the Islamic headscarf from schools for fear of a fundamentalist backlash is, on close inspection, highly questionable. Moreover, if fundamentalism is the real issue, then *foulards* should not only be excluded from public schools – they should not be tolerated anywhere. If Islam were (mistakenly) thought of as a fundamentalist religion, literally undermining the democratic tolerant state, the social order, and the lives of innocent citizens, then I do not see why only its religious symbols should be banned – and only in school – rather than the Islamic religion as a whole. Either the ban is called for because of the symbolic meaning of the headscarf – in which case it would not be justified on the basis of the self-defense principle (*hijabs* cannot be more dangerous for liberal institutions than revolutionary literature, which falls well within the boundaries of toleration) – or the prohibition should be defended on the grounds of the actual threat posed by the Muslim religion. But then it does not make sense to prohibit only the headscarf, and only in the public sphere. On closer inspection, then, the self-defense argument against the Islamic veil in school falls apart.

In conclusion, the position of the neutralist liberals, while helping to account for why the *foulard* case became a hotly disputed political issue, does not provide sound arguments for prohibition. All arguments such as those that we have just considered can be shown to imply some form of exclusion (or unequal inclusion) of the Islamic students in relation to the rest of the class. While Christian symbols are accepted as a matter of fact, Islamic symbols are contested because they are considered provocative. On the other hand, punk fashion is accepted even though it is provocative, but this does not count because punks are not a fundamentalist religious group posing a threat to democratic institutions. And yet the self-defense argument has never prevented the publication of revolutionary material, even when terrorism was an actual danger in European countries. In fact, France has always been extremely tolerant of terrorist refugees from Italy, for example, and French intellectuals, now so critical of the veil, were very critical of Italian anti-terrorist laws. So even the self-defense argument may imply a form of discrimination against the Muslim students when compared with (domestic) terrorism.

RESTATING THE PROBLEM

If limits to toleration of the *foulard* at school are unjustified, then the Islamic veil ought to be tolerated; but in order to be a satisfactory so-lution, toleration should be adopted for the right reasons, that is, not by dismissing the core questions underlying the issue, as I have already argued. So far, I have carefully considered the reasons against the veil in school, coming to the conclusion that none is sufficient to justify its prohibition, basically for reasons of fairness. As we have just seen, pater-nalism, the argument based on the separation of church and state, and the self-defense argument should apply equally to many other symbols, forms of behavior, and attitudes in our culture which, unlike the Islamic veil, are accepted as a matter of course. This is why the application of these arguments to this particular case appears clearly unfair. But, at this point, if toleration were adopted by default, no position is taken seriously and it would clearly not be the correct solution for either party involved in the conflict.

Having so far carefully listened to the (inconclusive) reasons against toleration, I think we should now try to make sense of what was really involved for the Islamic students and why they resisted the action of school officials. Why could they not accept the idea that French schools are secular, that religion has no part to play in them, that no one wanted to convert them and that their creed, together with its symbols and rituals, was perfectly acceptable outside the school, but that inside they had to be and behave like all other students? Why could they not be content with the idea of being like everyone else in the class? Was their insistence a sign of real religious fanaticism or of a perverse determination not to integrate – of refusing Frenchness? Of course, all these reasons might have constituted motives for the girls' insistence; but, as political theorists, we do not need such extreme motives in order to understand their behavior. Their minoritarian position and their less than full inclusion into French citizenship constitutes the relevant reason from a normative point of view. If considerations of justice would in fact warrant their conduct, whether or not other motives may have prompted the actual behavior, is normatively irrelevant. Political theory should therefore concentrate on the issue of justice.

The girls belong to a cultural and religious minority whose presence is now more visible in France, but whose members are far from being fully included in social and political terms. The inclusion offered by liberal democracy, by means of equal rights, fails in its goal. In fact, rights are given to individuals qua individuals, whatever their differences. Access to the public sphere of citizenship is therefore granted by disguising one's differences and group membership – in a word, one's collective identity. This kind of individualistic–universalistic inclusion is not satisfactory to members of minority groups who are publicly accepted only despite having characteristics that deviate from those of the majority. To be sure, public blindness to differences is intended to prevent institutional prejudice and bias. But this original anti-discriminatory goal has now been shown to create new forms of discrimination. The implicit requirement that different collective identities be invisible applies only to social groups that do not form part of the majority in society. The collective cultural or ethnic identities of the majority are not even seen as different, but as normal; they constitute the norm in society and set its standards. Because of this they do not need to be disguised in the public sphere. On the one hand, they no longer appear as different; on the other, being the norm, they set the standards against which all other differences are judged. Speaking French, in France, is not perceived as speaking a particular language, but, quite simply, as speaking. Members of the majority – white, Catholic, French-speaking, heterosexual males – need not disguise their collective identity: it is what defines the norm in the public sphere. At the same time, it makes no sense for them to make a public statement concerning their normal way of life. The majority, on the whole, simply takes its normality for granted, and has no experience of the sense of exclusion that pertains to minority groups. So the discrimination implied in the neutrality principle, interpreted as *laïcité*, is double-edged. First, despite being a universal principle, it applies differently to majority and minority members; second, it prevents minority members from being fully included in the polity, given the impossibility of disguising their collective identity.

Considering the case of the *foulard* against this background, there is no way that the three girls could simply have been content to be "like all the other students," because by giving up their scarves they would not have been treated as equals or given the same consideration and respect. Non-religious or Christian students are not asked to change their dress and behavior in order to be accepted at school. This is, indeed, an instance of how equal treatment can sometimes treat different people unequally. Hence, the insistence of the three girls on wearing the headscarf is not necessarily a sign of religious fundamentalism. It may well have been a quest for full inclusion by seeking public acceptance of their cultural difference. Their demonstration could be seen as a plea for justice, inclusion, and equal respect; in order to be seen and heard publicly, they had to make a very positive statement, causing others to take notice of behavior that is normally expected to stay hidden in the private sphere. I think that, quite independently of the actual motives of the girls, democratic institutions need to take this implicit quest for full inclusion seriously. The liberal principles of openness, inclusiveness and, more crucially, of equal respect provide a basis for viewing such requests as legitimate. If toleration is positively meant as a symbolic gesture of public acceptance of a difference linked to a minoritarian identity, it must meet the underlying claim of full inclusion advanced by the Muslim girls. But clearly, in order to satisfy the girls' claim, toleration must be adopted in such a way that it permits its symbolic meaning as recognition to be appreciated.

Here, however, a liberal doubt can be raised. The arguments against toleration might be insufficient, as previously shown, and the quest for inclusion might be legitimate from the standpoint of liberal democracy, yet the above kind of toleration might still be inconsistent with liberal practice, and might be ineffective in bringing about inclusion, producing instead the perverse effect of political fragmentation and cultural divisiveness. This liberal objection partly restates the worry already implicit in the self-defense argument for the *foulard* prohibition, namely the worry about the breach of liberal neutrality as crucial to the persistence of liberal society. But I have already shown above that such a worry is misplaced, given that, on the one hand, the public sphere is already inhabited by majoritarian identities, and, on the other, that neutrality need not to be dismissed, but only reinterpreted. Toleration in its symbolic meaning of public recognition of collective identities and social differences is not incompatible with liberal politics and liberal neutrality, but only with one of the possible interpretations of liberalism. Public or institutional blindness is only one of the possible interpretations of liberal neutrality (much as *laïcité* is only one of the interpretations of public blindness), though it is probably the most common. Using Ronald Dworkin's distinction between constitutive and derivative principles,[14] one can say that liberal neutrality is constitutive, and institutional blindness derivative. Only if neutrality is interpreted as institutional blindness is public recognition of social differences obviously incompatible with a crucial liberal principle. For this reason, in fact, feminists and supporters of multiculturalism have strongly attacked liberalism and, in particular, liberal neutrality and the public/private distinction.[15] They argue that since liberal neutrality is tailored to a particular identity which disguises diversity under the pretense of universality and impartiality, we must do away with the very idea of public space, impartiality, and general rules. Despite their radical tone, however, feminists and multiculturalists are not prepared to give up the liberal principles of individual liberties, a free press, or equal worth and respect, which are intrinsically linked with some form of the public/private distinction.

By contrast, I argue that liberal neutrality should not be done away with, but simply reinterpreted. It is meant to be an anti-discriminatory principle, aimed at preventing advantages or burdens from being unfairly attached to religious creeds, moral values, or cultural alternatives. Institutional blindness is a strategy for fulfilling this anti-discriminatory aim, but, as it currently operates in some circumstances, it clearly involves some form of discrimination and less than equal respect. In these cases, institutional blindness should give way to a public recognition of

---

[14] See Dworkin, "Liberalism."
[15] For an example of this attitude against the public/private distinction, see Young, *Justice and the Politics of Difference.*

minoritarian differences, which does not mean giving undue attention to individual characteristics that should be irrelevant from a political point of view. It would also not imply being discriminatory, as some liberals have remarked. The fact that the members of a minority group are excluded from full participation in democratic citizenship because they are "different" makes those differences politically relevant. While in an ideal world they should not count in political life (and should not need to be concealed either), at present they do actually count as factors of exclusion. Therefore, recognizing them in the public sphere is a way of neutralizing the undue burden they place on their bearers. It is another way of equalizing all differences in the public arena, hence of being neutral and impartial.

Similarly, equal treatment is only a derivative of the principle of equal respect. Sometimes equal respect requires equal treatment (as in grading tests at school); sometimes it requires equivalent treatment – that is, policies that are equally sensitive to different identities, as in the Islamic headscarf case and in the question of maternity leave; and at other times it may suggest differential treatment, as in affirmative action policies, as a compensatory measure for past and persistent exclusion. Leaving aside for the moment the question of whether equivalent and differential treatments do achieve their intended goal, from a theoretical point of view, all three kinds of public policy are required by the principle of equal respect. Which one is in order in any given situation varies according to the circumstances, but, in any case, it is not an ad hoc decision. Given the circumstances, only one kind of public policy satisfies the equal respect principle and the anti-discrimination clause. In sum, tolerating the headscarf in public schools does not mean giving special attention to Islamic students, but giving them the same consideration as that granted to non-religious and Christian students.

Finally, is public toleration of the Islamic headscarf likely to be an effective way of promoting the full inclusion of Muslim students or will it give rise to a divisive and hostile attitude, setting the rest of the class against them and contributing to their further segregation?[16] I think that the public toleration of social differences will constitute a step towards full inclusion of minority members only if it is grounded on reciprocity. Unilateral toleration may in fact be viewed as a condescending or paternalistic

---

[16] This is the "objection from futility," according to Albert Hirschman's typology (*The Rhetoric of Reaction* [Cambridge, Mass.: Belknap Press, 1991]), which is raised by those who are skeptical about symbolic politics constituting the stuff of recognition. See, for example, Michael Walzer, "Minority Rites," *Dissent*, Summer 1996, pp. 53–5.

gesture by those being tolerated; it might be better than suppression or repression, but it is far from satisfactory. In turn, any uneasiness about being tolerated might engender a feeling of resentment in the majority. Thus, if headscarves are to be tolerated in school because of the principle of equal respect, then liberal democracy, in turn, is entitled to ask new minorities for political loyalty to its democratic institutions. Such a reciprocal request is not only justified on ethical grounds, but also for pragmatic reasons. If toleration is to be instrumental in promoting the full inclusion of members of marginal, oppressed, and minoritarian groups, it must be the premise for a cooperative attitude among different social groups. In a case like that of the veil, prohibition cannot but reinforce social hostility between the Muslim community and the majority, yet toleration is only a first step towards cooperative pluralism. If it is perceived as a mere modus vivendi, it may simply conceal hostility and conflict. What, however, can be done to avoid the resentment of the majority and the dissatisfaction of the minority, apart from granting toleration? Asking those who are tolerated to reciprocate is one possible answer. In this way, two results can, in principle, be achieved. First, minority groups will not be treated condescendingly, as passive recipients, but as responsible, active members of the polity. Second, majority members will be able to view toleration not only as a public indulgence, but as a strategy of inclusion, implying a corresponding responsibility and obligation by the minority. The typical asymmetrical relationship linking the tolerator and the tolerated, which makes toleration such a difficult and ambiguous virtue, is consequently transformed into an equal partnership: nationals accept immigrants, with their different traits and cultures, as part of the normal variety of a pluralist society, and immigrants in turn, as loyal citizens, accept democratic institutions.

5

Should we tolerate racism?

Arguments for toleration are easier to deal with than claims for limiting toleration of offensive practices. As we have seen above, the argument for public toleration of difference can be grounded on the lack of
public respect implied by the principle of public blindness, given that
the latter applies unilaterally to minority differences and cannot ensure
that newcomers or excluded groups satisfy even the minimal conditions
for becoming fully functioning citizens. Moreover, public toleration of
differences, given its symbolic nature, can be attributed neutrally (being
content-independent) and impartially (being generalizable to all differences, once the harm test is passed). By contrast, the argument for limiting freedom of expression for the sake of toleration is generally more
complex. Even if its fundamental premises are sound, it nevertheless implies the limitation of some individual right and also forms of preferential
treatment. Briefly, the argument can be summarized as follows.

The starting point must be the common knowledge that liberal
democratic institutions and governments have taken a stand against exclusion and discrimination not only in the most obvious formal sense of
a lack of rights, but also in the broader sense of a lack of public respect,
dignity, and consideration which are due to everyone and seen as necessary conditions for being a good citizen. Without such a starting point,
the whole argument against the toleration of offensive practices does not
hold up or make sense in a given social context.

Second, once public toleration and its symbolic meaning have been
granted, some behavior and practices are found to be offensive to the
collective identities of those from previously excluded groups, perhaps
damaging the self-confidence and self-esteem of the newcomer,[1] and having the effect of unsettling the process of inclusion of the whole group.

[1] See Altman, "Liberalism and Campus Hate Speech," pp. 302–17.

More serious consequences might arise too, which, if unchecked, could easily multiply and might even lead to systematic intimidation and attacks on what are in effect still minority groups, undermining their inclusion in the public domain. Such a development – if it remains unchecked – would suggest that there is still some freedom for individuals and groups in the society to act in an offensive way. This, in turn, implies that institutional indifference to social intimidation, humiliation and stigmatization of minorities has not yet been overcome. This second step of the argument stresses that offenses against newly admitted identities are not only damaging to the individual who is the target, but are also likely to jeopardize the whole process of inclusion. Hence, non-toleration of offensive practices implies something more than merely protecting the individual victim from intimidation and harassment. It is a symbolic public gesture against discrimination in general.

Third, once the symbolic meaning of non-toleration is grasped, we can proceed to explain why the dignity of such groups is entitled to protection, while similar offenses to majority members should be tolerated. Why is it that ethnic insults should be forbidden, while insults to capitalists, for example, should be tolerated? Why should the self-esteem and self-confidence of people of African or Asian origin suffer more than that of other categories of citizen and taxpayer? The answer is connected with the need to repair past injustice, past exclusion, and discrimination. It considers the difference in self-esteem and self-confidence between an established member of society and a newcomer. As a rule, an offense against the collective identity of the former is not only compensated for by high social standing, but does not threaten their inclusion in the polity. By contrast, the latter is generally in a very weak social position, as their previous exclusion and discrimination will have left persisting prejudices. In this case the offense is more serious, not for psychological but for structural reasons of social standing and rank. Since the victims' objective weakness can be ascribed to the effects of past injustice, there are reasons for giving special consideration to the collective image of previously excluded groups, as a form of redress.

Fourth, this argument in terms of justice can be supplemented by another based on the principle of consistency. Liberal institutions and governments granting public toleration of differences have taken a step toward comprehensive inclusion. If, however, intolerant attitudes are widespread, including attitudes and actions that are offensive to the collective identities of different groups, and undermine the process of inclusion, some limits should be placed on any such intolerant expression, given public commitment to a tolerant and open society.

This argument is obviously open to criticism and objections at various stages in its long and complex development. There are objections of principle – i.e. against any kind of special consideration or preferential treatment given to minority groups in order to ensure liberal justice; and against any limitations on the rights to liberty of the members of the majority, even for the sake of equality and social justice. Then there are criticisms on points of fact – i.e. on the connection between the public protection of weak identities and their inclusion as a stable part of society. Finally, there are pragmatic objections about the perverse consequences of such policies, and there are many difficulties in applying this argument concretely: from a precise definition of what counts as an offense or as exclusion, to what it means to be a member of a particular group. I will try to see how this general argument applies to the issue of racism which, in principle, should make the argument easier, given the general view that racism is morally and socially intolerable.

Many of the arguments in favor of limiting the toleration of certain attitudes, practices, and behavior appeal to alleged racism as their justification. Although racism is universally condemned, it is still widespread in more or less direct forms, and thus jeopardizes the ideal of a multicultural society where inclusion is based on the recognition of differences, rather than on the full assimilation of minorities to the social mainstream. Racist attitudes and behavior, even if not directly translated into attacks and open discrimination, constitute an insidious danger to the politics of recognition. But in fact, in liberal democracies, they often escape legitimate political intervention, belonging instead to the sphere of spontaneous social interaction which, as a rule, pertains to individual freedom. It seems that government cannot interfere in this area without giving up the basics of its liberal tenet; besides, people cannot effectively be forced to choose their friends or partners by legal command. And yet, can racism, which is the exact opposite of toleration, be tolerated? Are we to give up any attempt to check racist attitudes which undermine the very project of a multicultural society?

In this chapter I take up this general question by considering some of the examples which have been publicly debated in different contexts in recent years, such as the outlawing of racist groups in EC countries, the hate speech controversy in the US and the prohibition of historical revisionism issued by the German Supreme Court. Analysis of these examples will show that the project of toleration as recognition is harder to pursue when it touches on the everyday interaction of individuals and groups. Some liberal thinkers consider that this area falls outside the realm of politics, which should exclusively concern matters of justice; even without reference to a thick conception of politics that focuses on human happiness, quality of life, and common good, however, a liberal conception of politics cannot but see that racist attitudes do in fact affect justice. A just society cannot escape the issue of social exclusion, whether it is the result of material deprivation or marginalization, humiliation, and stereotyping. Racist offenses, whether physical or verbal, are not generally aimed at individuals randomly, but specifically because those individuals are members of groups which are socially and culturally subordinate in society. In this way, racism prolongs and fosters asymmetrical power relationships. Therefore it seems that the expression of racist attitudes does not simply concern individual freedom, which might be entitled to toleration, but contributes to injustice and requires some sort of public intervention.

The examples which I am going to consider are instances of the need to limit toleration, on the one hand, and of the difficulty of defining such limits, on the other. They are also instances of the peculiar opposition that exists between racism and toleration as recognition. I will start by asking whether or not racism is tolerable in general, and then proceed to see whether a general theoretical answer can be applied to different cases.

Racism, in its broadest definition, is articulated in a variety of doctrines and beliefs: from the classical doctrine that argues for the superiority of one particular race, to a more practical hostility and resentment towards different ethnic or cultural groups.[2] The target of racist attitudes does not even necessarily belong to a different race in the conventional sense. Just as the concept of race, which actually has no scientific foundation,[3] is the result of a social construction, so any different group can be construed in racial, or at least ethnic, terms. The most obvious example concerns

[2] For general definitions of racism, see: Léon Poliakov, *Le Mythe Arian* (Paris: Calman-Lévy, 1971); Pierre-André Taguieff, *La force du préjugé* (Paris: La Découverte, 1988); George Mosse, *Toward the Final Solution: History of European Racism* (New York: Howard Fertig, 1978).

[3] That the concept of race has no scientific basis is contended by molecular biologists who have shown that there is no correspondence between groups traditionally defined in racial terms and genetic findings, and that the number of DNA similarities and of individual variations among humans is such as to make the concept of race empty and distorting. See A. Piazza, "Biologia senza razze," *Sisifo*, 26 October 1993, p. 7, and Luca and Francesco Cavalli-Sforza, *Chi siamo. La storia della diversità umana* (Milan: Mondadori, 1993).

the Jews, seen by Nazis as an inferior race, although their identity is basically religious and cultural. Despite the variety of its forms, racism always leads to some sort of segregation among groups, and usually also implies a hierarchical ranking. The idea is that each group should stay in its own place, geographically and socially, either because one group is considered naturally superior, or because differences between the groups are considered incompatible, and the idea that they might mix is distasteful.

However phrased, racism seems to be the very opposite of toleration – indeed, the very essence of intolerance. Toleration is the social virtue and the political principle that enables the peaceful and civil coexistence of different people and groups on the same footing within the same society. Racism, on the other hand, if unchecked and translated into action, leads to the separation and domination of certain racially defined groups over others which are deemed inferior. Furthermore, toleration is an expression of equality of respect: a reciprocal respect, which is politically granted to all by means of positive measures against discrimination. It is, in fact, the ideal cement of pluralist democracy. Equality of respect does not cancel out the many divisions and contrasts which arise from all possible differences within a maximally pluralist society, but it places them in a framework of moral acceptability, lifting the veil of contempt, humiliation, and shame that is linked to minoritarian differences.

Racism, on the other hand, reinforces the feeling of dislike and distaste produced by cultural differences, grounding it on the alleged superiority of a certain race or civilization or group. It is not that racism in all cases necessarily and explicitly affirms a disrespect of so-called inferior groups. There is, in fact, a form of respect which is compatible with racism: namely, the unequal respect paid in any hierarchical society to those who, at each level of the hierarchy, perform their role dutifully and exhibit the virtues appropriate to their station – for those situated at the bottom and at the margins of society these might include humility, devotion, and gratitude. It is simply that racism precludes equality, reciprocity, and mutual respect. Consequently, from a racist viewpoint, someone belonging to a supposedly inferior race can be accepted, if at all, only as a subordinate, and respected only if he or she is willing to accept this situation. And this is clearly opposed to the goal of toleration, whose aim is to free people from the burden of their differences and identities.

Thus, racist attitudes, apart from their undesirable practical consequences, which might include violence and real discrimination, display an intolerance which is intrinsically harmful, both directly for those who are striving to be accepted on an equal footing, and, more generally, for the process of including such minorities within a pluralist democracy. This is due to the fact that, whether or not it is explicitly spelled out, underlying any racist attitude is a devaluation, diminution, or even dehumanization of those who are the target of racism. Such humiliation can be the premise for cruelty, slavery and, at worst, genocide. But even if racism does not lead to violence and/or discrimination, the fact that members of a racially defined group are considered unworthy of equal respect because of some ascribed and morally indifferent characteristic is, without doubt, a moral wrong, and is intrinsically humiliating for its targets.

Since the defeat of Nazism and the revelation of the Holocaust, there is little doubt that racism has been regarded as morally wrong across all cultures and moral codes. In fact, despite many examples to the contrary in practice, few people today easily accept being called racist. The general condemnation of racism produces a tendency to disguise racist attitudes and behavior under different labels. So although racist hatred and discrimination are still widespread, a direct defense or open endorsement of racism are rare, limited to small fanatical groups, since it is generally unacceptable in public discourse.

Should we therefore tolerate racism? We have seen that if translated into political action it can have dramatic negative consequences, leading even to the destruction of liberal justice. But even if it does not actually threaten the stability of the liberal order, racist attitudes and behavior, scattered throughout society, are intrinsically harmful directly and indirectly to those who are targeted. Even leaving aside potential harmful consequences to the system and to individuals, racism embodies attitudes which directly contrast with the most fundamental principles and cherished values of liberal democracy, denying equal respect and moral worth to all citizens. Finally, it is universally regarded as a moral wrong. According to the political morality which sustains liberal institutions, racism appears to belong in the category of the intolerable. Briefly, it seems to fall outside all the limits fixed for toleration both as a political principle and as a social virtue. Within the political domain, racism is excluded from toleration in the name both of the harm principle and of the self-defense of the liberal order. In social intercourse the toleration of racism simply amounts to indulgence, for toleration is a virtue only if it refers to behavior which is disliked or disapproved of by the tolerator, but which is not universally seen as a moral wrong.[4] Therefore it would seem to follow not only that racist attacks and acts of discrimination should be prosecuted, but also that racist movements and parties should in some way be legally prevented from spreading and gaining power, by using democratic procedures. Moreover, given that racist attitudes are acknowledged to be both harmful and morally wrong, they should also be excluded from toleration, whether political or social.

However, when philosophical reasoning is applied to public affairs, any argument for a particular application of a general principle seems dramatically underdetermined; more specifically, the question of racism is a good instance of the so-called pragmatic paradox of toleration.[5] The more tolerant a society, the more liberal it is, but also the more exposed to the risk of being overtaken by intolerant forces. If liberalism is to be preserved, toleration must be restricted; and the stricter its limits of toleration, the safer liberalism, but the less liberal the society. The balance between self-defense and oppressive politics is a difficult one, and is a matter of contextual sensitivity, not of the uniquely correct implementation of principles. The limits to toleration are thus necessarily the result of a pragmatic accommodation: principles are balanced against shared understandings of acceptable state interference, of actual risks to the system, and of what counts as harm. In sum, in deliberations on specific cases, the above argument showing racism as intolerable provides reasons for questioning toleration of racism, rather than straightforwardly justifying intolerance.

AN EASY ANSWER: LIMITS TO THE HARMFUL
CONSEQUENCES OF RACISM

Let us consider different types of instances of racism in order to understand when the argument against toleration applies, and to what extent, starting with cases where government intervention is the obvious answer.

---

[4] According to an influential strand of analysis, toleration would be a moral virtue when applied to forms of behavior or attitudes that fall somewhere in between matters of moral indifference and matters that are universally regarded as morally wrong. This point has been made especially clear by Horton, "Toleration as a Virtue."

[5] The pragmatic paradox of toleration is discussed by Norberto Bobbio, "Le ragioni della tolleranza," in P. C. Bori, ed., *Eguali e diversi nella storia* (Bologna: Il Mulino, 1986), pp. 243–57, and "Tolleranza e verità," *Lettera internazionale*, 15, 1988, pp. 16–18. The pragmatic paradox must be set apart from the ethical paradox, analyzed by Cohen, "An Ethical Paradox," which has to do with the prima facie moral and logical impossibility to accept what is subject to disapproval.

Comparatively non-controversial cases occur when racism leads directly to violent attacks, harassment, or to any behavior explicitly aimed at excluding or discriminating against someone because of his or her race. In the first case, violent racist behavior constitutes a clear infringement of the harm principle. Even if the definition of harm is a matter of interpretation, there is a shared understanding that physical coercion definitely constitutes harm of the worst kind. It represents the classic example of violation of rights: the violation of the right to physical security. Thus violent attacks on anybody, for whatever reason, are legally prosecutable; in this respect, violence need not actually be linked to racism for it to be prohibited. It can be argued that racism produces further psychological damage by humiliating the person attacked, and by indirectly harming all members of the group in question. However, when violence is at issue, whether or not as a result of racism, toleration is definitely excluded.

Similarly, in cases of racist discrimination or exclusion, even if no actual physical harm is involved, there is still little doubt that coercion occurs and that the right to liberty of the victim has been violated – even according to the strictest reading of libertarians such as Hayek or Nozick.[6] So in this case, too, racist actions should be legally prosecuted because they violate rights and any such violation is prosecutable, whatever its motivation. Here, however, we can establish a connection between racism and prohibition. In the open society, exclusion from jobs, higher education, certain levels of welfare, and so on, can occur unintentionally, as a result of competition and market allocation. Whether this is considered just and justifiable is controversial, but in any case it cannot be said to constitute a direct violation of the right to liberty of the excluded. If, by contrast, racism is the reason for the exclusion (and if this can be proved), it cannot be seen as an unintentional result of competition and market allocation, but as an intentional act of discrimination, an obstacle intended to prevent someone from having access to certain resources or opportunities. In other words, if proved, racist attitudes constitute an intention to exclude and, hence, a positive violation of rights. The violation of a right is in this sense dependent on the racist attitude, but the difficulty lies in the proof. Leaving this problem aside, toleration for such an act is clearly out of the question.

It should be noted, however, that, even though in this case there is a direct link between the racist motivation and legal prosecution of the act (a link which is absent in the former case of violent attack), prohibition does

---

[6] See F. A. Hayek, *The Constitution of Liberty* (London and Chicago: Routledge and University of Chicago Press, 1960), and R. Nozick, *Anarchy, State and Utopia* (New York: Basic Books, 1974).

not concern racism per se, but the intentional exclusion which results. In other words, it is the harmful consequence which is punishable, not the attitude or the belief that produces it. In a sense, this is obvious and right; in a liberal society, it is harmful actions and not intentions that should be punished.[7] But, at the same time, this throws a different light on the classic principle that toleration should be restricted in the face of intolerance. There is no doubt that racism is intrinsically intolerant, and yet it can and should be stopped only when it results in harmful actions, and such actions are legally prosecutable whether or not they are consequences of racism. It now becomes clear in what sense the non-controversial principle that tolerance should be restricted in the face of intolerance is actually indetermined. The subject of public non-toleration is not the intolerant doctrine per se, but its actual or potential harmful consequences for third parties and for the system as a whole. Going back, then, to the original question, "Should we tolerate racism?," the apparently obvious answer in the negative must be modified to: "Yes, unless harmful consequences are or might be the result."

The point needs further elaboration. In cases of violence or open discrimination induced by racist attitudes, harm and the infringement of rights are not contingent or unexpected consequences of action, but the direct outcome of clearly defined attitudes and motivations. Legal intervention, in such instances, recognizes racism as the origin of the harm.[8] And yet an explicit link between violence and racist attitudes does not seem sufficient to extend the prosecution of racism to the level of beliefs and motivations which are not actually acted upon.

In order to disentangle the issue, I would draw a distinction between racist conduct which is intrinsically harmful, independently of its underlying motivations, and conduct which is harmful in virtue of the racist attitude that underpins it, such as verbal abuse or racist propaganda and demonstrations. In the first case, the crucial reason for fixing limits to toleration stems from the harmful effects of the conduct and not from the motivations behind it. If the same action were done for different motives, it would not be tolerated in any circumstance, because the outcome entails a violation of rights. The second case is theoretically more

---

[7] For example, in the Italian criminal code, as well as in some international treaties, there are laws against genocide, against racial, ethnic, and religious discrimination, and also against incitement to genocide, racial violence, and discrimination. There are no laws against racism. See the *Criminal Code of the Italian Republic*, law of 9 October 1967, no. 962; law of 13 October 1975, no. 654; laws of 26 April 1993 and 25 June 1993, no. 205; law of 6 March 1998, no. 40, art. 41.

[8] This circumstance is taken into account in the Italian criminal code, where the subjects of sanctions are always harmful actions, but where such actions are also clearly referred back to their racist motivations.

intriguing: there, it seems that the argument showing racism as intolerable can at last find proper application, given that the expression of racist attitudes is what directly constitutes the wrong. The point of contention now is whether a verbal wrong counts as harm, and justifies limits to toleration.

When the direct consequence of racist conduct is obviously harmful, as in the cases considered above, racist acts are excluded from toleration. Difficulties arise either when harmful consequences are only potential, or when it is arguable whether racist acts are in fact harmful.

Let us now consider potentially harmful consequences of racism. We have seen that racist doctrine, if systematically developed and embodied in political organizations, can produce a society deeply at odds with liberal and democratic values. If racist organizations were to gain support and, making use of democratic procedures, become politically powerful, democracy would be threatened, and it would probably be too late for any legal ban to be effective. However, it is, in practice, very hard to trace a line between a possible risk that might in theory arise as the result of propaganda and an actual risk. Should the publication of racist propaganda be forbidden, for example? Or should only publications that call for illegal action be forbidden? Again, this is a difficult line to draw. And what about racist organizations and associations themselves: should they be outlawed? It is very hard to find a general criterion for decision-making in such instances; on the one hand, given the difficulties involved in preserving the liberal order with minimal state interference, public decisions will largely depend on the perception of risk represented by racist groups. On the other hand, the perception of risk is not independent of whether racism is a burning political issue in that society. This is generally the case when the groups which are the target of racism raise their voice against oppression, discrimination, and humiliation, and when their protest gains wider support in society at large. But if racism is only episodic, or not clearly opposed by its victims, it is not usually associated with any risk to the political order, even though it may be common practice in that society. Moreover, the perception of risk will be balanced against the level of state intervention considered acceptable.

The point is that while the three contextual variables just mentioned (perception of risk, racism as a political issue, and the acceptable level of state intervention) can account for the decision actually made, it is less clear that they can also provide a justification for it, whether the decision be prohibition or toleration. In fact, a mistaken perception of risk can lead to a wrong solution. From a normative viewpoint, apart from extreme cases, any choice is genuinely underdetermined, and the decision will eventually be fixed by extra-ethical considerations. In general, the argument against toleration of racist movements on the basis of self-defense of the liberal order cannot easily arrive at a satisfactory answer, given that the extent of the threat to society as a whole is a matter of inherent uncertainty, and is hence intrinsically always contestable *ex ante*.

As the self-defense argument against the potential dangers of racism appears highly underdetermined within contemporary democracy, the harm that results from racist abuse seems to provide stronger grounds for intervention, insofar as in such cases the abuse is not simply an intention, but is indeed real. That a small Nazi organization might win enough support and gain political power in a liberal democratic state is hard to believe, but there is little doubt that a Nazi march displaying racist slogans in public is insulting and humiliating to those who are targeted. In fact, it is on the grounds of the (alleged) harm produced by racist abuse that much of contemporary debate concerning the limits to hate speech has developed. However slim the possible risk to the social order, it cannot be denied that racist marches and slogans offend those at whom they are aimed. It is no accident, then, that in contemporary arguments against toleration of racism reference to racist offenses plays a more prominent role than reference to the risks to the liberal order.

THE CASE OF THE ITALIAN CONSTITUTIONAL CLAUSE AGAINST FASCISM

As an example of the general evolution of the reasons against the toleration of racism, from democratic self-defense to racist abuse, I will refer to the clause in the Italian constitution, created in 1948 just after World War II, which forbids the reestablishment of the Fascist Party in Italy.[9] Of course, fascism is not the same as racism, but given that a racist doctrine is clearly a part of fascist ideology and that the fascist regime subscribed to the racial laws against Jews in 1938 and took part in the Nazi persecution of Jews during the war, I contend that it is not unreasonable to cite fascism as an example of racism. Widely agreed upon amongst all parties contributing to the new charter, the provision forbidding fascist and racist ideology, organization, or party was included in the constitution

---

[9] See XII Disposizione transitoria e finale, Comma 1 of the Italian constitution.

and, in 1952, was translated into an actual criminal law, later modified in the context of anti-terrorist legislation in the 1970s.[10] It was clearly meant to defend the new republic against the risk of a fascist resurgence. The memories of the tragedies brought about by the fascist regime were still fresh, while the risk of a right-wing putsch was perceived as real – and with good reason. During the Cold War it was always conceivable that former fascists, in a country which now had the largest Communist Party in the west, might take the opportunity to win support in a bid to counter communism. After all, elsewhere in Europe fascist regimes still ruled in Spain and Portugal and a fascist coup took place in Greece in the 1960s.

In fact, the anti-fascist law was not used in the 1950s to stop a neo-fascist party from being founded, even under a different name; the only time it was seriously applied in the second half of the twentieth century was in the 1970s, when it was used to outlaw two small extreme right-wing groups, clearly linked to fascist terrorism in a period of great political tension and real danger for the democratic order, which was under attack from both left- and right-wing terrorism.[11] Once the wave of terrorism had passed, and a stable democratic order was reestablished, the anti-fascist rule was used, though not often, under a different interpretation, as a means of defining as criminal and punishing the racist behavior of Nazi skinhead groups against Jews and immigrants – i.e. the two main racist targets in the country. In general, nowadays, the law tends to be implemented by judges and legal scholars as an instrument against racist harassment and offenses expressed by some Nazi-inspired football fans or juvenile organizations. Thus, what was originally intended as a defense of democracy against fascist attacks, in the days when there was a perceived risk to the political order, is now used as a legal weapon against racist abuse. The actual harm resulting from racist attacks has overtaken the potential danger of racism to the democratic order.

Yet although potential violence towards ethnic groups is currently perceived as a more urgent reason for stopping racism than the self-defense

---

[10] Note the definition of a fascist organization as provided by a 1952 statute: fascist organizations are those (a) pursuing anti-democratic goals; (b) threatening and exalting violence as a proper means of political struggle; (c) advocating the suppression of fundamental liberties; (d) denigrating democracy; and (e) making racist propaganda. Such a definition emphasizes the anti-democratic, violent, and subversive nature of fascism, but leaves room for interpreting the statute in a more precise anti-racist sense.

[11] For a proper reconstruction of those events and of the political atmosphere, see F. Ferraresi, *Threats to Democracy* (Princeton: Princeton University Press, 1996).

of democracy, it must be underlined that the level of intervention that is permissible is not the same in the two cases. While the self-defense argument can justify the outlawing of racist organizations, the possibility of racist abuse can, at most, provide justification for the prohibition of marches. In general, only well-defined sorts of racist behavior can be regulated on the grounds that they are offensive or are instances of discriminatory behavior. But at this point another problem makes it difficult to intervene politically in the matter of racist offenses. Can verbal abuse and humiliation derived from certain (racist) attitudes and speech codes count as doing harm; that is, can they provide a warrant for the withholding of toleration and the imposition of limits to freedom of expression? This question, which underlies most contemporary cases concerning hate speech and racist attitudes, implies a genuine theoretical, ethical, and political dilemma between the commitment to combat racism and its harmful consequences for civil coexistence and the principle of freedom of expression. Whether or not the dilemma can be solved, and if so in what way, however, is more dependent on contextual variables, such as the political culture and legal tradition of the country concerned, which implicitly define the priority or the balance between the right of freedom of expression and the right to personal dignity, than on conclusive normative arguments – as the following discussion on hate speech will show.

In European political and legal culture, offenses, racist or otherwise, constitute a definite harm because they violate the right of personal dignity. Criminalizing them is not, therefore, seen as an undue restriction on freedom of expression – although, as a matter of fact, these criminal laws are not commonly enforced (with the exception of cases of libel and defamation by the media).[12] In this way, a pragmatic solution has been worked out: on the one hand, there is the need to protect individual dignity, which is entrusted to the criminal laws against racist abuse – whose implementation, limited to a small number of paradigm cases, is more symbolic than a strict and general legal enforcement would require. On the other, there are legal provisions which are rarely enforced and which, therefore, in practice have not significantly impinged upon the right to freedom of expression or imposed any noticeable restrictions on everyday language (which, as a result, retains many racist expressions). Yet, in this way, a symbolic recognition of the intolerability of racism is

---

[12] A useful reconstruction of the difficult balance between the priority of the First Amendment and defamation law is offered by S. H. Shiffrin, *The First Amendment: Democracy and Romance* (Princeton: Princeton University Press, 1990), pp. 30–1 and 42–4.

granted, notwithstanding a general practice of tolerance and the fact that there is no censorship on everyday language. Before assessing any such solution properly, let us reconstruct the arguments used in the hate speech controversy.

HATE SPEECH

Let us first try to summarize the problem in its theoretical dimension. The issue is raised when members of minority groups that are traditionally subjected to various forms of racism start resisting racist insults, provocation, and harassment in general, and calling for political intervention. Certain particular circumstances are necessary for this to become an issue at all, least of all a controversial one. First, the sociopolitical background must be a liberal democratic society where racism is politically banned and publicly condemned. In other words, for a racial group to raise its voice against racist insults (and by this I do not mean segregation, physical attacks, or open discrimination), it is first necessary that the society be democratic and committed to anti-racism, and that segregation and discrimination be publicly rejected and actively fought against. Only when the barriers of segregation and of discrimination have been legally removed, and only when the ideal of equal citizenship independent of race, language, origin, and religion is firmly entrenched in that society, can the problem of racist offenses and humiliation be reasonably approached. Here we are facing the now familiar problems that arise from aiming at the full inclusion, beyond the mere legal extension of equal rights, of groups that have previously been objects of discrimination. The same demand for recognition of equal citizenship underlies claims for public toleration of differences and claims for stopping toleration of racist offenses. Second, when the issue of offensive racist expression is raised, the group in question – or rather its spokespersons – must have already reached political visibility and the problem of its full inclusion must be acknowledged in the political sphere. This does not mean that members of that group have already achieved full inclusion and are recognized as equal citizens and members of the community. It does mean, however, that minorities which demand rules against hate speech or prosecution for racist insults are often perceived by the majority as vociferous and as unduly aggressive, despite the persistent disadvantages and marginal position of most people in such groups. This fact contributes to making the two rival positions more polarized and, in general, the whole issue more controversial.

Last, but not least, arguments in favor of ruling out racist offenses become an issue only in liberal democracies which are committed to the priority of free speech over other liberal rights, such as the protection of personal dignity. That is the case in the United States where the First Amendment provides a constitutional protection for free speech and where the priority of this right over others appears undisputed, which simply could not make sense in the European context. If, as in my earlier example about Italian anti-fascist laws, a liberal democratic constitution acknowledges that the right to free speech can be restricted not only by harmful consequences which are independent from the content of the speech, but also by its potential clash with other individual rights (such as the right to personal dignity and public respect), thereby including criminal laws against libel, defamation, injury and offenses, then the problem of racist offenses is easily faced by extending and specifying those general rules.[13] That is the case in most European countries, where a growing awareness of racist abuse against groups that have been traditionally subject to racism (Jews, gypsies, immigrants) has found a response in legal provisions which, theoretically, are just a special application of general rules against abuse, and, politically, have never been subject to controversy. If, by contrast, the constitutional framework fixes a clear priority of the right to free speech over other liberal rights, then arguments to stop racist abuse are not easily accommodated within the legal and political culture. The lack of legal provision against general abuse, moreover, creates a further difficulty. Laws against racist speech, in fact, appear not only to clash with freedom of speech, but also to raise the issue of differential treatment: why should only racist abuse be forbidden?

I do not want to discuss here whether the priority of free speech over other liberal rights makes for a more liberal society or for a more contentious and aggressive one. Nor do I want to discuss the issue of whether the reference to the First Amendment is more ideological than principled, more unilateral than universal, given that such a priority did not prevent the USA from becoming embroiled in the McCarthy campaign, which was certainly not inspired by the ideal of free speech. I contend that when there is a (potential or actual) clash of rights, liberal theory is genuinely unable to decide on the correct solution. In other words, there are reasons, which are not conclusive, both in favor of the priority of free speech and in favor of a balance between the two conflicting rights. As a

---

[13] Libel is also acknowledged by American laws; but it is arguable whether or not public officials are protected from libel; see *New York Times* v. *Sullivan* from which an absolute protection of free speech in the political/public domain seems to derive. See Shiffrin, *The First Amendment*, pp. 49–50.

result, a decision is generally reached on extra-normative grounds, such as the legal or political tradition, the harshness of the conflict, historical antecedents, etc. Here, I want to engage in a theoretical reconstruction of the issue of hate speech, assuming the priority of free speech and trying to see if in such a framework an argument in favor of outlawing racist abuse can nevertheless be accommodated.

The priority given to free speech can be argued on different grounds: for example, on the grounds of a Millian consequentialism, according to which the damage suffered by society as a whole if one dissenting voice is silenced is far greater than the harm produced by single cases of abuse towards individuals. On this basis, toleration of racist abuse is endorsed as the lesser evil.[14] On the other hand, priority can be based on the crucial importance of free speech for the working of democratic institutions. This is indeed the notion endorsed in the case *New York Times* v. *Sullivan*,[15] where it was stated that debate on public issues should be uninhibited, robust, and wide open in order to allow a proper working of political democracy as self-government. From such an argument the central meaning of the First Amendment derives and entails that "prosecution for libel on governmental matters has no place in the American System of jurisprudence."[16] In this case, legislation against abuse is regarded as a dangerous weapon in the hands of politicians and of the ruling class who may use it to check criticisms and censor a free press and voices of dissent. In any case, let us assume that, for whatever argument, the priority of free speech over other rights is a shared value and from such a standpoint let us inspect the debate around hate speech.

In this context the issue is focused on whether racist abuse should count as harm and can justify limits to freedom of expression. In the literature on hate speech, much attention is devoted to (a) arguments for and against abuse as a form of psychological harm, and (b) the tracing of analytical distinctions between speech as a form of expression, with or without value, and speech as a mere utterance in order to give a justification for restriction of some kinds of speech acts without in general questioning the priority of free speech. I do not find these lines of argument very promising, and will therefore approach the issue of hate speech against

---

[14] Mill, *On Liberty*.   [15] 376 US 254, 273, 1964.
[16] See, Shiffrin, *The First Amendment*, p. 50. Shiffrin's critical analysis of this problem shows, however, that the priority of free speech is not and cannot be absolute: "In truth, it turns out that nothing is sacred . . . Freedom of speech is an important value, but when it comes into conflict with other important values, like order and reputation, accommodations are made" (pp. 44–5).

the background of my general argument of toleration as recognition – that is, starting from a reinterpretation of these claims as requests for inclusion, as another step in the process of full inclusion of members of oppressed groups. More precisely I will try to see if this view of the arguments against hate speech makes them easier to accommodate in a liberalism that is dominated by the priority of free speech.

The argument against government interference goes as follows: common language cannot be, and in a liberal society ought not to be, politically controlled and purified of all offensive words and expressions. In social intercourse verbal harassment and insults of many kinds are actually quite common for a variety of reasons. Although they are offensive and to some degree harmful to people, they are usually considered both unavoidable, given the volatile nature of speech, and also tolerable in comparison with a systematic policing of speech by the government. Obviously, speech can be forbidden if it is thought to produce harmful consequences, but this should as a rule be independent of its content and message.[17] For example, a rock concert can reasonably be forbidden (and has, in fact, been forbidden) in St. Mark's Square, Venice, on the grounds that the valuable and fragile space could not stand the assault of thousands of youngsters and their left-over rubbish, cans, bottles, etc. The likely damage to the environment does not follow from the kind of music, the text of the songs, or the general message of the concert. But intervention is legitimate because freedom of speech is constrained by reasons independent of the content of the speech. In the case of abusive speech, on the other hand, the offense and any damage produced by words is intrinsic to speech; therefore any prohibition of abusive speech would require a political assessment of its content, which would open the way to unacceptable public interference in a basic individual freedom. This argument holds for racist offenses, insults, and verbal harassment, given that (a) in order to be defined as racist, their content must first be assessed, and (b) since generic verbal abuse is considered tolerable, verbal racist abuse cannot be subject to different and special treatment. After all, so the argument goes, what is important is to fight real discrimination and inequality instead of insisting on words.

However, no absolutist position in favor of free speech is tenable on close inspection. Despite the First Amendment, laws forbidding speech are widespread in any legal system: "laws against perjury, blackmail and

---

[17] See Schauer, "The Phenomenology of Speech and Harm." That speech cannot legitimately be limited because of its content and message, but only for independent reasons, rehearses the Lockean argument that religion can be limited but not for religious reasons. See Locke, *Letter Concerning Toleration*.

fraud prohibit speech. Much of contract law and securities law abridges speech. Indeed no one has ever contended that citizens are free to say anything, anywhere, at any time."[18] In all these cases speech is prohibited because of its content. The notion of content-neutral regulation, which is regarded as permissible, is intended to prevent governmental bias toward the point of view expressed, and it is assumed that content-neutral regulation grants this effect. However, many uncontroversial speech prohibitions, such as those mentioned above, do not meet the condition of content-neutrality; it does not follow from this that they are expressions of governmental bias. On the other hand, some content-independent predicaments may in fact stem from an implicit institutional bias against rock music, for instance. Briefly, the condition of content-neutrality cannot work as an absolute guideline for public decision on speech regulation. If this is the case, and if the First Amendment does not and cannot absolutely rule out *any* intervention on speech, then there is no a priori reason why we cannot enter into a discussion of the content-specific nature of racist abuse and evaluate its harmful effects.

As for the special treatment objection, different and special treatment is exactly what is claimed by minority groups with reference to offensive racist speech. The claim is supported by a double argument. In the first place, minority groups targeted by racism have previously suffered exclusion, discrimination, and oppression, the consequences of which still affect the opportunities and the social standing of their members. Past or persistent injustice gives the members of these minorities an entitlement to claim special help in the difficult process of attaining inclusion in society as equal social partners; this help must take the form of a public stand against racist insults, as a form of public protection against contempt directed at their identity. In the second place, racism has been acknowledged as intolerable in general terms, so racist insults have a special status compared to other forms of insult, and highlight a sort of social aggressiveness and hatred which are not just occasional and contingent, but patterned in a fashion which is harmful not only to the individual victim but to the whole group and to social relations at large. Putting together past injustice and persistent marginalization with the specificity of racial hatred, the argument in favor of making offensive racist speech a special category of intolerable speech has significant force.

If accepted, this argument would be valid only if the content of the speech in question was actually diagnosed as racist. But given that the

[18] Shiffrin, *The First Amendment*, p. 14.

restriction we are discussing here concerns only a specified class of offensive speech – namely insults – the limits imposed on the content of speech would be similar to other kinds of speech regulation already accepted in democratic legal systems, such as those adopted for the language of public officials or in courts. Insults to the court or to the judges are forbidden because of their intentional content. However, given that the kind of speech which is forbidden is very specific and the context well defined, government intervention is restricted to very special circumstances and the limits to freedom of expression are actually small in comparison with the value of public authority which is thus (symbolically) protected. In these cases, restrictions to speech are considered acceptable vis-à-vis certain values if they are kept closely within the bounds of well-defined classes of speech and specific contexts, thus avoiding any risk of a slippery slope or any danger that government interference with freedom of expression might become too easy. It is not by chance, for example, that the issue of hate speech regulations in the United States is always raised with reference to specific contexts: university campuses, the workplace, etc. In other words, it has been acknowledged that there is some basis for limiting racist abuse; such limitation can find reasonable accommodation within liberal politics, since restrictions to individual freedom of expression which it would impose are small and any political interference would be well defined and limited to a particular class of offensive speech acts (insults, verbal aggression, and harassment) within specified contexts.

There are also pragmatic considerations: even if the argument in favor of restriction were granted, would the anticipated advantages balance the risks and the costs? As we have just seen, in order to minimize restrictions to freedom of expression, speech regulations which are not content-independent should be limited to well-defined classes of offensive language (insults to specific people) and to special contexts (schools, campuses, etc.); therefore, only a relatively small proportion of racist offenses could actually be prohibited. This being the case, one may wonder whether speech might not, after all, be better left totally free. If regulation could in any case only be applied to a very few instances, and if everyday social communication cannot sensibly be fully cleansed of racist expressions, then government interference, though limited, may not be worthwhile, and toleration may turn out to be the more convenient policy, given a lack of viable alternatives.

This observation is not final, however, because the argument in favor of restrictions has both a literal and a symbolic meaning. Literally, it is demanded that citizens in a still weak social position be spared the humiliation of racist abuse. But, more importantly, the claim concerns the stabilization of the public presence of identities that have previously been excluded and discriminated against, a process which is undermined by the persistence of unchecked racist speech. The destabilizing effect of widespread racist speech is symbolically reinforced by its public tolerance. The argument for restrictions is thus aimed also at institutionalizing some form of public stand against racism which symbolically delegitimizes it. And, as I have argued before, for the claimants the symbolic result is more significant than the literal one. From the point of view of the claimants, even if racist offenses cannot generally be banned, the regulation of a well-defined class of speech within specified contexts can be symbolically important.[19]

Let us go back to the question of whether speech regulations are worthwhile, all things considered. One position held by many liberals accepts that there is some merit to the argument for the regulation of hate speech, but also recognizes that the problem cannot be solved by legal intervention in matters of speech and expression. The solution must be found within civil society, in a process of mutual education which eventually establishes non-racist speech codes. Whether or not speech codes can be deliberately modified by participants is another interesting issue which, however, I do not intend to discuss here. I simply want to remark that, according to this position, offenses caused by racist speech are acknowledged to be a problem for the civil coexistence of people from various groups and origins. It is held that offensive speech should not be morally tolerated, and can legitimately be socially sanctioned, but it is not a subject for legal censorship, because in that case the remedy would be worse than the original problem.[20] This view takes both the arguments in favor of restriction and the risks attendant on a legal ban on racist speech very seriously, but overlooks one important aspect of the issue, namely the symbolic meaning of legal restriction, as explained above. If this symbolic implication is taken into account, one can see that the regulation of racist speech need not be general nor need it purify all speech of racist expressions or statements in order to take account of the

---

[19] On the symbolic value of some hate speech regulation see: R. C. Post, "Racist Speech, Democracy and the First Amendment," *William and Mary Law Review*, 32, 1991, pp. 267–388.

[20] See Dworkin, "Women and Pornography."

considerations I have raised above; a legal stand against racism has a symbolic meaning which is highly desirable in itself and which is missing in societies in which racist offenses are negatively sanctioned by well-meaning people in informal social ways – no matter how practically effective this form of action is.

Within the context of the priority of free speech, a possible accommodation between the two sets of reasons can link a limited legal restriction, intended as a response to the symbolic needs of the victims of social hatred, and an active campaign for a refusal on the part of society as a whole to tolerate racist speech. The informal social rejection of racist speech can perhaps be effective in eliminating it from society altogether in the long term. In this respect, it may be suggested that any legal regulation be confined to the language of public officials and civil servants, including teachers, doctors, and nurses, for example. In other words, if, as I have argued, what is really at stake is the symbolic meaning of legal restriction, as a protection of discriminated identities, and if a public stand against racism is more important to the claimants than the (impossible) general policing of common language, then one way of attaining this goal without threatening the principle of free speech and without finding oneself on a slippery slope to illiberalism is the limitation of legal regulation of language to the use of language in the performance of public roles. Such regulation should basically state that the public official or civil servant, while on duty, should always treat everyone with due respect. Insults, humiliation, and the diminution of others are thus explicitly banned from the behavior and language of public officials. In this way, no special provision needs to be made for racist offenses and no special protection for weak groups needs to be envisaged. The general regulation must simply be enforced with reference to potential racist offenses by public officials.

Let us summarize the reasoning so far. There are good reasons for taking the demand for a policing of racist offenses seriously. The danger that the state might engage in illiberal policing of language should, however, also be given careful consideration. Consequently, restrictions on speech should be limited to well-defined contexts and classes of speech. Only a limited number of racist offenses could therefore come under the purview of the legal system, but, despite this limitation, the regulation of hate speech can nevertheless be worthwhile for its symbolic value. If the meaning of the regulation of speech is mainly symbolic, the demand for such regulation can be reconciled with the protection of free speech by limiting legal regulation to the language of public officials. In that case, no special provision for racial minorities would be required, simply a general code regulating the behavior and speech of officials in the public sphere, so as to embody the ideal of neutrality and of equal public respect. It may be noted that in the US, after the PC campaign, public officials have become very careful in addressing the general public; hence that such a provision would turn out to be useless and empty. Yet, it is unlikely that infringements of the principles of equal respect by officials and other persons acting in their public capacity will never occur, and in view of the symbolic importance of this issue, even a few cases of racist speech would suffice to require that legal proceedings and a public debate be initiated.

No such accommodation, however, takes into account an important, highly provocative and offensive category of hate speech: namely, racist demonstrations in public spaces, displaying racist symbolism and slogans, with open aggression and direct threats to their victims. One has only to think of the meetings of groups of white supremacists, where hate, spite, and disdain for non-whites are stated and shouted in the most provocative way so as to be offensive not only to their victims, but to all non-racist people as well. Can the victims of such provocation be content with the symbolic stand against racism, as outlined above, involving a regulation of public speech codes? In fact, such measures do represent a symbolic response to the demand that racist insults be banned in everyday life situations, but they are altogether inadequate in cases of racist demonstrations. Are those to be considered expressions of dissident views to be protected against the moral disapproval they elicit in most citizens, let alone in their victims? This is, of course, one of the positions expressed in this controversy, for example, concerning the much-debated case of Nazi marches in the Jewish neighborhood of Skokie in the United States.

Before discussing this position, let me summarize some relevant differences between racist insults and racist demonstrations. In the latter, racist abuse is not contingent or casual, but planned; it is part of a political scheme, and, moreover, it is explicitly meant to single out whole groups as targets for racial hatred, rather than being directed at particular individuals. These considerations should intuitively make racist demonstrations a more obvious subject for legal restrictions than abuse directed at some individual. Yet, under a strictly liberal reading, they make room for the opposite argument. In fact, racist demonstrations are seen to present more difficulties for restrictions than individual cases of racist insult insofar as, first, they actually express a politically extreme viewpoint and not simply an outburst of rage, hence they seem obviously entitled to the constitutional protection of the First Amendment; and, second, since they aim not at specific individuals, but at whole groups, the harm they are supposed to induce cannot easily be proved in court, and can be seen as a matter of mere speculation. As a result, the common intuition about the greater offensiveness and intolerability of public demonstrations is twisted in favor of the priority of free speech. For this reason, the debate around racist demonstrations in the USA is mainly focused, first, on whether expression as such, or only valuable expression, is entitled to constitutional protection, and, second, on whether racist assaults or attacks are the direct result of public gatherings. The burden of the proof must then shift to show a direct causal link between racist marches and racist attacks, a link which is difficult to establish, though there is no doubt that such open displays of racism do excite racial hatred and aggression.

I contend that the liberal argument in favor of free speech is in such instances questionable, but for different reasons. I think that for free speech to have absolute, unquestioned priority it must be the expression of a (more or less valuable) viewpoint; proposals to limit free speech need not depend on a demonstration that the harm done by the forms of speech in question is measurable. If the speech under consideration concerns a public incitement to commit crimes, such as murder or rape, then this should, as a rule, be declared intolerable, a crime in itself. In the case of racial hatred the risk to the security of the racial groups in question is exacerbated by the special offense racism represents to the targeted groups and to society as a whole. The risk of opening the way to censorship of political demonstrations at large is relatively small given that the groups which are to be considered victims of racial hatred can in principle be easily identified. Moreover, other contextual variables should be considered in the public decision, for example the place of the march. In any case, the risk of a slippery slope argument should be balanced against the greater risk of letting incitement to crime go unchecked. All in all, I hold that demonstrations by such groups as Nazis, white supremacists, or Ku Klux Klan members ought not to be tolerated. This would be unlikely to be the start of an illiberal slippery slope, but would emphasize some very basic liberal principles, amongst which is toleration itself. This is where the argument on the intolerability of racism properly applies, since the harm which cannot be tolerated in this case is intrinsic to the very expression of racism, not simply to independent harmful consequences of racist acts. This is because the incitement to racial hatred implies not only deep offense to its victims, but offense to society at large equivalent to an incitement to criminal acts.

In conclusion, hate speech which is an issue only in the context of the constitutional priority of free speech over other rights raises two different kinds of problem – racist insults to single individuals and racist demonstrations. These call for different responses. In the first case, I have argued that some limitation of the legal regulation of speech to well-defined contexts can meet the symbolic quest of public protection of weak identities so as to support the full inclusion of their bearers, which racist insults intend to undermine; in the second case, public declaration of racial hatred constitutes a more fundamental offense and threat to basic societal bonds, which cannot be tolerated any more than incitement to rape or torture.

THE GERMAN SUPREME COURT'S DECISION ON HISTORICAL REVISIONISM

So far, we have considered racist abuse in the form of direct insults or open provocations such as slogans shouted at football stadiums and in public demonstrations. When dealing with racist viewpoints and ideology presented as theories, we need a different argument. Racist ideology, no matter how offensive, does not consist merely of insults; it is part of an argument which, although biased and tendentious, formally appears to be open to discussion and criticism. There is little doubt that racist ideology, phrased in rational prose, pretending to be part of an academic discourse, might sound more offensive and humiliating than a racist insult shouted by a drunken student at night. Yet it does not follow that censorship and repression are legitimate in these circumstances: there might be good independent reasons for avoiding any kind of censorship of any theoretical discourse and scientific research. In this case, it may be preferable to leave to the scientific community and to public opinion the task of finding an appropriate response in the form of criticisms and denunciation of falsity, forgery, and bad faith. After all, the scientific community and the free press can be much more effective than any censorship in excluding a *soi disant* racist theory; it can do this simply by applying the usual critical and argumentative standards.

I will face this question by looking at the case of the verdict on historical revisionism given by the German Supreme Court in 1994, which issued a legal condemnation of the expression of a revisionist thesis. As is widely known, in recent decades some historians have been attempting to deny or minimize the reality of the Holocaust, rejecting the existence of the final solution for the Jews and of the gas chambers themselves. This thesis has obviously caused great controversy, not only among historians but amongst the public at large. And it is clear that the denial of the Nazis' responsibility in the disappearance of six million Jews is offensive not only to Jewish people, but to all sincere anti-racist democrats. The question is, does this justify legal repression of a position in a debate about history, no matter how controversial it may be?

The following circumstances led the Supreme Court to this much de-bated verdict. The National Democratic Party, which is beyond doubt a neo-Nazi organization in Germany, called a cultural meeting in Munich for 12 March 1991, where a well-known English revisionist historian, David Irving, was supposed to discuss the collective guilt wrongly, in his view, attached to the German nation because of an instrumental and biased use of the history of the Third Reich. The subject of the debate would have been a rejection of the allegation of the collective guilt of the German nation, by means of a complete reappraisal of the Nazi experi-ence, which is the general purpose of the revisionist school of historical thought. Once the announcement of the meeting was made, the city of Munich decided to intervene in order to prevent any offense to Jewish people. The German legal system, like other European codes, includes criminal laws that are meant both to punish and prevent offenses and psychological injury, as a means of protecting certain rights, such as the rights of personal dignity, respect, and honor; indeed, an influential ten-dency in judicial interpretation has led to an extensive application of such laws to cover revisionist statements. So, in this case, based on such an interpretation, according to which the set of criminal laws defending personal dignity have been renamed "provisions against the lie about Auschwitz," the city government of Munich ordered the organizers of the meeting to omit any reference to the denial of the Holocaust in order to avoid breaching the law. The meeting's organizers appealed against this directive, firstly to the government of Upper Bavaria, then, succes-sively, to the Administrative Court of Munich, of Bavaria, and of the Federation, and, finally, after their appeal had been rejected by all these courts, to the Federal Constitutional Court.

Their appeal was grounded on the fundamental right to free expres-sion which, so the meeting's organizers maintained, had been breached by the preventive directive of the city of Munich. Carrying out this direc-tive, they argued, would subordinate the right to freedom of expression to personal rights. The appeal was based on the following argument. Although the prevalent judicial tendency had encouraged an extensive interpretation of laws so as to punish those who denied the Holocaust, in acting in this fashion the courts were behaving contrary to the federal constitution. In fact, so the argument went, an attempt to enact a specific law prohibiting revisionist statements had already failed in 1984, because the Bundesrat had judged it constitutionally unsound. Therefore the prevalent judicial position on the topic should be seen as a way of bypassing the constitutional ban on a specific law on revisionism, which would contradict freedom of opinion. On the basis of this reasoning, the Supreme Court was formally asked to give directives as to the legitimacy of the extensive application of the laws to the denial or minimization of the persecution of the Jews, as propagated by historical revisionism.

The response of the Supreme Court is based on a distinction between opinions, which have constitutional protection, and from which freedom of expression is derived, and facts. Opinions are the expression of a subjective judgment, and are not, as such, subjected to a true-or-false test; by contrast, facts can be proved to be either true or false, and statements of fact express an objective relationship with reality. Following this strongly positivist epistemological stand, the court went on to say that facts are entitled to constitutional protection only as long as they are the premises for forming opinions, but obviously such protection ought to stop short of statements of fact which cannot possibly contribute to forming any opinion. This is especially the case when facts are inaccurate or positively false. The court also acknowledged that a clear-cut distinction between statements of fact and opinion is difficult to ascertain and intrinsically contestable, and that, as a rule, constitutional protection should cover expressions as a whole, comprising both statements of fact and value judgments. Such protection, however, should not be limitless – for example, there must be legal provisions in place to protect people's honor and dignity. In this sense there is no absolute priority of the right to freedom of expression over personal rights, and in case of serious abuse to a third party the expression of opinions must be checked. Besides, when offensive opinions are founded on facts that have been proved false, the personal rights ought to prevail. Given that the statement that Jews were not subjected to massive extermination by the Nazis was, considering all the evidence, false, it cannot claim constitutional protection. As a result, the appeal was rejected and the condemnation of revisionism reaffirmed on the grounds of its falsity.

The legal and political culture behind this verdict is obviously very distant from the American one, where the controversy over hate speech has erupted. In the American context, offending and insulting people, if not clearly libelous and if it does not cause specifiable harm to the victim, count as a tolerable harm in comparison with the harm which an infringement of free speech would produce from the point of view both of liberal principles and of practical consequences to society as a whole. Therefore, the conflict between the right of freedom of expression and the rights to personal respect, honor, etc. has already found a settlement in the affirmed priority of free speech. And that is why the case for hate speech is so difficult, because it is a challenge to a shared priority which is also a guideline in the settlement of conflicts of rights. If, by contrast, such a priority is not stated, then personal rights can define limits to freedom of speech, making it relatively easier to face the issue of racist offenses. But it is still to be seen whether these limits should be extended from direct insults and provocation to the expression of positions presented in the form of historical interpretations. In the German case, another more straightforward solution would have been the prohibition of the meeting as an instance of a racist public demonstration, displaying racial hatred of the Jews which cannot be tolerated in any democratic state, least of all Germany. But, in fact, the city of Munich based its prohibition on a very different argument, taking advantage of recent judicial decisions against revisionism, and thus viewing the meeting not so much as a Nazi demonstration, but as a cultural political event, a questionable one given the legal provisions against the propagation of lies about Auschwitz.

Under this description of the event, people can as easily be offended by a historical thesis as by a scientific theory (such as evolution, for example, which some see as an offense to human dignity by linking humans with monkeys), but this is not a sufficient reason for prohibiting the theory or the views in a liberal democratic society, because offense has always been the reason behind all arguments for the enforcement of morals by moral majorities. For this very reason, the extension of rules against personal offense and injury to racist positions is not so straightforward, even in contexts where personal rights are acknowledged to impose some legitimate limits to freedom of expression. That is why the Federal Court's decision had to make reference to the distinction between facts and opinions, on the basis of which constitutional protection can be denied to statements of facts which are evidently false. Obviously the dichotomy between facts and opinions, corresponding to that between objectivity and subjectivity, truth and falsity, belongs to a very questionable epistemology, but we do not need to get involved in that here in order to assess the ethical and political dimensions of this verdict. What I want to stress is, rather, that the court had to take this stand in order to conclude that historical revisionism is a false doctrine, devoid of any truth value. This conclusion, in turn, had to be reached in order to create a firmer basis for the prohibition than the simple fact that historical revisionism is a racist doctrine that is especially offensive to Jewish people and true democrats. Thus the crucial reason for the legal ban of revisionism was, for the Supreme Court, its manifest falsity. However, I argue that this justification, instead of providing stronger grounds for the prohibition of racist theories than mere offenses, clashes with liberal neutrality and makes the verdict altogether unsound from a liberal and democratic point of view.

While I hold that the strongly offensive nature of revisionism for Jewish people – supplemented by a general argument to the effect that racism is intolerable and by a special argument about Jews as special victims of racist crimes in the context of German history – might have offered a contextual justification for the verdict (though not one beyond dispute), the argumentative strategy adopted by the court has unacceptable implications for liberal democracy. Indeed, political toleration should never depend on a judgment about the truth of the belief in question.

In fact, the theory of toleration was worked out in order to stop governments meddling in disputes concerning the truth and to find ways of coexisting despite disagreement about what beliefs are true. More specifically, toleration was originally conceived for preventing governments from imposing their "truths" and prosecuting what they held to be "mistakes." Indeed, the potential subjects of toleration were originally only religious beliefs and not facts open to empirical evidence. But it should be underlined that in the seventeenth century religious creeds were thought to be matters for truth judgment. The supporters of toleration, and particularly Locke, have stressed that the proper circumstances for extending toleration were disagreement about the true religion. A policy of toleration did not depend on holding that objective truth was impossible to attain but on the epistemological and ethical impossibility of imposing the truth by means of violence and persecution. Hence, toleration is not derived from a skeptical argument so much as from the undesirability of imposing the true faith. John Stuart Mill later added to this argument the open defense of mistakes (which had already been sketched by Milton) as a crucial test for the truth to be tried out. For Mill, truth can be acknowledged as such only if it has been challenged and has then overcome opposing positions. The latter, though mistaken, have an important role in making it possible for the truth to emerge. Therefore censorship or repression of mistakes and false beliefs are not only useless, because truth cannot be imposed by force, but also harmful to the open-ended process of discovery of new knowledge.

For this reason the argument from falsity advanced by the German Supreme Court, instead of offering firmer grounds for the prohibition than the argument from offense, fails to provide a sound reason for limiting toleration of historical revisionism according to liberal standards. It was probably adopted because it seemed to be more politically impartial than the argument based on racist offenses, but it is, in fact, intolerant. The argument from falsity, being independent of the context – i.e. the special case of Germany and its Nazi past – equally applies to all cases of false beliefs. It would follow that a public meeting on creationist theories should also be legally forbidden, and the risk of starting out down the slippery slope is clear to see.

If, from the viewpoint of the public ethics of liberal democracy, the German Supreme Court's decision can be contested even in a political culture that is not influenced by the First Amendment, any discussion of whether racist theories should be tolerated or not becomes less straightforward. The issue becomes especially pressing when such theories are considered not simply as views to be debated in journals and conferences, but as doctrines which can be taught at school. If we consider the above verdict in relation to teaching in state schools, then some further reflections are in order.

If the state has no business meddling in scientific debate or academic discussion, and cannot declare one theory to be true and another false, it must nevertheless face the issue of school curricula. Can public schools teach racist doctrines? Can they teach false doctrines? And should the government be neutral on this matter? The discussion of curricula in relation to multiculturalism has shown that what is taught in public schools is definitely a matter for a political ruling, and is not culturally neutral. Whether cultural neutrality can or cannot, and should or should not, be achieved is an open question. In any case, I think that the public education of a liberal democratic state cannot be neutral with reference to the fundamental political values and principles sustaining liberalism and democracy. For example, it cannot be neutral between democracy and dictatorship, between law-abiding and law-violating behavior, between equal respect and discrimination in social intercourse, and so on. In other words, it cannot be neutral in relation to justice. Similarly, it cannot be neutral with reference to truth, as far as truth can be ascertained. Neutrality is out of place in relation to justice because of the principle of self-defense (justice and shared political values are needed to sustain the stability of the liberal democratic order) and also for reasons of consistency (democracy cannot logically promote a regime alternative to itself). Moreover, with reference to truth, neutrality would contrast with the harm principle, given that if a patently false theory (e.g. the Ptolemaic system) were legitimately taught in school, the capabilities and opportunities of the students would be damaged. In sum, the teaching of racist doctrines as well as of patently false doctrines goes beyond the limits imposed by toleration, and should not be permitted in school. Also in this case, however, the implementation turns out to be complex if some undesirable effects are to be avoided. One thing is that in regulating schools the state should ensure that a concern for the political values sustaining democracy is expressed and that the curriculum includes the history of the Nazi horrors, the Holocaust, and so on, in the teaching program. To institute a system in which all school texts were examined by a censorship committee, mandated to suppress all supposed falsity would be a different matter altogether. I think that the freedom of expression of teachers and book-writers ought to be preserved in order to keep public education open-minded, critical, and innovative. Once the anti-racist attitude is clearly affirmed as a guideline in school curricula, the teaching should be entrusted to teachers and to texts of their choice, while public intervention can be justified only in case of a patent betrayal of that trust.

Although I have argued in favor of some limits to hate speech in relation to racist insults and public demonstrations, even in a political culture dominated by the priority of the First Amendment, when racism is embodied in theories, views or interpretations, no matter how offensive they may sound, freedom of expression should, as a rule, prevail. Criticism and deconstruction of racist ideologies should be left to the scientific community and public discussion. There might then be special justification, due to special historical circumstances, for the intolerance of certain doctrines because of their special power to offend victims of such tragedies as the Holocaust. But, in principle, the expression of any doctrine, view, or ideology should be allowed, just as direct racist abuse should be forbidden at least in the well-defined contexts. By contrast, teaching racism in school should not be tolerated, because it violates the principle of equal respect and equal treatment, and also because it discriminates against those students belonging to the targeted racial groups. This position cannot sensibly imply censorship on teaching and school texts, but justifies interference only when the anti-racist guidelines for teaching are ignored.

CONCLUSION

I started out by arguing that racism belongs to that class of attitudes and forms of behavior considered intolerable in liberal democracy, not simply because of its potential risks and the actual harm it may cause to people, but also because of its underlying assumption, which is in direct opposition to basic democratic principles and values. This argument, however, cannot be used directly as a basis for the prohibition of racist acts and attitudes, because an argument of this kind is inadequate when it comes to actual political implementation. So I have made a survey of various kinds of racist behavior in order to see when, how, and to what extent toleration ought to be restricted.

First, I have considered those racist acts that are directly violent and those that result in discrimination and exclusion. Both imply a violation of fundamental rights, and should therefore be legally prosecuted. Physical violence, or intentional exclusion from resources and opportunities, are intolerable not so much because racism itself is intolerable, but because people's rights are violated.

At this point, the following question is in order: if there is not a clearly identifiable breach of rights, should racism be tolerated, despite being acknowledged as intolerable? Here we are confronted with the pragmatic paradox of toleration and the difficult balance between the liberal imperative to use a minimum level of coercion and the necessary limits to toleration. A political ban on racism could imply that racist organizations should be outlawed or dismantled and/or that racist speech, propaganda, and theories be censored. Government intervention affecting political associations, as it interferes with a basic liberal right, needs to be justified by the self-defense of the political system, which in turn must be shown to be in real danger. The argument providing this justification is complex, because the danger is always to some extent hypothetical in a stable democratic system.

By contrast, racist speech and propaganda do constitute an offense against members of racial groups which have endured exclusion, marginalization, and discrimination. And yet, can offenses of this kind justify censorship of speech codes? The argument for restrictions on forms of speech has a dual justification: on the one hand, as a redress for past and persisting exclusion which justifies the special protection of certain groups, and, on the other, the fact that racism is intolerable in democratic systems. The possible damage to liberalism caused by the indiscriminate regulation of speech, however, should also be taken into account. Which right – freedom of expression or non-discrimination – should have priority, though, is genuinely undetermined and generally defined by extra-normative contextual elements, such as the legal and political tradition and historical circumstances. I have tried to show that even in a culture where free speech ranks first, there is room to impose legitimate limits to hate speech. In this context, however, restrictions need to be limited to well-specified classes of speech and well-defined contexts, in order to avoid an escalation – i.e. only direct insults to people and public racist demonstrations should be prohibited. Even though the restrictions would in such cases be limited, they would nevertheless be important to the claimants because of their symbolic meaning as public stands against racism.

As far as the expression of racist views and theories are concerned, government intervention is out of place, as the scientific community can take the appropriate measures by means of criticism. However, whereas racist views should be tolerated in the realm of academic discourse, and even in public discourse, they cannot be tolerated in school curricula. Public education is an area to which the teaching of democratic ideas is entrusted, where political decisions are in order, and where students have to learn to live with a diversity of groups, cultures, and ideas, treating them all with equal respect. Racist views would directly contradict a democratic education. And yet, also in this case, the implementation needs to take into account the risk of impairing a free, open, critical, and innovative public education.

6

Same-sex marriages

INTRODUCTION

Finally, I will take up the issue of marriage between homosexuals, one that has been under discussion for some while now within both homosexual and heterosexual communities in many countries. Particularly in the United States in recent years marriage rather than partnership has been the focus of this discussion in the gay community. This is because in 1993 the Hawaiian Supreme Court declared the ban on same-sex marriages to be discriminatory under the Hawaiian constitution. At the same time the court became engaged in a further debate in order to assess whether this discrimination was justified by a compelling state interest. If the final verdict declared this form of discrimination to be unjustified, that would mean that Hawaii would lift the ban on same-sex marriages.[1] A wide debate involving legal, gender, and cultural studies has developed around that very controversial verdict,[2] and meanwhile many American cities have extended the same benefits enjoyed by heterosexual partners to homosexual partners, indirectly recognizing such unions.[3] More recently, the state of Vermont has recognized same-sex partnership, extending most of the benefits of heterosexual families to homosexual couples.[4]

[1] The Hawaiian case is analyzed by W. N. Eskridge, *The Case for Same-Sex Marriage* (New York: The Free Press, 1996).
[2] See, for example, K. Weston, *Family We Choose. Lesbians, Gays, Kinship* (New York: Columbia University Press, 1991); Mark Strasser, *Legally Wed: Same Sex Marriage and the Constitution* (Ithaca: Cornell University Press, 1997); Morris B. Kaplan, "Intimacy and Equality: The Question of Lesbian and Gay Marriage," *Philosophical Forum*, 25, 1994, 333–40.
[3] This was the case in Hollywood (1985, implemented in 1989); Santa Cruz and Madison (1986); Los Angeles (1988); Seattle and New York City (1989); San Francisco (1990); Washington D.C. (1991); Chicago and Baltimore (1993); New Orleans and San Diego (1994); Denver (1995). These dates come from Eskridge, *The Case for Same-Sex Marriage*.
[4] So far, the Vermont legislation (2000) is the most advanced among the various provisions for gays and lesbians couples in the US and in Europe, except for the Netherlands.

In Europe in February 1994, a European Parliament resolution proposed that member states recognize same-sex marriages;[5] since then many countries, following a verdict of the European Court of Justice in Luxembourg, which extended employment benefits from heterosexual to homosexual partnerships, hence opening the way for legal recognition of gay couples,[6] have adopted legislation which recognizes same-sex partnership, either explicitly (as in the case of Holland and Scandinavian countries), or implicitly, by means of the legalization of civil unions, heterosexual and homosexual alike (as in France). So far, however, no country has properly granted the right to same-sex marriage, and so far the recognition of same-sex partnership has not included the right to adoption by a gay couple.

My argument is that the fight for same-sex marriages is the direct and final development of the stand against public intolerance of gays and constitutes a further and important step in their inclusion. In this chapter I will argue that the public toleration of homosexual identity leads to a revised and extended conception of the family which makes the notion of same-sex marriage just and reasonable. I consider the acceptance of same-sex marriages to be an example of the kind of revision of societal standards which would follow naturally from construing toleration as recognition. When toleration as recognition legitimizes differences and identities as viable options within liberal society, then societal standards and conventions ought to be redrawn so as to make room for the newly accepted identity. This is a crucial aspect of what marks the difference between normal liberal views of toleration and the revised conception for which I am arguing. The issue of homosexuality is paradigmatic in this respect: while many liberals would argue that full citizenship for homosexuals does not require any special revision of liberal toleration, they would not be ready to admit same-sex marriage as a direct consequence of the toleration of homosexual identity.

THE GAY MOVEMENT AND TOLERATION AS RECOGNITION

The gay movement represents an especially interesting case of the claim for toleration as recognition because it brings forward the issue of visibility in a way that does not arise in the case of ethnic or cultural differences. While a foreign accent or a different skin color cannot easily be

---

[5] See Eskridge, *The Case for Same-Sex Marriage*.
[6] See *Grant v. South-West Train Ltd.*, 19 July 1996, quoted by Robert Wintemute, *Sexual Orientation and Human Rights* (Oxford: Clarendon Press, 1996).

hidden, sexual orientation is not directly perceivable unless the person particularly wants to disclose it. Consequently, immigrants and national minorities have been invisible insofar as they have been physically excluded from the public arena, kept at the margins of liberal society, employed only in the humblest occupations, and hence seen only as an underclass, whether or not they have been endowed with citizenship rights. In their case, the issue of visibility is intrinsically intertwined with their actual presence in public which constitutes the crucial first step for their full inclusion.

Given that ethnic identities cannot be concealed, they cannot easily be included despite their differences, because their presence in public implies the visibility of their differences. By contrast, gays and lesbians have always been able to be full and active citizens in society: they have ready access to important positions, honor, status, and power, as long as they keep their sexual orientation "in the closet." Their public presence does not necessarily mean the acknowledgment of their different identity. In the case of homosexuality, the ambiguities of liberal toleration, built around the public/private divide, become particularly prominent, given that the distinction between the private individual with his or her differences, and the citizen, the public persona, stripped of all particular characteristics, is perfectly feasible and has allowed homosexuals to be included as long as they disguise their sexual orientation in public. Once the legal ban on sodomy between consenting adults has been lifted (and in many countries this happened only recently, while in others the ban is still in force[7]) liberal toleration is basically fulfilled. At that point, homosexuality is tolerated like any other lifestyle that concerns personal freedom, and should not count as a factor in public life, so that, for example, no legal barriers prevent homosexual citizens from running for president or becoming prime minister. If homosexuals are still socially despised and humiliated, this may be regrettable, but it does not impinge on liberal toleration, because it falls outside the political domain and is a matter for social campaigns and long-term education. From the standpoint of liberal toleration, once homosexual sex has been legalized, gays and lesbians become full citizens on an equal footing with heterosexuals, even if they still face difficulties and humiliation in their private and social life. Something can obviously be done, and has in many cases already been done, to fight discrimination against homosexuals in employment,

---

[7] See "Appendix III – United States: States Without and With Laws Prohibiting Private, Adult, Consensual Oral or Anal Intercourse," in Wintemute, *Sexual Orientation and Human Rights*, pp. 268–9.

housing, and so forth, but this is because social discrimination is unjustified in any case.[8]

But I would argue that discrimination against homosexuals is not simply caused by uncivilized attitudes spread throughout society, attitudes which political institutions can fight only on a case-by-case basis. There is in fact a link between the widespread negative view of gays by members of society and their long past of public invisibility, between the social abhorrence of gays and the absence of their identity from institutions and public life. Their invisibility as homosexuals reinforces their social powerlessness and facilitates an exposure to attacks and various forms of humiliation. By contrast, public visibility works as a form of public recognition and would empower gays and lesbians in social life as well. Only then could homosexual citizens be said to enjoy both the rights and the status of citizenship in the full sense. But this process of inclusion finds a de facto obstacle in liberal toleration and neutrality, because liberal toleration admits homosexuality only as a private choice and does nothing to take down the invisibility barrier. I argue that public neutrality not only requires that their difference be discounted in public treatment, but, also takes for granted, that it be concealed altogether.

An example of the public invisibility requirement is the ban on homosexuality in the military in the United States and in Europe. I argue that this ban is not simply an instance of intolerance, a breach of liberal toleration, but is in fact permitted by the usual working of liberal toleration along the public/private divide. If homosexuality is tolerated as a private taste which is implicitly required to be invisible, then the ban of gays from the military is explained by the fact that the army is an institution where people do not simply work together, but actually live together, hence where private and public lives are not so easily distinguishable: only a ban grants invisibility. That the whole point is invisibility rather than actual exclusion of gays is confirmed by President Clinton's proposed solution "no one asks, no one tells" which reaffirms the equality of all citizens, but without reference to, or indeed despite, sexual orientation. Some people might try to defend the ban on the basis of neutral reason such as the protection and the safety of homosexuals from potential attacks in communities such as the army. I shall come back to this neutral argument and its shortcomings, but it is easy to see that there is always room to articulate intolerance in terms of some neutral reasons.

---

[8] Wintemute, ibid., considers discrimination on the grounds of sexual orientation as a distinct type of discrimination and argues that freedom from it should be recognized as a human right (pp. 6–10).

In other words, the ban on recognition of homosexuality in the military is neither a simple infringement of liberal toleration nor is it justified by acceptable neutral reasons. It is best understood as a consequence of the invisibility implicitly connected with liberal toleration. Many liberals may comment that only a parochial notion of liberal toleration would imply invisibility, while liberal toleration, at its best, in its proper and fuller understanding, can never justify invisibility. Now it may be that a most advanced interpretation of liberal toleration would indeed reject public invisibility as an intolerant drawback, but then such most advanced interpretation would in fact coincide with toleration as recognition. Toleration as recognition is precisely meant to fulfill the promises of liberal toleration, while doing away with its actual embodiments in exclusionary forms.[9]

Other instances of the invisibility requirement are provided by gays who, in many countries, have become important politicians but usually at the price of keeping secret their sexual orientation. If the latter happens to be disclosed, a scandal often results, and their career is jeopardized. Even in a morally tolerant society such as Italy, where the sexual life of politicians, be it heterosexual or homosexual, does not provoke public scandal but merely becomes the subject of gossip, the strong division between private and public nevertheless keeps homosexuality well out of the view of the public. Thus it happens that while heterosexual politicians are often pictured with their families, spouse or children, the public life of gays intentionally excludes any reference to their life outside Parliament and party conventions.[10] Can this separation promote more civilized attitudes toward gay and lesbian citizens?

According to liberal toleration, in its usual interpretations homosexuals have rights, not as full-blown individuals, but only as desexualized persons. Their sexual life is tolerated at the price of being kept under cover, which in turn means that their different identities are excluded from the viable alternatives that make up the norm.[11] It is no accident that the gay movement has focused on the issue of coming out and on gay pride: the particular intolerance they have suffered has directly to do

---

9 I am grateful for this point to the participants of the conference "Toleration and Identity," George Washington University, 23–24 March 2001, especially Stephen Macedo and Russel Hardin.

10 Weston, in *Families We Choose, Lesbians, Gays, Kinship*, points out that the sexual identity of straight people is indeed embedded in all kinship relationship.

11 "What is remarkable about these 'public aspects' and 'other public manifestations' is how frequently heterosexual persons engage in them, and how much such persons take their ability to do so, and therefore to be open about their sexual orientation, completely for granted" (Wintemute, *Sexual Orientation and Human Rights*, p. 15).

with the compulsory invisibility of their emotional life.[12] Therefore the gay movement, while fighting against legal barriers that prohibit homosexuality and exclude them from the full enjoyment of rights, has also explicitly raised the issue of public recognition of their identity and opposed the imposed invisibility of their difference. The rise of the gay movement in the USA, in fact, is symbolically dated from the Stonewall riots of July 1969,[13] when gays responded to an attack against a gay bar, Stonewall's Inn, with two days of public demonstrations, shouting their sexual preferences in the streets. For the first time, gays marched as gays protesting against intolerance, and understood that they could not be citizens on an equal footing with heterosexuals if they were compelled to live in disguise or were confined to ghettoes, easy preys to violent attacks. The coming out movement and the gay pride strategy have been their claim for toleration as recognition.

Some liberals would object that public invisibility is not a requirement and that liberal toleration and neutrality do not compel anyone to disguise their sexual orientation or emotional life. In fact, toleration and neutrality imply, first, that sexual orientation is a matter of personal freedom as long as it is expressed between consenting adults, and, second, that public action should be neutral regarding sexual orientation; hence, that gays should not be excluded because of their difference from any public institution or employment. If, in the real life of contemporary democracy, gays are in fact often prevented from full access to public institutions, such as the military, that is either justified in neutral terms or represents a case in which the demands of neutrality are not fulfilled; under a proper interpretation, neutrality does not require difference invisibility in the public sphere but difference blindness in public treatment. However, I argue that neutrality as public blindness will never properly make up for the history of homosexuals' invisibility. In the first place, looking again at the military example, alongside justifications for the ban which appears bluntly unacceptable, such as the immorality or corruption represented by homosexuality, some neutral reasons can be advanced as well, such as that appealing to the very protection and safety of gays. If justification is neutral with reference to the moral evaluation

---

[12] Indeed, this is the argument underlying the position in favor of outing: "Social acceptance of homosexuality as a natural and universal variation would end most of the emotional difficulties as well as the fateful significance of what is otherwise described as coming out," in W. Johnasson and W. Percy, *Outing: Shattering the Conspiracy of Silence* (New York and London: The Hawarth Press, 1994).

[13] See Angela Wilson, "Introduction," to *A Simple Matter of Justice* (London: Cassel, 1995).

of homosexuality, it has fulfilled a crucial condition for being acceptable according to liberal toleration, but it may not be acceptable for toleration as recognition. The ground for toleration as recognition is equality of respect and equal respect is a stronger requirement than mere neutrality. A rule that excludes homosexuals from public institutions runs counter to the principle of equality of respect. Moreover, what is presented as protection for a discriminated group cannot work as justification for differential treatment if this treatment is imposed on, and opposed by, that very group. In other words, toleration as recognition provides wider and more straightforward reasons for rejecting any form of discrimination implying exclusion and humiliation of an oppressed group. Although this kind of discrimination can in principle be avoided on the basis of liberal toleration, taken at its best, this is less straightforward (and in practice it has not worked in that direction), and is more exposed to neutral justifications that implicitly appeal to exclusive social standards, which public blindness is not equipped to detect. In the second place, but more importantly, toleration as recognition is sensitive to exclusionary social standards and enables liberal institutions to detect forms of exclusion which public blindness tends to obscure. In fact, whereas in many contemporary societies liberal toleration and public blindness to differences have exhausted their impetus for motivating social and political change, in that they have succeeded in removing the institutional barriers that limited the personal freedom of homosexuals or caused them to be treated differently, toleration as recognition commits liberal institutions to the further task of making room for the newly admitted gay identity. I will try now to show how this commitment is entailed by toleration as recognition, but does not follow from the usual conceptions of liberal toleration. What makes the difference is the positive attitude towards social identities whose bearers have been excluded from full membership in society: while liberal toleration leaves people free to express themselves, toleration as recognition intends to do something more, usually symbolically, in order to make an excluded identity a normal presence in the public space of society and a viable option. As I have said, toleration as recognition basically consists in a set of fundamental reasons, which in turn allow for the symbolic meaning of acceptance to be attached to toleration in the literal sense. If these reasons – usually declared in a legal judgment or in public regulations – are of the kind "everyone can lead the sexual life of his or her choice and should not be discriminated against because of it," liberal toleration of this form cannot by itself provide the recognition gays seek. And gays who do not want to live in the closet have to bear the burden of coming out without any institutional support. By contrast, if the ground for toleration is spelled out as "same-sex preference should be included in the normal range of alternatives from which citizens can freely pick without being discriminated against, marginalized, or humiliated," then toleration implies a symbolic stand legitimizing the public presence of gays and lesbians.

Given that the alternative in question is a matter of harsh moral controversy, it must be stressed once more that recognition, in this sense, does not imply any promotion or endorsement of homosexuality, nor any tacit assertion that homosexuality is morally good. On this point the discussion is especially heated, given that all public stands which are not merely negative forms of toleration are objected to by conservatives, who oppose homosexuality because, they argue, it promotes perverse forms of behavior. Moreover, communitarian political thinkers, such as Michael Sandel, deny that homosexuality can be legitimized independently of a moral judgment on its inherent value.[14] I hold that both conservatives and communitarians are wrong on this point; to be consistent they ought to reject toleration and the rights of personal freedom altogether. There is a third way between toleration of homosexuality as a necessary evil and recognition of its moral value: that is, the inclusion of gayness as a viable option in liberal society and of gay identity as part of the "normal" range. Even in the more traditional sense, toleration implies that the forms of behavior and practice to be tolerated violate no rights and harm no third party. This judgment does not require a content evaluation of the behavior in question, since it is possible to make an independent judgment about whether or not the form of behavior violates rights or harms a third party. Once this judgment has been made and a policy of toleration adopted, liberal institutions have no right either to encourage or to discourage any one of the acceptable behavioral options; yet I contend that keeping homosexuality out of the public view or ignoring it in all public norms and standards is a form of discouragement. Thus it is not toleration as recognition that implies a positive moral evaluation and promotion of homosexuality, but, rather, it is the usual view of toleration which works to discourage homosexuality. If a group has a history of oppression, invisibility, and humiliation, as do homosexuals, their difference needs to be positively accepted as a normal option within the mainstream of a

---

[14] Michael Sandel, "Moral Argument and Liberal Toleration: Abortion and Homosexuality," *California Law Review*, 77, 1989, pp. 521–38. See also the criticisms to Sandel by M. S. Moore, "Sandelian Antiliberalism," *California Law Review*, 77, 1989, pp. 539–60.

pluralistic society, and this recognition, whatever form it may take, is not a positive evaluation of the morality of homosexuals, but is a public declaration that their lifestyle, which harms no one, has a right to be one of the many options in society, alongside, for instance, that of the priesthood.

So far, I have dismissed the idea that toleration as recognition entails an appreciation of homosexuality as morally good, but I have still to spell out its implications for public conventions and societal standards. If the whole point of toleration as recognition is to treat homosexuality as a normal option and to include homosexual citizens on an equal footing with heterosexuals, then once their public presence is declared acceptable and has become visible, public conventions and societal standards cannot pretend that homosexuality does not exist. All standard patterns of conduct that are concerned with emotional life, intimate relationships, and domestic arrangements are thus immediately called into question; they may all have to be rethought so as to take account of homosexuality. And the institution of the family, which represents the classical locus of intimate life, is obviously in the forefront.

Before considering the possible transformations of the family, I am going to take up the fundamental conservative objection to any revision of societal standards in order to make room for homosexuality. This position considers any public action that aims to lift the stigma of homosexuality as a form of reverse discrimination. Without going into the pros and cons of reverse discrimination as such, I contend that this conservative stand is wrong, because lifting the stigma and thereby putting an end to the humiliation experienced by homosexuals does not amount to reverse discrimination. Instead, it allows citizens who violate no laws and pay their taxes to enjoy the same liberty to form recognized long-lasting relationships as anyone else. Treating homosexuals decently means revising common social assumptions about emotional relationships so that they are no longer modeled and based exclusively on heterosexual conduct. If liberal institutions acknowledge only heterosexual relationships, preferably bound by marriage, they are not acting impartially, but are clearly reinforcing and reproducing social prejudices concerning homosexuality.

However, the point of the conservative objection does not concern reverse discrimination per se, but is, rather, grounded on the view that the social stigma on homosexuality exists for a reason. Behind this view is the conception of toleration as a moral virtue, i.e. the suspension of the power of interference with behavior of which we disapprove morally.[15] In this sense, homosexuality is a proper subject of toleration because it is a morally objectionable form of conduct, which, however, does not infringe on the harm principle, and can therefore be permitted for various reasons (social peace, respect of others, compassion of others, and so on). Yet, under this moral interpretation, toleration can be no more than passive acceptance or negative submission to its subject, which does not get rid of the moral disapprobation of the practice. I have argued that this conception of the moral virtue of toleration is in order only in interpersonal relations, and is altogether out of place in politics, where toleration is a principle of ensuring civil coexistence of conflicting differences, by maintaining a regime of equal liberty and equal respect. But, this argument aside, at this point liberals can object that the immorality of homosexuality cannot be granted, as conservatives argue, because it derives from certain moral codes which are by no means universally shared in pluralistic societies.

The conservative response to this remark makes reference to two lines of arguments: that of the natural and healthy intimate life and that of the moral majority.[16] Though usually intertwined, these arguments are at two different levels: the first is a substantive argument explaining why homosexuality is immoral, and the second is a meta-argument which holds that a moral majority has a right to shape the moral environment of a society. The first argument says that only one form of sexual intercourse is natural – that which leads to procreation, given that procreation is the reason why there are two sexes. Different inclinations go against natural conduct, and are hence a form of perversion. Moreover, heterosexual sex is the basis of the institution of marriage and the family, which constitute the only healthy way of rearing children and reproducing society, and the fundamental cell of the political community. Hence a community has a strong interest in defending its most basic institution and the conduct that sustains it, imposing a corresponding duty on the conduct of individuals. By contrast, the moral majority argument does not get involved in the moral evaluation of homosexuality, but states that in a political community the majority has the right to make political decisions, legally binding on all, as much on crucial moral matters as on the political economy. This position appears to reject toleration altogether, and thus seems flatly incompatible with individual rights to liberty, but, in fact, it is more subtle. It does not say that the majority has

---

[15] See chapter 1.

[16] The moral majority argument is presented by Devlin, *The Enforcement of Morals*. See Hart's response in *Law, Liberty and Morality*.

a right to impose its moral choice on all society, but rather that it has a duty to prevent the harm that might befall younger generations if they are exposed to what is held to be immoral and socially perverse behavior. Hence, the moral majority argument is presented as a specification of the self-defense argument, spelled out by Mill as a legitimate limit to toleration.

I shall not expatiate on liberal responses to these two arguments, because they are widely known and discussed. I only want to point out that, first, the claim that heterosexual sex alone is natural is not supported by animal behavior research, which finds that homosexuality exists among animals of all species, very likely to the benefit of biological evolution; and, second, the moral majority argument is a tricky defense of traditional morality, given that the rate of divorce and of single-parent families in contemporary democracies suggests that the majority probably holds very different moral views on these subjects and is actually already in the process of constructing new forms of the family.

MARRIAGE OR PARTNERSHIP?

There are two possible ways of reshaping conventional relationships in order to make room for homosexuality: either by legitimating different forms of intimate relationship outside the family or by transforming the very institution of the family so as to include same-sex relationships. Both have been explored, the first more directly and the second more hesitantly. Both result in a radical reinterpretation of traditional morality and of the acceptable forms of sexual activity, emotional commitment, and parenting.

In my view, although the first solution is usually considered to be the more radical and more in line with a liberation project, a redefinition of the family to include gays and lesbians is a better response and a step forwards in the promotion of liberal justice. It must be stressed that the argument in favor of same-sex marriage should not prevent individual gays or lesbians from deciding simply to live together without marrying. What it does is give them a further option that has hitherto been closed to them. Although the legal recognition of partnerships outside marriage may answer the same needs as marriage and may grant the same benefits, there are two immediate reasons in favor of marriage. The first is symbolic: recognition is achieved through symbols, and symbolic actions, as I have argued, are very real indeed. The difference between partnership and marriage lies exactly in the symbolic implications of marriage, in its public declaration of a mutual commitment between bride and groom, ritualized in a celebration.[17] If this symbolism were meaningless, as some argue it to be, there would be no point in choosing to marry rather than just living together, or vice versa. Marriage will display stronger symbolic effect than the legalization of partnership, stressing both the visibility and the normality of homosexuals' difference, hence smoothing the process towards the full legitimation of homosexuality. I shall return to this shortly.

The second point concerns the adoption and fostering of children: if same-sex marriages were legalized, the right to adopt and foster would immediately follow, but this would not be the case with legal partnerships. On the one hand, recognized partnerships, whether homosexual or heterosexual, do not automatically give the right to adopt or have access to artificial insemination; on the other hand, same-sex partnerships have been recognized to a certain extent, in terms of certain benefits being extended from heterosexual to homosexual partnerships, an extension that has stopped short of adoption. Think, for example, of a recent case involving a well-to-do British gay couple who wanted a child: in the USA they succeeded, by means of *in vitro* fertilization and with a surrogate mother, and the partner who was not the biological father was able to adopt the baby. When they returned to Britain with their baby, they were stopped at the point of entry, because the baby was unknown and not legally theirs. How the case will eventually be settled is still to be seen, which suggests that the recognized partnership strategy is not a completely straightforward solution to the issue of adoption.

At this point, we should consider whether the claim to normality put forward by some members of the gay and lesbian movement, that is, the claim that homosexual relations be seen as a normal option within society, thus giving gays access to the same opportunities as the rest of the population, makes any sense in a strategy of gay liberation.[18] As I mentioned before, same-sex marriage is not a goal that is shared and sought after by all within the gay community. The reasoning behind this position can be reconstructed as follows. The basic argument of the

---

[17] "As a matter of political symbolism we ought to be able to marry the persons we love. Without the right to marry, gay Americans are second class citizens." Eskridge, *The Case for Same-Sex Marriage*, p. 63.

[18] This problem is explored by Kaplan, "Intimacy and Equality: The Question of Lesbian and Gay Marriage"; Wilson, *A Simple Matter of Justice*; Weston, *Family We Choose: Lesbians, Gays, Kinship*; Eskridge, *The Case for Same-Sex Marriage*.

gay and lesbian movement can be found in the critique of heterosexual sexuality, typically expressed within traditional marriage, which constitutes the norm of civilized life and excludes what is different as deviant. Homosexuality is seen as the extreme deviance, because it is not simply an uncivilized mode of sexuality, but is considered to be perverted, to go against nature. If this is the position that sustains the exclusion of homosexuality from society, the goal of gay liberation should not be that of conforming to the dominant standards and gaining access to the dominant institutions, which are tailored precisely so as to leave them out; the goal instead should be to assert their different sexual inclinations loudly, to affirm their value, rejecting any impossible or undesirable compromise. In this way, gays and lesbians would be free to invent and to experiment in the field of sexuality, just like the avant-garde within the arts, becoming the leading group of a sexual and cultural revolution, overcoming the oppression that is an intrinsic characteristic of the patriarchal family. The subversion of the rules and the roles that make up the traditional heterosexual family opens up forms of sexuality and of emotional life which will benefit not only gays, lesbians, and bisexual people, but also women and children who have traditionally played dependent roles in the patriarchal family. The conclusion of this argument against the family as the main locus of oppression is the rejection of the very idea of same-sex marriage. "Since when is marriage a path to liberation?," asks, for example, Paula Etteltrick, arguing that gender hierarchy is entailed by, and hence inseparable from, marriage.[19]

In a sense, this radical position shares the conservative stand on the internal logic of the concept of marriage. I will return to this shortly. The point I want to consider now is whether the desire to be recognized as different, yet at the same time normal, expresses an attitude of cultural conservatism by those homosexuals who invoke the right to marry.[20] It must be said that this issue is located outside the proper focus of my work which does not aim at affirming any political line on this question, but rather at judging dominant standards and conventions from the viewpoint of the excluded, and at arguing for the reform of these conventions guided by principles of justice. I have no essentialist idea about what the "right" identity for gays is or about what form of life best realizes that identity; from the viewpoint of political theory, the problems are oppression, exclusion, and humiliation by liberal institutions, on the one hand,

---

[19] Paula Etteltrick, "Since When is Marriage a Path to Liberation?" in W. Bubenstein, ed., *Lesbians, Gays and the Law* (New York: The New Press, 1993), pp. 401–5.
[20] This point is taken up by Kaplan, "Intimacy and Equality."

and the imposition on individuals of norms and conventions either by the moral majority or by self-proclaimed leaders of the minority group. It is up to the individual, whether gay or not, to decide between sexual freedom or stable relationships at different stages in life, and whether to live in a very conformist or a very non-conformist way. The problem is to prevent homosexuals from being compelled to be non-conformist, because no other option is open to them. The argument against the normalization of homosexuality is analogous to that for outing, i.e. for publicizing someone's homosexuality against his or her will.[21] While this move can be understood as a form of political strategy against free-riding, and thus as an action similar to picketing in strikes, it cannot be accepted as a justifiable step for gay liberation, because no one can be coerced to become free. Besides, being gay, like being black or being a woman, is a collective identity which does not exhaust the individual's social identity: it should be up to the single member to define the terms of his or her membership. Some may be more committed to gay liberation, others may be more interested in their professional life or in a political career; some may prefer sexual promiscuity, others monogamy. I have no intention of portraying any ideal type of gay life to be promoted by political institutions, but simply of exploring the conditions in which individual homosexuals might flourish. In short, the radical objection to arguments in favor of homosexual marriage is unjustified from the point of view of justice.

Moreover, I believe that the radical objection mistakenly undervalues the potential innovative strength of same-sex marriage. Same-sex marriage cannot exist without a radical transformation of the institutions of marriage and the family. On this point, conservatives are right: the access of gays to legal marriage involves turning upside-down a central pillar of societal standards – namely, the family, which is "naturally" composed of a man, his wife, and children. In this respect, a non-institutionalized, subversive sexuality, which is kept well within the limits of inner-city ghettoes and involves only small numbers of people, is relatively easy to tolerate: it can be viewed merely as some form of contemporary Bohemianism. What is much more threatening is the idea that the family, the core of all traditions and the channel of cultural transmission, might be redescribed in such a completely non-traditional manner, yet keep its traditional label and, as a result, its central social location.

---

[21] See Johnasson and Percy, *Outing: Shattering the Conspiracy of Silence.*

There is, however, a more moderate position within the gay movement which takes issue with same-sex marriage; according to this argument, same-sex marriage appears, on the one hand, to go too far, hence is unrealistic on pragmatic grounds, and, on the other, forms part of a politics of identity which is regarded as politically hopeless, because it does not share the goals or priorities of any political movement.[22] According to this position, what is important is not symbolic politics, but real resources; so, if the gay movement really wishes to put an end to discrimination because of sexual orientation, it must aspire to create a situation in which gay couples have the same benefits as heterosexual couples. The fight for marriage is, by comparison meaningless, because nothing can be gained by gays and lesbians through marriage which could not also be gained in a recognized partnership, at least in real, material terms. Investing all that energy for the sake of a mere symbolic recognition is beside the point for a political movement, and, moreover, risks sparking off a backlash from the majority. This argument interweaves pragmatic and political considerations. I shall not deal with the pragmatic dimension here, but the political considerations adduced boil down to a distinction between real benefits and unreal symbols. The point is that the whole politics of the gay movement has aimed at symbolic recognition, asserting the visibility of homosexuality in public, the importance of coming out, and so on. Real politics, however, cannot be set apart from symbolic politics in the general strategy of the gay movement, which is built around the assertion of the legitimacy of gay and lesbian identities. And, furthermore, it is not true that legal partnership and same-sex marriage are equivalent in terms of material benefits and implications: as I said before, adoption is not usually a viable option for non-married or same-sex partners.

In conclusion, neither the radical nor the moderate position against same-sex marriage argues convincingly that legal partnership is the correct aim to pursue and that marriage is a cultural step backwards and, therefore, a pointless goal.

THE LOGIC-OF-MARRIAGE ARGUMENT

So far we have considered, first, the objection of conservatives, who oppose any suggestion that homosexuality be accepted as a normal option

---

[22] See Lance Selfa, "What's Wrong with Identity Politics?" in D. Morton, ed., *The Material Queer* (Boulder, Colo.: Westview Press, 1996), pp. 46–8.

and that gays be given public recognition and the same rights as heterosexuals and, a fortiori, who oppose same-sex partnership and marriage;
second, the objection against same-sex marriage advanced by radical sections of the gay movement, in the name of subversion and a refusal to
submit to cultural domination; and, third, the more moderate objection
against identity politics. In the literature on the subject, however, the
most common objection to same-sex marriage cannot be easily assigned
to any clear political position; it covers the entire left–right spectrum.
It constitutes a specific argument against the marriage of two people of
the same sex, grounded on the very logic which is alleged to govern the
meaning and the proper use of the notion of marriage. By its very logic,
so the argument goes, marriage is the long-term union of a man and a
woman for the purpose of having and raising children. Just as a table
is not a window, so marriage cannot take place between two people of
the same sex, who cannot procreate. In other words, the argument in
favor of same-sex marriage is incoherent. Being gay can be a perfectly
right and meaningful option, and gays should have equal rights and be
free from discrimination, harassment and homophobia, but, as a mute
person cannot become an opera singer, so gays cannot get married: they
cannot get permission to do something that they are not capable of doing.
After all, ought implies can.[23]

I hold that this argument is really crucial for the issue because it appears to be independent of any substantive stand on the intrinsic value
of homosexuality, and it cannot be directly linked with any specific political view. In fact, this argument can underpin, respectively, conservative,
liberal, and radical objections to same-sex marriage, making the debate
all the more insidious.

The logic-of-marriage argument can be adopted in two senses: the first
points out the logic of the notion, which excludes the union of same-sex
partners; the second points to the nature of the thing, which entails that
marriage is a union between a man and a woman. The first sense has
a more liberal nuance, because it does not refer to a substantive norm
about intimate relationships, but simply appeals to a formal semantic
norm governing the use of the word marriage. The second sense refers
to a normative conception of what marriage is, and hence implies a substantive judgment. However, we shall see that the first, morally neutral

---

[23] This argument is critically examined by Strasser, *Legally Wed: Same-Sex Marriage and the Constitution*,
and by Eskridge, *The Case for Same-Sex Marriage*.

sense in fact collapses into the second. The meaning of words is constantly subject to change and evolution so that there is nothing incoherent in a semantic shift, unless one holds a theory which directly links words with things, and things with essences. In that case, the original meaning of an expression fixes once and for all the future uses of the term, because the nature of the thing defines the original meaning; thus we are back to a normative conception of what marriage should consist of in order to be defined as a marriage. But it must be conceded that not all semantic shifts are necessarily possible or coherent. Semantic changes are not totally arbitrary; they find their limits and justification in the very possibility of being recognized and thus adopted by the speaking community. Seen in this light, it may happen that extending the notion of marriage to same-sex couples is indeed incoherent. The question to ask, then, can be reframed thus: in the cluster of meanings and familiar uses of the word 'marriage'– as opposed to partnership, friendship, blood relationship, love affairs, and so on – is there something which presently prevents us from understanding, making sense of, and using the phrase "same-sex marriage"? Before answering, it must be noted that what in each case actually gives sense to a word is not its internal logic, but, rather, the external cultural variables which open the way to possible semantic extensions and analogies, while at the same time banning other possibilities. Incidentally, following this reasoning, I hold that the response to the logic-of-marriage argument based on historical records is not appropriate, because it suggests that the meaning of a term is given in its original definition.[24] That is why it is thought to be essential to show that, from the very start, the word "marriage" was meant also to cover same-sex unions. But if shifts of meaning are regarded as part of the evolution of a culture and a language, there is no need to prove that same-sex marriages were recognized in the past. Yet it must be argued that the cultural and social transformations that have taken place in our emotional lives make the very idea of same-sex marriage understandable and coherent to us.

Marriage has traditionally been understood as a stable intimate union between a man and a woman, usually with the intention of having and raising children. Procreation has always been a traditional function of marriage, though not exactly its sole reason for being, given that infertile marriages have always existed. In contemporary advanced societies,

---

[24] Eskridge, *The Case for Same-Sex Marriage.*

moreover, procreation has been positively separated from sexuality; this development has been made possible by innovations in contraception, but also by changes in cultural attitudes. Sexual activity is thought to be an important aspect of life for *any* adult, whether married or not, while the decision to have children is regarded as a further and more significant choice, given the high levels of responsibility involved in parenting. As is well known, not only are there married couples who cannot have children, but there are others who do not wish to have children, although their marriage is perfectly valid. And though marriage is still the typical framework for having children, it is by no means the only one, nor is procreation its exclusive function.

Moreover, new reproductive technologies have made it possible for infertile couples to reproduce by artificial means; this possibility further emphasizes the distinction between the sexual act and reproduction. If the definition of marriage does not involve procreation, and if the institution of marriage does not require procreation to be legally valid, then what appear to be essential are the stability and intimacy of a union. But there is nothing to suggest that homosexual couples cannot achieve these essentials just as easily as heterosexual couples. Hence, there is no impediment intrinsic to the common understanding of the notion of marriage which precludes gays or lesbians from this option. Moreover, if reproduction has become, at least in principle, independent of sexual activity, gay couples can also have children by means of *in vitro* fertilization, surrogate mothering and adoption. Without getting involved here in the discussion on such reproductive technologies, reproduction is in principle not ruled out for homosexual couples. However, this very possibility raises another question: is it right that children be raised by homosexual couples? The question is very delicate and constitutes the hardest aspect of the discussion on same-sex marriage, since the choices and lifestyle of the couple have a direct effect on an innocent third party who may turn out to be disadvantaged compared to children born and raised in traditional families.

Up to this point, the focus has been on justice for gays and lesbians and on the transformation of the conventional idea of marriage so as to include them and to stop homosexuality from being a burden, and to make it just one of the viable options in society, compatible with the full enjoyment of citizenship and personal rights. From the point of view of justice for gays and lesbians, I have argued that same-sex marriage should follow from the public recognition of their presence achieved by toleration. I have not argued that marriage itself will finally provide homosexual couples with the full status of citizens; I hold, rather, that marriage should be accessible to homosexuals if their sexual orientation is to be regarded as a viable option on the same footing as that of heterosexuals. The point is not to define an ideal lifestyle for homosexuals, whether or not this involves marriage,[25] but to provide them with the same opportunity as heterosexuals to pursue their ideal of the good life, within or outside the gay community, in a marriage or in a partnership. They should not be compelled to experiment with subversive and unconventional forms of intimacy, because homosexuals are as likely to be conformist, quiet, work-oriented and well disciplined as they are to be non-conformist, rebellious, or promiscuous. Thus, on the one hand, same-sex marriage represents an incredibly vivid recognition of the legitimate presence of homosexuality in the mainstream of society, and, on the other, it constitutes an opportunity to live a certain kind of quiet and disciplined intimate life for those who look for stable, committed relationships. But if same-sex marriages satisfy homosexuals in one respect, they may still turn out to be an undesirable environment in which to bring up children. And if this is the case, harm to a third party must be an important consideration, thus coming down in favor of the idea of a legal partnership for homosexuals but with no right to adopt or foster.[26]

The argument against allowing homosexual couples to adopt or giving them free access to reproductive technology appeals to children's rights and runs approximately as follows. Children have a right to be loved, cared for and educated by responsible parents, and to be raised in a normal, healthy family – that is, a family composed of a father, mother, and possibly other siblings, living in a civilized and decent way. The presence of a maternal and a paternal figure answers the deep emotional and psychological needs for stability, identification, and separation of the self, enabling an individual to grow up into a normal, healthy adult. Given this need for stability, together with the dominant model of the family, the child of same-sex parents would feel his or her condition to be different and strange compared with that of other children, and would run the risk of being excluded, discriminated against, and ridiculed by school-fellows and others. It has to be said that in real life any number of circumstances can occur to upset the ideal: parents might separate, or one might die; they might be irresponsible, too poor, culturally inadequate, or abusive.

---

[25] This seems to me the approach by Kaplan, "Intimacy and Equality," p. 336, and Mark Blasius, "An Ethos of Lesbian and Gay Existence," *Political Theory*, 20, 1992, pp. 642–72.

[26] On this issue, see Stephen Hicks and Janet McDermott, eds., *Lesbian and Gay Fostering and Adoption* (London and Philadelphia: Jessica Kinsley, 1999).

The list of possible domestic horrors and crimes is seemingly endless. However, so the argument goes, such misfortunes are unplanned, and do not constitute a reason to stop wishing the best for children. When public officials (judges, social workers, psychologists, etc.) are in a position to make a decision about a child's future life, they should attempt to grant him or her conditions that resemble the ideal as closely as possible, avoiding any family situation which is clearly inadequate and an obvious sources of problems. Therefore, allowing a homosexual couple to adopt or foster would not be in the child's best interests as long as it is assumed that such a family falls short of providing the ideal circumstances for bringing up children.

However, this argument assumes what must actually be demonstrated – that is, that the dominant model of the family provides the ideal environment for raising children. But this assumption can no longer stand up to critical inspection. In fact, the traditional family is considered the ideal for rearing children, because it is considered the natural locus of intimacy and reproduction. Nature is here taken to have a normative, as well as a descriptive character. On the descriptive side, however, child-rearing has undergone so many different changes through history and across human cultures that appeal to the purportedly natural foundation of the nuclear, monogamous, heterosexual family is clearly without force. In many cultures and in different historical periods children were raised in a totally female environment, with no male presence. At adolescence, girls, who stayed on with the women, were separated from boys, who were entrusted to male instructors for a manly and often military education. I am not thinking of far-off and exotic cultures, but of recent western history, which gives the lie to the "natural" argument in favor of opposite-sex parenting. To put it differently, this apparently natural need was an extremely late discovery in western history; this suggests that we can in fact dispense with it. Moreover, the record of child abuse, violence, and rape singles out the family as the main locus of such crimes; these records should make us reflect on the biased character of the ideal vision of the natural family. In other words, there is no evidence that the model of the heterosexual family is either the natural or the ideal place for rearing children. It is rather the cultural dominance of the traditional model of the family that makes it "ideal" in the eyes of the majority; but it is also for this very reason that homosexual families may turn out to be a problem for children. It is precisely because such families are not considered part of the norm – the "natural" model of the family – that they engender in their children and their peers a sense of abnormality, which might easily translate into a sense of exclusion. When divorce was rare and viewed as a social disgrace, the children of divorced parents had to suffer as a result of the shame, as well as having to cope psychologically with the disruption of the family. Now that divorce is commonplace, children still have to cope with the fact that their parents are separated, but they are by no means regarded as strange, to be kept at a distance because they might possibly be morally infected. Indeed, having divorced parents is now considered part of the normal condition of growing up. I am not recommending divorce as a sound educational policy; I am just pointing out that, by admitting its existence, the liberal state has acknowledged an individual's personal freedom to revise their intimate commitment, which cannot be enforced against the two parties' will. In this way, the state has consistently given up any perfectionist ideal of marriage and family, limiting its paternalistic intervention in favor of children to cases of unquestionable harm: abuse, violence, or physical deprivation, a position which often clashes with the argument in favor of privacy for the traditional family. At this point, if liberal institutions want to be consistent, same-sex marriage ought to be acknowledged. All that a political community can do for children is defend them from parental or external violence and provide them with an education, because any attempt to impose a particular model of family life as the natural and ideal environment in which to bring up children is unjustified, and implies an interference with personal liberty that is not in line with liberal institutions; indeed, instead of preventing harm, it is likely to do more harm to children of unconventional families, by maintaining prejudices in society. Hence, preventing homosexual couples from adopting is based on a biased definition of the ideal and natural environment for children; furthermore, it is unsupported by historical and empirical evidence and does not take into account the perverse effects that the cultural domination of traditional families may have on children raised in unconventional settings.

CONCLUSION

To sum up: same-sex marriage is a paradigmatic example of what toleration as recognition implies concerning social standards and public conventions. I have, first, shown that liberal toleration is insufficient to grant full inclusion to gays and lesbians who, as a rule, already have citizenship rights and access to public office, though only in disguise – that is, only if their sexual orientation is invisible. Hence their claims to full inclusion have focused on the issue of visibility and of the public acceptance of their different sexual orientation, so as to enable them to become full members in the polity without giving up their different identity. Liberal toleration, even at its best, if not discouraging, does not help to overcome invisibility and to make the public presence of gays and lesbians legitimate. This is because the reasons grounding liberal toleration are only negative ("homosexual orientation does not harm anyone; hence it belongs to the area of personal liberty where political interference is unjustified") and do not allow the symbolic meaning of recognition to be attached. The crucial test for liberal toleration's insufficiency concerns the issue of exclusive social standards. The negative reasons backing toleration do not commit liberal institutions to any special revision of exclusive societal standards, such as the family. It is no accident that the arguments put forward by various groups in favor of revising societal standards are made in the name of principles other than toleration, such as non-discrimination and equal rights. By contrast, if toleration is positively meant as recognition of the public presence of homosexuals as part of the normal range of viable options in society, then a revision of the norm must follow as a specific commitment.

Yet, one might say: "what's wrong with combining traditional liberal toleration with anti-discrimination and equal rights? Why should we abandon the familiar language of liberal theory and embark on the slippery slope of identity politics if, after all, the same result obtains with a two-step strategy?" I would respond first that the traditional liberal strategy is more complex and less straightforward than my revised conception of toleration as recognition: the second step in the liberal position does not follow from the first and requires a totally separate argument. Second, I would argue that the liberal view overlooks the issue of recognition as a crucial element of compensation for previous humiliation and exclusion. Recognition is not a good to be distributed according to principles of justice, but a symbolic act which can be attached to other actions, depending on the meaning and the reasons sustaining those actions. The particular nature of the reasons cited to legitimize a decision then becomes crucial both for qualifying the attitude expressed in certain public acts and also for making possible certain kinds of subsequent action. The point is that an argument from non-discrimination and equal rights can take a very different course and have a different outcome depending on whether or not it is informed by sensitivity to social differences. Sensitivity to social differences, however, constitutes the background of the whole reasoning for toleration as recognition. If sexual orientation is simply discounted as the ground for public action, then homosexual citizens appear to enjoy perfectly equal rights because, like everyone else, they can get married, albeit only to a member of the opposite sex, given the common understanding of what constitutes a marriage. On this reading, the discrimination and the corresponding humiliation suffered by homosexuals simply become invisible, just as their sexual orientation is supposed to be invisible in the public sphere. In order effectively to sustain the argument for same-sex marriage, non-discrimination and equal rights should be placed in a larger debate focused on differences and on forms of exclusion that follow from difference blindness. In other words, the reasoning which leads to an understanding of toleration as recognition needs to be retrieved here so that equal rights are interpreted as equivalent rights, i.e. as the equal empowerment of different individuals. In conclusion, if toleration does not include the reasons for recognition, a separate appeal will need to be made to those reasons in any case in the form of an argument for equivalent rights. Thus, toleration as recognition constitutes the most effective and direct way of securing the legitimization of the public presence of homosexuality, and it implies the revision of exclusive social standards as well.

I have argued that a fair revision – one that makes room for gays and lesbians in liberal institutions – must lead to the acknowledgment of forms of same-sex marriage, in which gay couples have all the rights and benefits given to heterosexual couples (including adoption). This represents the most vivid form of public recognition. Despite all objections from conservatives, liberals, and radical homosexuals, none of which is finally persuasive, same-sex marriage must be recognized if homosexuality is not to be seen as a mark of an unnatural or perverse orientation. Reasons of political opportunity may suggest that it would be better to postpone this argument, and that other forms of political activism are likely to do more for the inclusion and acceptance of homosexuality in society. But this can only be decided contextually. Furthermore, the argument in favor of same-sex marriage can only be delayed; it cannot be abandoned altogether if gays and lesbians are to be treated with equal respect and dignity.

7

Toleration and identity politics

THE ARGUMENT FOR TOLERATION AS RECOGNITION

In this final chapter I want first of all to summarize the normative conception behind toleration as recognition, and then to consider some objections to it. The first and most common objection is that toleration as recognition is incompatible with liberal politics and a risk to the liberal order. Though the allegation of incompatibility is not incomprehensible in that public toleration of differences will lead to a redrawing of societal standards, and, consequently, worsen the majority's status, I argue that toleration as recognition is nevertheless compatible with liberal principles and does not infringe any right or fundamental value.

A second common objection concerns further claims for recognition, which are considered dangerous consequences of the public toleration of differences. Even though toleration as recognition can ultimately be made compatible with liberal politics, it opens the way to the arena of identity politics, whose tendencies towards particularism and tribalism are deeply at odds with liberal justice. In response, I will map out the key arguments in the politics of identity, sorting out the different claims and assessing whether adopting toleration as recognition commits the government to meeting further claims as well. Then I outline a general strategy for dealing with demands for recognition which suggests that from the perspective of social justice only some can be met, while others should be rejected and most can be negotiated.

Finally, two non-conventional objections to toleration as recognition will be taken up, the first questioning symbolic politics as such, and the second pointing out that social standing and reputation are positional goods and not, therefore, in principle generalizable. I will try to respond to both these objections and to reaffirm the value of toleration as recognition.

The conception of toleration as recognition shares with the standard conception of neutralist liberalism the view that toleration is a matter of justice.[1] But, in this case, the question does not primarily concern equal liberty, but equal terms of inclusion. Inclusion here is meant not only in the formal sense of having citizenship rights, but in the substantive sense of enjoying the status of full membership in society. It is not a resource to be distributed, but, rather, designates the capability to make use of citizenship rights and social opportunities; therefore it makes a difference to how people are socially and publicly regarded. I argue that people marked by differences which are tolerated in the private sphere but which are invisible or marginalized in public life, and subject to prejudice, stigmatization, and discrimination in social interactions, cannot be fully participating members of social and political life on the same footing as the majority. Briefly, exclusion is the result of being different from the norm, which leads to unequal access to social goods and unequal membership in society. Inclusion is crucial for social justice, and a precondition for being a functioning political actor and a subject to whom social goods are distributed, and yet the issue of inclusion cannot be grasped from the constitutional perspective adopted by neutralist liberalism. From the constitutional standpoint, all citizens are equally included and all differences are equally different, while the distinction between majoritarian identities and other identities is ignored. Only by means of a (non-reductive) analysis of those differences which raise genuine issues of toleration in contemporary democracies can the problem of unequal inclusion for the bearers of different identities emerge. Issues of toleration derive from inequalities in social standing, public respect, and social and political power among the various groups living in a pluralist democracy. It is these inequalities which make disagreements on the conception of the good and culture especially intractable.

Given this reading of the social circumstances in which toleration becomes a pressing issue, the normative approach in terms of compatibility between values, norms, and practices in democratic society proves superficial and incapable of dealing with the problem of inclusion. If toleration is subscribed to on compatibility grounds, as liberals imply, it tends to be granted only in its literal meaning of non-interference, which is not the real issue at stake. In other words, the argument from

---

[1] On the link between toleration and justice, see my "Tolérance et justice sociale."

the compatibility viewpoint supports toleration for the wrong reasons, not even touching on the question of exclusion. Public toleration should instead be granted for the right reasons, that is, because of the symbolic meaning of recognition and inclusion of difference within the normal range of viable options and possible alternative ways of living, all coexisting equally in society. Public toleration should reverse the invisibility and marginality of different identities which public blindness, far from dispelling, in fact reinforces. And in order to play this symbolic role, an argument for toleration as recognition is vital.

The reasons for public toleration are to be found in such crucial liberal principles as equality of respect, inclusion, and openness. But if liberal justice provides the appropriate normative grounds, we must then ask whether toleration as recognition also belongs to liberal politics, or moves beyond it, undermining other liberal values, institutions, or rights. The discussion mainly concerns the notion of recognition that appears to contrast with the liberal ideal of neutrality and impartiality, introducing a specific content evaluation of differences (implying the abandonment of anti-perfectionism), as well as questioning the partiality and discretion of the political authority (given that recognition cannot be granted generally and universally, but only to specific claimants).[2]

I have argued that toleration as recognition reverses the common practice of neutrality towards differences. Under the current interpretation, neutrality implies a distant, non-differentiating public stance on various opinions, values, practices, and lifestyles. By contrast, toleration as recognition implies public concern, positive attention, and consideration for differences. Public concern for differences is necessary in order to reverse their previous invisibility, marginality, and stigmatization. Moreover, while neutrality is intended to be universal, positive consideration cannot be given in general, but only to a specific difference. And this marks a significant shift in liberal politics.

Such a shift in public attitude toward differences can, however, be reconciled both with the anti-perfectionist intention, and with the anti-discriminatory ideal implied by the principle of neutrality. The concept of recognition adopted in this framework does not imply any endorsement of the intrinsic value of any specific difference, but simply its acceptance within the range of normal viable options and alternatives of

---

[2] The liberal criticism of the politics of recognition is repeatedly made with few variations. Among recent stands, see David Miller, "Group Identities, National Identities and Democratic Politics," in Horton and Mendus, ed., *Toleration, Identity and Difference*, pp. 103–25, and Brian Barry, *Culture and Equality. An Egalitarian Critique of Multiculturalism* (Cambridge: Polity Press, 2000).

society. Provided that the difference in question does not infringe any rights, its public recognition is content-independent, and, even though it must be granted to each difference separately, it can be generalized to all claimants. Content-independence and impartiality are thus reconciled with a positive public consideration of differences. In conclusion, having shown that toleration as symbolic recognition is grounded in an argument from liberal justice and, moreover, can be realized without preferential treatment or violation of rights, there seems to be no reason why it should not be considered the appropriate normative response to demands for recognition of differences within the framework of liberal democracy.

In fact, toleration as recognition tends to be opposed from various sides (more so in countries where the secular ideal of *laïcité* embodies the principle of neutrality than in others), because, despite its symbolic nature, it engenders real transformations in societal norms. The inclusion of differences in the public sphere implicitly leads to the redrawing of the standards of civility, propriety, and normality, constituting a worsening of the majority's social position, given that the latter loses its monopolistic position of control over societal conventions and norms. This very fact helps to understand how the liberal argument for toleration in terms of compatibility can work against the public toleration of differences. Differences are incompatible if they constitute a threat to the liberal order and/or if they harm other people. As we have seen, the public presence of minority differences often does represent a threat to public conventions, implicitly questioning societal standards. Moreover, the transformation of public conventions would lead to a worsening of the majority's position. Hence, the public acceptance of social differences is in many cases incompatible with the status quo, and that is why it is easy to justify limits to public toleration of differences in terms of a threat to the existing order.[3] On the other hand, within the theoretical framework I propose, concern for such incompatibility is overridden by a consideration of the way in which the monopolistic control of societal standards by the majority is embedded in forms of social domination. When a palpable injustice is at issue, neither the persistence of the status

[3] This argument based on incompatibility duplicates the argument against social reforms based on the criterion of Pareto optimality, which rules out any change which would worsen the position of any individual. It is not by chance that Pareto optimality, as opposed to various conceptions of liberal equality (such as Rawls's and Dworkin's), has been the mark of laissez-faire liberalism. Consider, for example, J. Buchanan and G. Tullock, *The Calculus of Consent* (Ann Arbor: University of Michigan Press, 1962).

quo, nor the worsening of the situation of the privileged group can be invoked to block action aimed at reestablishing justice.[4]

The argument for toleration as recognition can go so far. Now, however, we must consider the consequences. Indeed the symbolic inclusion of differences in the public space by means of toleration is only the first move towards the full inclusion of minorities, because it is the first step in what is commonly called "identity politics" or "the politics of recognition." The term identity politics usually means the political commitment to a multicultural society in which various groups and minorities live together peacefully, without giving up their collective identities and differences in either the public or the private sphere.[5] Identity politics implies different political measures and policies aimed at the public recognition of minorities' collective identities, of which toleration as recognition is just the first step. It is a step which I have shown to be compatible with the principles and rules of liberalism, though it requires a different political attitude, positively acknowledging instead of ignoring differences. Yet the issue is whether the whole of identity politics would then follow directly as a result of accepting my views about toleration as recognition. While, in fact, toleration as recognition is, all things considered, a justified and also a reasonable demand for bringing about the visibility of minorities, a demand which avoids complex distributive questions and does not stretch liberal theory too far, it may also open the way to many other, much more questionable, minority claims, advanced in the name of the politics of recognition. And once the latter has received legitimation by a public toleration of differences, we find ourselves on a slippery slope, with no clear limits. Thus, in order to avoid the endless and divisive demands from the politics of recognition, it is better to be cautious with public toleration as well.

In order to counter this objection, I shall first look at identity politics, considering various different types of claim that are made in its name;

---

4 On the point of justice with reference to the accommodation of cultural differences, see W. F. Schwartz, ed., *Justice in Immigration* (Cambridge: Cambridge University Press, 1995).

5 Multiculturalism is sometimes used as a descriptive notion, meaning a society where a plurality of cultural groups coexist with all their tensions and conflicts. But on this definition, multiculturalism is simply a synonym for pluralism. Sometimes, multiculturalism is used as a normative ideal of a pluralist society in which the various groups and cultures do not need to become assimilated to the dominant model or merge into a melting-pot, but where each group can keep its special identity. The normative meaning, which is the one to which I subscribe, is, for example, put forward by Raz, "Multiculturalism. A Liberal Perspective." In the literature on multiculturalism, there are also positions in favor of a revision of traditional modes of inclusion, yet against identity politics: see, for example, M. Martiniello, *Sortir des ghettos culturels* (Paris: Presses des Sciences Politiques, 1997).

I shall then sort these claims out and assess how far they go in stretching the framework of liberal democracy; at the same time I shall ask which of them can lay claim to being direct, indirect, and merely alleged consequences of toleration as recognition. Finally, I should be in a position to answer the question whether the commitment to toleration as recognition of differences leads to a similar commitment to other forms of recognition.

THE POLITICS OF RECOGNITION

Claims for the public recognition of minority identities can be grouped into roughly six categories:

1) Claims for public toleration of social differences, which I have been discussing so far.
2) Claims for limiting toleration of practices and forms of speech that are seen as offensive to the dignity of members of newly included groups, and which thus damage their collective image and public presence. These are also issues of toleration, but in such cases those who have fought for toleration as recognition are in fact demanding limits to toleration as non-interference, as part of the same politics of inclusion.
3) Claims for revising public conventions that are based on a majority culture, and which exclude minority members from certain activities, such as public festivities, some aspects of school curricula, work practices, schedules, etc.
4) Claims for special policies aimed at providing minority members with more opportunities and resources so as to balance social disadvantages, such as affirmative action policies and reverse discrimination programs.
5) Claims for special support for minority cultures in order to prevent them from being swamped by the majority culture and, also, to provide minorities with the opportunity to practice their way of life.
6) Claims for collective rights to group autonomy and collective liberty.

The latter claims, which present liberal politics with great difficulties, should be kept separate from the others, because collective liberty and group autonomy are not necessarily aimed at fairer terms of inclusion for minority members, but instead state the will to separate, albeit only in cultural terms, from the larger society.[6]

---

[6] The distinction between claims to a fairer inclusion and claims to autonomy and separation corresponds to a similar distinction drawn by Kymlicka ("Social Unity in a Liberal State," *Social*

This provisional and open list ranks claims from the less to the more demanding for liberal politics; one can easily see from this that identity politics is not an all-or-nothing affair, but requires each claim to be examined and assessed on its own terms. I shall now proceed to do this with reference to each claim's link with public toleration of social differences and to argue against the slippery slope objection to toleration as recognition.

Among claims which are a direct development from toleration as recognition, the first includes demands to limit toleration in instances involving offensive behavior and speech. As we saw in chapter 5, the quest for special protection against offenses and humiliation stems from the very same reasons as the quest for toleration as recognition of differences. Against the risk of continued marginalization as a result of being stereotyped and humiliated, newly admitted groups ask to be positively protected from offensive behavior which undermines their public image and, thus, their social acceptance.

The reasons supporting claims for public protection are thus a direct development from those that favor public toleration, and the final goal is precisely the same: i.e. full inclusion. In this sense, it would seem reasonable to suppose that once the state has granted public toleration of differences, it should consistently also meet claims for special protection. But, in fact, the decision to provide public protection is more complex, since it encounters difficulties from which public toleration is free.[7] The first and major difficulty is that public protection from offensive practices collides with a fundamental liberal principle, namely freedom of expression. Freedom of expression can sometimes be curtailed, but only if adequate justification is provided. In this case, the argument is based on justice, showing that harassment and stereotyping not only induce humiliation and shame in one's identity, but work together to push that identity to the margins of the public sphere and of civil society. Yet this argument is highly controversial because, on the one hand, it is far from clear that all forms of speech that are offensive to some minority constitute harm[8] and, on the other, free speech would then be limited on the

---

Philosophy and Policy Foundation, USA, 1996) between two patterns of cultural diversity: multiethnic diversity and multinational diversity. Ethnic and national minorities are sorted out by their different claims, respectively, to integration and to separation. Another distinction which partially overlaps with mine and Kymlicka's, is that between pluralistic and totalitarian communities. This distinction concerns demands for internal loyalty; compare Michael Walzer "What Rights for Cultural Communities?"

[7] For a more detailed discussion of this topic, see chapter 5.

[8] See the detailed analysis of harm by Joel Feinberg, *Social Philosophy* (Englewood Cliffs: Prentice Hall, 1973). He, however, admits offenses as one of the three kinds of harm.

grounds of its content (thus violating the content-independence condition for restrictions).[9] Finally it is contestable that the alleged damage can be effectively repaired by imposing restrictions on freedom of expression (rather than allowing more speech expressing the opposite viewpoint).

But even assuming that limiting freedom of expression can be made acceptable, a second difficulty must be considered – that is, differential treatment.[10] Political protection from offensive behavior applies only to certain groups, imposing limits on the freedom of other citizens in relation to that group. This difficulty might be overridden by an appropriate argument appealing to redress for past injustice. But at this point practical difficulties arise concerning how long a previously oppressed group can invoke past injustice for obtaining special protection, and how far limitation of toleration of offensive speech and behavior should be extended in order to minimize constraints on freedom. As far as the definition of a group as oppressed is concerned, one possibility might be to apply a revised version of the principle of unmodified diversity, as advanced by Bruce Ackerman in relation to the compensatory transfer of goods to disadvantaged parties.[11] Disadvantaged parties are entitled to a compensatory distribution of goods if no one in society is prepared to exchange his or her position with them, and the distribution should cease as soon as the exchange of positions is considered worthwhile. Similarly, oppressed groups would be entitled to special public protection if no member of the majority group was prepared to change places with them. However, the test of unmodified diversity is not very reliable when applied to the identification of oppressed groups. While some advantages and disadvantages of membership in a group can be easily measured and compared in economic terms, other aspects involve matters of identity which are non-comparable (or not easily comparable) values. In sum, I think there is no clear-cut analytical criterion for sorting out which groups, among those that have suffered past exclusion, are entitled to extra legal protection from offensive behavior, apart from a very contextual analysis of past history and the present records of its members' social situation. The definition of the scope and the areas to which protection should apply is equally difficult. In order to minimize restrictions

---

9 See Schauer, "The Phenomenology of Speech and Harm."

10 There are many liberal arguments leading to the conclusion that procedures of equal treatment are not ends in themselves, but instruments for ensuring that people are treated as equals. If this is the proper goal of liberal equality, then, according to the circumstances, it may require either equal treatment, equivalent treatment, or preferential treatment. On this point, as examples, see J. Rawls's difference principle in *TJ*; Dworkin, "Liberalism"; Fiss, "Groups and the Equal Protection Clause."

11 Ackerman, *Social Justice in the Liberal State*.

on free speech, offensive behavior needs to be specified as a definite kind of action and speech within limited and well-defined social areas. In this respect the decision must inevitably be contextual, but in reality the implementation of measures for public protection of minorities proves to be even more difficult and problematic. In general, I think the situation can be made easier if public protection is understood in its symbolic sense, as a public stand against prejudice and stereotyping, and a bias towards minority traits and supposed characteristics. If this is more important than the actual banning of offensive language and action (which in any case can never be complete in a liberal democratic state), then some symbolic measure may be contextually devised which acknowledges the valid reasons the members of a given minority have for claiming special protection and is flexible and open to compromise in all aspects of the practical implementation of remedies for symbolic exclusion, as I have argued in chapter 5.

Amongst the direct consequences of public toleration are also the non-symbolic transformations of social standards, which I considered when discussing the exemplary case of same-sex marriage. The acceptance of differences in the public sphere easily leads to a number of changes in behavioral norms so as to accommodate the newly included groups. This kind of transformation, which characterizes a multicultural society, can, for example, concern:

1) the revision of the "canon" in state schools to include the history, literature, and arts of different cultures and also of women;
2) changes in the menus of school cafeterias, taking into account the dietary requirements of Muslims, Jews, Buddhists, and vegetarians;
3) revisions in public festivities, work practices, and schedules;
4) a modification in the public standing of homosexual couples and the idea of the family.

I argue that such transformations follow directly from the public recognition of differences. Indeed, their symbolic inclusion in the public space – and in the range of viable options and "normal" alternatives available in a pluralistic society – would be inconsistent with those public conventions which are (maybe unconsciously) grounded on majoritarian social standards. The latter have always been assumed to be shared, non-controversial and to have only innocuous associations: Sunday has been chosen as the obvious weekly holiday in societies where the Christian tradition is dominant; although in contemporary democratic societies this choice is definitely more a question of convention than of religious orientation, it may be perceived as exclusionary by people of different religions within those same societies. For reasons of consistency, the state should accommodate differences within the public life of society and modify societal standards that are exclusive in effect. As we have seen, the resistance of the majority to these transformations is strong, but, though it can be rationally explained, it cannot be justified in terms of fairness. The argument against revising public attitudes and conventions develops as follows: the holders of different creeds are, in general, immigrants; they have therefore chosen to come to their host countries, however constrained by unfavorable circumstances their decision was. Thus it is up to them, as guests, to adapt to the conventions and habits of the natives ("when in Rome, do as the Romans do"); they have no right to upset society.[12] However, this argument overlooks a number of issues: first, there has always been some internal minority of a different faith and with a different way of life – for example, Jews and homosexuals, who for a long time were not in a position to challenge Christian or heterosexual conventions, no matter how excluded they felt. Therefore it is not only immigrants who demand a revision of the acceptable norms. Second, immigrants are not tourists: they have come to work and to find a new home; they are contributing to the development of the country of which their children will probably be citizens. Therefore their views must be taken into account, and they should be helped to integrate. Third, the power to control social norms should not be seen as a legitimate expectation, but as a privilege. The revision of such norms might look to the majority like a real loss, but, being a privilege, cannot be rightly protected.

It does not follow, however, that all social conventions have to be radically revised: that would probably engender too high a level of uncertainty to be tolerable. Rather, the argument implies that minority claims for changes in standards ought to be acknowledged and listened to carefully, then negotiated as to their practicability. For example, changing the weekly holiday from Sunday to some other day would create enormous practical problems in all sectors of social life, from business to school (and,

---

[12] Michael Walzer, in the chapter on "membership" in *Spheres of Justice*, makes a forceful argument against treating immigrants as *Gastarbeiter* and, while he maintains that the state has a right to decide on access policies, he argues that once immigrants have been admitted they must be treated as citizens and members of the political community. But he argues in favor of local accommodation policies rather than cultural neutrality. See "New Tribalism." On the problem of societal standards and minorities see also W. Kymlicka, *Multicultural Citizenship* (Oxford: Oxford University Press, 1995).

in fact, to my knowledge no one has ever argued for such a change). In order to accommodate differences, however, a number of less drastic measures could be taken – from liberalizing shop opening hours to making working hours more flexible, and so on. Transformations could be negotiated because, once again, what is at issue is the symbolic act of recognition rather than a particular desire to change public holidays. What is resented is the political indifference to the exclusive implications of the organization of public life; a shift in public attention and consideration for differences is the real aim of the politics of recognition. The changes themselves are signs of a revised public attitude, which recognizes different identities, but the content of those changes is much less important than the recognition itself, and can therefore be subject to negotiation on practical grounds (cost, difficulties of implementation, side-effects, etc.).

In sum, the commitment to a public recognition of differences, implied in public toleration, entails an undertaking to question and revise those conventions which are based on what the majority considers to be the norm, so as to take into account the views of minorities. These revisions will not alter economic conditions or affect the real power of members of minority groups, but will highlight a new sense of public concern and sensitivity which should eventually erode the stigma of marginality and oppression associated with minority membership. This transformation is demanded – and valued – for its symbolic meaning, because it constitutes a further step in the politics of recognition. The specific content of the change in social norms is less important than the existence of a political will to reform and take account of the position of minorities. If this reading of recognition is correct, then negotiation for new conventions is both justified and acceptable for minority groups. Although the recognition of identities is not negotiable, the ways in which recognition is expressed most certainly are.

As an indirect consequence of toleration as recognition, a number of claims for securing special resources, opportunities, protection, and support may be put forward by individual members of minority groups. The justification for this preferential treatment is the past discrimination and oppression which make membership of some groups a continuing disadvantage and burden. I will argue that the link between this kind of claim and public toleration can in some cases be very tenuous. In general, the commitment to toleration as recognition does not entail undertaking to meet these claims, most of which should not be considered as an extension of the politics of recognition. They should be taken on their own terms, and assessed according to the principles of distributive justice. Indeed, they are properly distributive claims, in that the recipients are to be individual members of disadvantaged groups qua members; yet, because of the crucial reference to the group, these claims are also seen as intertwined with the politics of identity. Identity is fundamental for advancing the group claim to distributive goods, but, at the same time, the assertion of one's identity does not seem to be the main point of such demands. Their real aim is to reduce the burden attached to certain collective identities, and hence to neutralize identity as much as possible from political developments (at least prospectively). In fact, the reference to a group identity which is the subject of prejudice and stereotyping is often used as a special resource by the group's spokespeople in order to strengthen their claim and get a better deal in distributive terms.

The special distribution to individuals qua members, claimed in order to counterbalance some disadvantage that accompanies membership of certain groups, is meant to secure special opportunities or resources for people who would otherwise be deprived of the average chances available to other citizens. This is the kind of logic that typically underlies affirmative action.[13] The latter, despite its many critics, can at least in principle be reconciled with the principles of liberal justice, its goal being equality of opportunity for all citizens. I do not intend to discuss the merits and defects of affirmative action, since it is not directly relevant to my topic. I only want to remark that the demands for affirmative action or similar policies belong specifically to the domain of distributive justice, and should be assessed accordingly. Even if affirmative action is discarded as a plausible normative solution, the issue of disadvantages non-contingently attached to membership in certain groups is a problem which liberal justice has to face, either in a universal fashion or in terms of groups.[14] In passing, it should be mentioned that affirmative action has always been seen as a temporary remedy to fill the gap left by past oppression and persistent discrimination, and never as a collective right. In sum, while affirmative action is definitely a strategy of distributive justice, it is less clear whether it also constitutes a step in the politics of recognition. Though distribution can sometimes represent a form of recognition, implying

---

[13] The literature on affirmative action is huge and reaches far beyond the bounds of philosophy. The philosophical arguments are spelled out in Cohen, Nagel, and Scanlon, eds., *Equality and Preferential Treatment*; G. Ezorsky, *Racism and Justice: The Case for Affirmative Action* (Ithaca: Cornell University Press, 1991).

[14] The distinction between equality of individuals, of sections, and of blocs in society is treated in Rae, *Equalities*.

special concern for certain groups' prospects, many critics have pointed out that it can cause the self-esteem of its beneficiaries to suffer. The preferential treatment which they exclusively enjoy appears to sanction their inability to succeed and their fundamental inferiority. More generally, affirmative action seems to recognize the status of a group as inferior, while the whole point of the politics of recognition is that members of oppressed groups are recognized as equals.[15]

In this respect, I do not see any special connection linking toleration as recognition and the distributive claims leading to affirmative action or policies of reverse discrimination. In point of fact, affirmative action policies were proposed before identity politics became an issue, and were based on justice for disadvantaged individuals where differences were considered only as disadvantages. Thus distributive claims for preferential treatment of minority members should be assessed primarily in terms of distributive principles, and the commitment to public toleration of differences should not necessarily lead to affirmative action. It follows that opposition to affirmative action cannot be a sufficient reason to oppose public toleration of differences. As to the claims that public toleration will in fact multiply distributive demands for minority members, it may be true, but only contingently, because no precise causal link can be established between public toleration which pertains to the domain of the politics of recognition and affirmative action which belongs to distributive policies.

When resources, protection, and financial support are, by contrast, demanded for the group as a whole, identity and distribution intertwine in a more complex way. Demands, say, for bilingual education for immigrants, public support for religious schools, or finance for the building of mosques in western countries all imply distributive provisions for the community, not simply for its individual members (although those who make use of such opportunities and resources are of course individual members). Indeed, these demands are usually made on the grounds of some injustice that the group in question would suffer if the support, opportunity, or resource were not provided by public finances. But, in

---

[15] Steven Lukes maintains that recognition, being always a side-effect of some other action, usually implies some distributive measures. If that were the case, recognition would not be a distinct part of social justice, that is a part distinct from distribution, as claimed by Nancy Fraser; it would necessarily be a part of distributive justice. Yet if recognition's task is to help the building of self-esteem and self-respect, it is unclear whether the preferential distribution entrusted to affirmative action works for or against recognition. See Lukes, "Toleration and Recognition" and Fraser, "From Distribution to Recognition?"

this case, injustice does not mean material deprivation for individuals as a result of their membership, but, rather, the difficulties involved if the minority's culture and creed are to survive and, consequently, the problems faced by minority members who wish to practice their customs and pursue their own conception of the good. What is at stake is, on the one hand, the equal opportunity for groups to survive and flourish as distinctive cultural or religious communities, and, on the other, equal conditions for individual members to practice their preferred lifestyle.

It is, however, far from certain that cultures and communities as such have a right to survival, or that individuals, in order to follow their preferred lifestyles with equal ease, have a right to public support. Liberal justice proposes equal opportunity for individuals and favors equal freedom from obstacles over equality of outcomes as well as intentional neutrality over causal neutrality, as we have seen.[16] In other words, liberal justice on the whole does not consider discriminatory the fact that individuals, all equally free to pursue their preferences, are not equally able to attain the satisfaction of these preferences. Liberal theory, by and large, holds that once individuals have equal access to certain fundamental opportunities or primary goods or basic resources, justice is realized, even though some people may fail to lead the kind of life they would have preferred. These kinds of collective claims therefore appear to constitute a very difficult problem, putting the liberal framework under real pressure. In fact, we are dealing here with preferential distributive measures, for groups rather than for individuals, for enabling the persistence of minoritarian cultures and religions – and this implies that the liberal principles of impartiality, individualism, and neutrality are all infringed.

There are, however, two kinds of liberal argument which provide justification for the public support of cultures and churches in terms either of the inclusion or of the well-being of individuals. Briefly, the first kind of argument defends public provision to minority cultures on the basis of principles of liberal justice. Extending full rights to individuals, so the argument goes, does not put members of minorities on an equal footing with the majority and does not grant them equal standing and respect. In order to overcome this kind of injustice and to achieve the inclusion of minorities, there has to be a public recognition of differences. Without this, there will be a disparity in the treatment of the group as a whole, resulting in less than equal respect for its members. Recognition in these cases is pursued by seeking active support for minority cultures,

---

[16] See chapter 2.

support which constitutes a sign of the group's public presence and acceptance. In this sense, it is a development of the argument for public toleration, starting from the lack of status and respect suffered by minority or oppressed groups, and pointing to public recognition of differences and minoritarian identities as the way of achieving equal respect and consideration. Think, for example, of a situation in which public funds are made available for confessional schools of the dominant church, while no provision is made for other religious communities; members of the latter cannot feel respected by such lack of public consideration. The politics of recognition is, then, intended as a proper generalization from the individual right to equal respect and consideration, in line with the crucial principle of liberal justice and with ethical individualism.

The second liberal argument in favor of public support follows a different path of reasoning, though the practical outcome is more or less the same. It moves from the fundamental value of autonomy and aims at promoting individual well-being. The notion of autonomy adopted here does not stress the value of individual choice independently of its content, but, rather, the value of meaningful options which, whether they are chosen or received, the agent can endorse and make his or her own.[17] This is regarded as fundamental to individual well-being, placing a special duty on the government to promote the conditions for autonomy and well-being. The ability to make a meaningful choice, in turn, presupposes a background of shared understandings and values which comes from a common culture. Cultures consist of a network of meanings, practices, habits, and values which are necessary conditions for the development and practice of autonomy, providing people with viable options, whose sense and value are shared and which can be socially appraised. This line of argument, which fits into the framework of perfectionist liberalism, suggests that the individual has a right to an appropriate culture, which in turn may be thought to impose an obligation on the government to support minority cultures.[18] This argument, like all arguments for rights,

[17] The usual concept of autonomy was originally articulated by Kant (*The Critique of Practical Reason* ed. Mary Gregory [Cambridge: Cambridge University Press, 1997]) and by Mill (*On Liberty*); despite the many differences between their conceptions of autonomy, they shared the idea of a rational agent's independence from received views and his or her capacity for critical judgment and free choice. In this respect, autonomous agents can distance themselves from given circumstances and contingencies and decide on modes of conduct that run against the prevailing regime of preferences and values. By contrast, Kymlicka, Raz, and Margalit, though in a different fashion, conceive of autonomy only within a framework of shared practices, rules, meanings, and values: in a word, of culture. This point is analyzed in detail by Raz in *The Morality of Freedom* and in *Ethics and the Public Domain*.

[18] The right to culture argument is shared by a few liberal thinkers; see Kymlicka, *Liberalism, Community and Culture*; W. Kymlicka, "The Right of Minority Cultures. A Reply to Kukathas,"

includes a reference to justice as well. The injustice to be repaired here is as follows: lacking a right to culture, minority groups or members (there is an ambiguity on this point) are deprived of a fundamental opportunity – that is, the cultural context – which is "naturally" available to the majority. Cultural rights then amount to the same provision of opportunity for minority members.

There is a crucial difference between the two arguments. In the first, public recognition of differences is seen as instrumental to the universalization of equal respect and dignity and to the full inclusion of any individual. Consequently, the measures and policies are meant as contingent, contextually variable and negotiable provisions. By contrast, the claim for a right to culture implies a public defense of minoritarian cultures independently of any discrimination or exclusion suffered by members. Public support would have to take the form of cultural rights which might sometimes be assigned to individuals as members of groups and sometimes to the group itself.[19]

There are various reasons which lead me to favor the first argument from justice over the second for cultural rights. First, the first kind of argument subscribes to ethical individualism insofar as it considers group differences, collective identities, and cultures to be instrumental in achieving inclusion and equal respect for anyone, i.e. for liberal justice. The argument for cultural rights, by contrast, defends the value of cultures, differences, and identities for their constitutive link with individual well-being, hence above and beyond justice. This position throws a questionable light on the concept of recognition adopted by the theory in the case of public support for cultures. Here, distribution is necessarily intertwined with recognition, insofar as distribution stands for recognition of a specific cultural identity. If the claim is spelt out as the rectification of injustice and discrimination suffered by group members, recognition would not be used in the very strong sense which implies valuing, or even endorsing, the different culture. But if it is advanced as a group right, then the emphasis shifts: from redressing discrimination against individuals and reduction of their well-being, to the constitutive value of culture for

Political Theory, 20, 1992, pp. 883–905; Kymlicka, *Multicultural Citizenship*; W. Kymlicka, ed., *The Rights of Minority Cultures* (Oxford: Oxford University Press, 1995); Raz, "Multiculturalism: A Liberal Perspective"; Raz, *Ethics and the Public Domain*; A. Margalit and M. Halbertal, "Liberalism and the Right to Culture," *Social Research*, 61, 1994, pp. 491–537; A. Margalit and J. Raz, "National Self-Determination," in W. Kymlicka, ed., *The Rights of Minority Cultures*, pp. 79–92.

[19] In her criticism of identity politics, Seyla Benhabib fails to draw the distinction between these two arguments and rejects the quest for recognition as an essentialist quest for identity with an intrinsic tendency to eliminate others. See "Democracy and Identity. In Search of the Civic Polity," *Philosophy and Social Criticism*, 24, 1998, pp. 85–100.

identity and the intrinsic worth of culture for human happiness. Thus, recognition may easily come to have a strong meaning which, I have argued, is questionable and which I want to avoid.

Second, the cultural right argument exhibits theoretical shortcomings: the right to one's own culture does not follow from the moral right to culture. If autonomy is taken as the fundamental liberal value for self-realization and individual well-being, and if a link is established between autonomy and cultural practices, why should any particular culture be protected instead of the culture of the majority? Why cannot any particular culture create the condition for individual autonomy? In fact, the shift from the "right to culture" to the "right to one's own culture" is not justified, unless the argument is supplemented by special considerations of justice (such as the special burden of assimilation for some groups or the actual inability of certain minorities to assimilate in the dominant culture).[20] A way out of this impasse is attempted by asserting that each individual has a right to his or her own culture because each individual has a fundamental interest in his or her own personal identity, and this identity can continue to exist only in the context of one's original culture.[21] But this twist in the argument causes another difficulty, namely the reference to a very questionable conception of culture as an encompassing way of life which is surrounded by relatively impervious barriers. Cultures, however, are not only subject to continual changes and influence from others, especially in a global arena, but are also internally segmented and divided,[22] so that young people's personalities are more often forged by generational subcultures than by traditional values and practices – subcultures that are indeed international.[23] Thus the argument for cultural rights either cannot sustain the right to one's own culture or is dependent on a questionable concept of culture.

Finally, this argument makes use of the complex and problematic notion of group rights, to which I shall shortly return, which is bypassed by the argument from justice. And if public support to minority cultures could be provided without reference to group rights, I think it better to do away with such "an unnecessary complication."[24]

---

[20] This is indeed the position taken by Kymlicka in *Multicultural Citizenship*.
[21] This is the position taken by Margalit and Halbertal in "Liberalism and the Right to Culture."
[22] Similar perplexities about the fundamental right to one's culture are spelled out by J. Waldron, "Minority Culture and the Cosmopolitan Alternative," in Kymlicka, *The Rights of Minority Cultures*, pp. 93–129.
[23] For this argument, see R. Baubock, "Group Rights for Cultural Minorities: Justification and Constraints," *European Forum* (Florence: EUI, 1996).
[24] Tariq Modood, "Collective Rights: An Unnecessary Complication," *European Forum* (Florence: EUI, 1996).

In general I think that when claims of public support for minority cultures are at stake, the decision should largely be taken by reference to the particular context in question, and the extent and the nature of the support is a matter of negotiation. If the first step towards public recognition of differences has been made, by means of public toleration, then political authorities are entitled to negotiate further distributive claims, especially when assessing whether they are supported by reasons of justice or whether the claimants are simply being opportunist and using identity as a means of pursuing the group's interest. This latter possibility obviously exists, and is often used as an argument against acknowledging such claims. I think that such distributive claims should be considered from the normative standpoint of inclusion, recognition, and equality of respect, and adjudicated accordingly, i.e. by deciding whether financing cultures from public funds can promote inclusion and equal respect. Often, there are good reasons to take them seriously. But if they turn out to be simply strategic claims for furthering group interests and, more specifically, the power of the group's spokespersons, then they should be regarded as properly belonging to the familiar politics of interests, pressure groups, and lobbying, and treated accordingly.

In sum, distributive claims for cultural support, though usually belonging to the domain of identity politics, can sometimes be part of the politics of interests. As part of identity politics, the issues they raise have no direct bearing on public toleration, even if the public acceptance of differences engenders a more favorable situation for their advancement. The decision to meet them needs, therefore, to be grounded on an argument of justice to be contextually spelled out.

A DIFFERENT PATH FOR THE POLITICS OF RECOGNITION: COLLECTIVE LIBERTY

The liberal suspicion of identity politics is also due to the fact that not all claims for public recognition aim for a full and equal inclusion of minority members. Among the many demands for public recognition of differences in a multicultural society, at least two types must be mentioned whose goal is not the inclusion of minorities. First, as I have already mentioned, identity politics is sometimes pursued by minority representatives in an opportunist way, within a bargaining strategy whose aim is to get a better deal in the distributive process. This strategy involves lobbying from within the minority group, which functions, then, as a pressure group in the distributive contest; the minority identity becomes instrumental as a weapon in the struggle. This kind of politics is usually seen as threatening by liberal institutions, both because it involves special and preferential treatment and because it is viewed as leading to social fragmentation and resurgent tribalism. In my opinion, these worries are misplaced. Even though the tool used for advancing these claims is identity, in this case we are not in fact dealing with the politics of recognition, i.e. a contest between non-negotiable identities, where recourse to compensation is precluded by incomparability and incommensurability. Here, we are in the familiar domain of a conflict of interests, of political bargaining, compromise, and policy-making, where identity is simply a resource or tool, not unlike money or oil.

Second, and more interestingly, recognition of differences is also implied in claims for the collective liberty of a given minority.[25] Collective liberty is often grouped together with toleration under the heading of "minority protection," but while both aim at reducing group conflict and at improving the minorities' situation, their respective final goals are very different: toleration being conceived for a pluralistic society, while collective liberty leads to a plural society.[26]

By collective liberty, I mean the collective right of a social group to non-intervention of the state in its organization, practices, and communal life. The minority's quest for such non-interference usually implies the suspension of some legal procedures with reference to the group – for instance the law against polygamy or that for mandatory education. And this leads to the problem of unequal treatment of citizens under the law. Collective liberty may be articulated in a number of specific claims to rights, ranging from the demand of a group to be left alone and free to practice its own customary communal life, to that of a well-defined, regionally based autonomy, which may be partly financed by the state, designed to preserve a group's integrity not only in terms of its language and culture, but also its territory and traditional economy. Examples of the first kind of collective liberty are provided by groups such as the Amish and the orthodox Jews of New York; examples of the second kind are provided by Native American reservations in North America, Aboriginal territories in Australia, and by French and German minorities

---

[25] I have taken the expression "collective liberty" from Day, *Liberty and Justice*, pp. 185ff. See also Larry Gostin, ed., *Civil Liberties in Conflict* (London: Routledge, 1988), pp. 8ff.

[26] While a pluralistic society means the coexistence of different groups and cultures interacting on the basis of a mixture of conflict and cooperation, a plural society is composed of groups each leading a separate existence with a minimum of contact. Contemporary plural societies are typically those that impose racial segregation, while in the past the multinational empires, from ancient world onwards, were typical examples of plural societies. On the concept of pluralism versus a plural society, see V. Van Dyke, *Human Rights, Ethnicity, Discrimination* (Westport, Conn.: Greenwood Press, 1985); on multinational empires, see Michael Walzer, *On Toleration*.

in northern Italy. In all of these cases, the goal of the group in question is to separate itself from the rest of society and to defend its differences and special identity against integration and dissolution.

The demand for collective liberty creates various problems for the liberal democratic state: first of all, it is a claim to a right which actually appears to amount to something more than the liberal right to free association and seems irreducible to the individual liberty of the group's members,[27] which is why it is an issue. It leads to the question of group rights, which has recently received much attention in the theoretical literature on multiculturalism (for good reason, because it is indeed the most complex and controversial aspect of identity politics). The very concept of a group right is extremely problematic for liberal theory, because it seems to imply a collective agent whose will imposes itself on individual members of the group. The liberal democratic tradition has always favored individual rights, which are meant to protect the fundamental interests of individuals by extracting them from the sphere of political negotiation. Individual rights are universal, in that anyone is (at least in principle) entitled to them; universality, in sum, grants equal treatment before the law.[28] By contrast, collective rights, assuming there are any, present a number of difficulties for liberal democracy. The problem is not so much ontological or semantic, concerning the very existence of irreducible groups and the meaning of irreducible forms of collective action;[29] rather it is moral. It is not so much that liberal democracy assumes that only individuals

[27] J. P. Day argues the distinction between individual and collective liberty by means of the following example: the liberty of the Soviet Union, its independence and sovereignty, did not imply the liberty of its citizens; by contrast, the people of Hong Kong enjoyed individual freedom, though Hong Kong was not a free state. Hence, the collective liberty of a group is not the sum of the individual liberties of its members. Some, such as Habermas and republican thinkers, see collective liberty as the outcome of political rights of citizens, though Habermas then acknowledges that this purely political and democratic interpretation is usually sustained by cultural identities. See J. Habermas, *The Inclusion of the Other* (Cambridge: Polity Press, 1998). A number of liberal thinkers argue that it amounts merely to the right to free association, and the right to religious liberty. See, for example, C. Kukathas, "Are There Any Cultural Rights?", *Political Theory*, 20, 1992, pp. 105–39. The point is that if cultural groups are considered as free associations, then, just like any club or corporate body, they can impose restrictions and rules on their members, with the right to exit in case of disagreement. Since membership in cultural groups is ascribed rather than chosen, and encompassing rather than specific, this apparently liberal position may turn out to be illiberal concerning individual rights within the group. This criticism has been pointed out by Brian Barry, *Culture and Equality*, discussing Kukathas' position.

[28] On the liberal and democratic preference for individual rights and for an individualistic method, see V. Van Dyke, "Justice as Fairness: For Groups?", *American Political Science Review*, 69, 1974, pp. 607–14, and V. Van Dyke, "The Individual, the State and Ethnic Communities in Political Theory," *World Politics*, 29, 1977, pp. 343–69.

[29] These kinds of difficulty are the familiar stuff of the long-standing debate between methodological individualism and holism. A general survey of the arguments in this controversy of the 1950s and

can be moral agents and thus admits only them as subjects of rights; liberal thought has already extended its definition of those it acknowledges to have moral rights as "moral patients" – e.g. children, the mentally handicapped, even foetuses and animals.[30] The difficulty concerns the possible morally undesirable consequences for individuals of recognizing subgroups of the society as politically significant units:[31] the liberal state is torn between a commitment to protect minorities and the protection of the individual within the group. Furthermore, there is the difficulty of defining group membership in an informal social group. This is not simply a pragmatic problem, but may have moral consequences as well, insofar as responsibility for collective action in informal groups is a highly complex and controversial matter. On more pragmatic grounds, there is the difficulty of defining the extension of autonomy and of tracing the boundaries of a territory.[32] But what is probably even more disturbing for the liberal democratic state is that in claims for collective liberty the question of the integrity of the state may be raised, albeit only in a cultural and, in some cases, an administrative sense.[33] In some cases political secession can become a realistic and threatening possibility; it is, after all, only one step further than administrative and cultural autonomy.[34] In other words, the quest for collective liberty, however articulated, proposes a way of settling groups' contests by means of division and separation. Its aim is not the empowerment of members of minority groups within the context of a pluralistic democracy, but the defense of the cultural, religious, and linguistic distinctiveness of the minority. The final goal of collective liberty is to achieve a homogeneity of groups, and in this respect it runs in the opposite direction to a policy of toleration and the other multicultural policies mentioned above, which aim towards social heterogeneity and diversity, grounded on respect and reciprocity. The minority desires to be set apart in such a way as to be able to dispense with toleration altogether; in a sense it is a fundamentalist quest, based on the feeling of total estrangement from society at large, and often of enmity, which prevents any cooperative vision bridging the distance between the

---

1960s can be found in J. O'Neill, ed., *Modes of Individualism and Collectivism* (London: Heinemann, 1973).

[30] This is what R. Baubock thinks is responsible for the liberal suspicion of collective rights. See Baubock, "Group Rights for Cultural Minorities."

[31] See V. Van Dyke, "Collective Entities and Moral Rights: Problems in Liberal Thought," *Journal of Politics*, 44, 1982, pp. 21–40.

[32] See the discussion between Chaudran Kukathas ("Are There Any Cultural Rights?") and Will Kymlicka ("The Rights of Minority Cultures. Reply to Kukathas," pp. 140–6); also see Kukathas, "Cutural Rights Again. A Rejoinder to Kymlicka," *Political Theory*, 20, 1992, pp. 647–80.

[33] See Crick, "Toleration and Tolerance," p. 171.   [34] See Kymlicka, "Liberal Nationalism."

minority and the majority. That is why the presence of people who do not belong to the group in the territory assigned to the minority usually creates trouble.[35]

Claims for collective liberty also imply a demand for recognition from the state; yet it is a different kind of recognition which is pursued in this case. It is the recognition of certain collective rights, or immunities, i.e. the recognition of the minority's special status vis-à-vis the population at large. By contrast, the recognition underlying public toleration is aimed at having different identities and their bearers being accepted as part of liberal society, on an equal footing with others. Inclusion and not separation is the general goal of the politics of recognition considered above, from public toleration to the reform of societal standards and support for minority cultures. In all these cases, the assertion of collective identity is to be seen as the way forward to integration without imposing too heavy a cost on individuals.

A solution emphasizing collective liberty was historically first put forward as a way out of the religious wars at the beginning of the modern period in Europe, a solution known under the name of territorialism.[36] But while it implied collective liberty for given churches in specific areas, by the same token it excluded any individual religious liberty inside each region – where the people's religion had to follow the king's choice, according to the principle of "cuius regio eius religio." The illiberal character of territorialism could be said to exist in contemporary cases of group liberty: the individual member is usually put under pressure to conform to traditional rules and ways of life. There might be justification for this pressure, and yielding to it may run the risk of pluralistic encapsulation.[37]

As we can see, the issue of collective rights exhibits distinctive difficulties which can be avoided by the idea of public support for culture, which was considered above. The latter is controversial because it implies preferential treatment for groups in the distributive process, but, as we have seen, this problem may be overcome by a special argument from justice. In any case, public support for culture does not mean that group members are subject to different norms, not even in special areas, but simply that they have a better opportunity to follow their lifestyle if they choose to do so. Nevertheless collective liberty may be a necessary compromise in the case of strong ethnic or cultural conflicts. Finally, it should be noted that the demand for collective liberty, while it signals a

---

[35] See Walzer, "New Tribalism." [36] See Bainton, *Studies in the Reformation.*
[37] The notion of pluralistic incapsulation is found in Moon, *Constructing Community.*

high level of group conflict or hostility, is only open to certain kinds of
social group, namely those which can be seen to have a separate social
existence (typically ethnic or religious groups), and which are territori-
ally based. Thus, neither groups that are defined by gender or sexual
preferences nor immigrants who are spread throughout a host country
can plausibly claim collective liberty.

From the point of view of political philosophy, the issue is whether rights
to collective liberty can eventually be justified in spite of all the difficulties
they raise for liberal democratic theory and practice. First of all, these
claims cannot simply be dismissed, either for prudential reasons or for
reasons of principle. The acknowledgment of collective rights for group
autonomy is, in any case, to be preferred to a high level of intergroup
conflict which carries the risk of repression, on the one hand, and terrorism, on the other – an outcome which is detrimental to law and order
for every member of society. But there are also normative reasons for
endorsing some claims to collective liberty. Such claims can in fact be
presented as a generalization of the right to self-determination, which is
actually legally recognized in international treaties and law, despite its
ambiguous and problematic nature.[38]

Given that claims for group autonomy cannot simply be dismissed
as illegitimate, they have been treated by political philosophers in three
different ways. First, the strictly liberal position denies the existence of
irreducible group rights, since only individuals – not groups – can be
moral agents to whom responsibility can be assigned and who can, if
necessary, be appropriately punished.[39] But, if there are no collective
rights, it does not follow that interests shared in common by individuals
cannot be adequately protected by individual rights. According to
this position, the right to self-determination is an individual right to
a collective good (sharing culture and language), while the state is a
fictitious legal entity, reducible to its individual components. In this way,
claims to various forms of group autonomy and self-rule are to be met

[38] On the right of self-determination, see J. Crawford, ed., *The Rights of the Peoples* (Oxford:
Oxford University Press, 1988); W. Connor, *Ethnonationalism. The Quest for Understanding* (Princeton:
Princeton University Press, 1994); Margalit and Raz, "National Self-Determination"; Y.
Tamir, *Liberal Nationalism* (Princeton: Princeton University Press, 1993); A. De-Shalit, "National
Self-Determination: Political, Not Cultural,"*Political Studies*, 44, 1996, pp. 906–20; M. Freeman,
"Democracy and Dynamite: The Peoples' Right to Self-Determination," *Political Studies*, 44,
1996, pp. 746–61, who underlines the ambiguities of self-determination.

[39] For this position, see C. Kukathas, "Are There Any Cultural Rights?" and Y. Tamir, "Reflection
on the Nature of Collective Rights and Collective Punishment," *European Forum* (Florence: EUI,
1996).

by the individual rights of religious liberty and freedom of association, which are meant to protect a sphere of activity from government or third-party intervention in order to pursue collective goals and practices. Such a reductionist position, however, is not a satisfactory way out of the difficulties inherent in the notion of group rights, because it seems to ignore the very possibility of a conflict between individual and collective rights and interests. Reductionism implies that the collective right can be traced right back to its individual components, i.e. to individual rights, while the possibility of conflict between the two highlights the fact that such reduction cannot be done. If one views a national or ethnic minority as a voluntary association, it is difficult to understand the problems raised by internal dissent from the demand for group autonomy. What about someone who would prefer to live in the broader society than in the secluded limits of their own group, but who wants to carry on being a member of that group? The right of exit, normally demanded by the democratic state as a condition for granting rights of group autonomy,[40] is not a sufficient protection for dissident individuals who may be compelled to move out of their territory or to give up their cultural affiliation altogether. Their freedom turns out to be constrained by collective freedom: *pace* the supporters of republicanism, collective liberty and individual liberty are in fact two separate things.

Two other liberal positions take issue with reductionism and argue for the existence of irreducible collective rights, although the justification for recognizing these rights appeals to the fundamental interests of individuals. These forms of liberalism reject the equation of the collective liberty of a group with freedom of association. The reason for this is that ethnic groups cannot be considered voluntary associations because their membership is neither voluntary nor formally defined, as it is, for example, in clubs, and because collective liberty is not simply a composite of individual liberties, but entails the collective action of group representatives or spokespeople.[41] At this point, once the fundamental interest of individuals to speak their native language and to practice their traditions is acknowledged, it follows that it can be protected only through the rights of the corresponding groups.

---

[40] On the right to exit as an adequate protection of the individual from the group, see Margalit and Raz, "National Self-Determination"; Margalit and Halbertal, "Liberalism and the Right to Culture"; Kukathas, "Are There Any Cultural Rights?"

[41] This position is shared, with different nuances, by W. Kymlicka, J. Raz, A. Margalit, M. Halbertal, R. Baubock, V. Van Dyke, and B. Parek, "Discourses on National Identity," *Political Studies*, 42, 1994, pp. 492–504.

The point of departure of each of these two liberal positions lies precisely in their respective conceptions of non-reductionism. According to one position, group rights impose external restrictions on the state, which may not interfere with the organization and internal life of the group, but these rights should not be thought to impose internal restrictions on individual rights unless the survival of the group is in question. External restrictions are justified on the basis of the group's self-preservation vis-à-vis the larger society: for example, the general right to acquire land has to be limited in territory that is assigned to aboriginal people, so that their community and way of life can be preserved.[42] The other position holds that the right to a particular culture (and not just any culture) is the basis for collective rights for groups, which in certain matters can behave like the state – that is, they can enforce certain regulations on their members.[43] Without entering any further into this discussion, it seems to me that these positions are not actually very clearly delineated; indeed, on closer inspection, they appear to be almost indistinguishable. If a minority is granted the right to impose external restrictions on the larger society, it is because its cultural survival is problematic, hence the conditions for imposing internal restriction obtain as well.

I do not think that any of these three positions on collective liberty is convincing from a normative point of view. The first, denying legitimacy to irreducible group rights and responding to claims for collective liberty by appealing to religious liberty and freedom of association, seems to me inadequate for settling intergroup conflict; it is likely to lead to policies that disadvantage minority groups. Besides, I cannot see how the public use of a language could be considered an individual right, since not only is it a public good to be enjoyed in communal activities, but it also requires the existence of an institutional structure whose beneficiary is the group. If most people in the subgroup decide to adopt the common language of the majority of citizens in the society, the survival of the minority language would be in danger, and such action would impose a certain result – the dissolution of the minority idiom – on those who want to go on using their own language, too. But if the decision of the majority can be imposed on the minority, then the right to one's language is not an individual human right, given that individual rights are, by definition, independent of decisions by the majority. The other two positions, which acknowledge the legitimacy of collective rights but

---

[42] Kymlicka, "Reply to Kukathas"; L. Green, "Internal Minorities and their Rights," in Kymlicka, ed., *The Rights of Minority Cultures*, pp. 256–72.

[43] Margalit and Halbertal, "Liberalism and the Right to Culture."

given them an individualistic justification, exhibit the same difficulties that we have noticed concerning the right to culture, from which they in fact derive. On the one hand, the individual's interest in the existence of a cultural context is really fundamental, but it is, in a way, too trivial to serve as the foundation of a specific collective right; on the other, it is doubtful that an interest in one's own culture – in the stability of traditional practices and collective life – can be protected by a specific right, because it would involve a manipulation of social evolution and excessive group interference with individual liberty in order to preserve traditions and customary ways of living.

Moreover, all three normative positions bypass the question of which groups are entitled to collective rights,[44] assuming it to be generally evident. Raz and Margalit have pointed to a certain dimension which is a necessary condition for group rights to be recognized by the larger society. It is a pragmatic consideration which stresses that a legitimate claim to group rights should imply the ability of the group to sustain an encompassing, comprehensive form of life. Once this condition is fulfilled, however, can any religious or ethnical group qualify as a candidate for autonomy, or only such groups as have suffered conquest, oppression, invasion, and repression? Obviously, a history of oppression and domination strengthens the claim for reparation – this is precisely the logic underlying the acknowledgment of aboriginal rights in countries such as Canada, Australia, and the USA, as well as the recognition of Israel as a state. However, these two criteria do not help to solve many situations: what is to be done when confronting minorities which have no history of oppression or discrimination, but which simply do not want to merge with the majority culture, wishing rather to lead a separate form of life, as in the case of the Amish in Pennsylvania? Is the lack of past oppression a sufficient condition to dismiss a specific separatist will? Moreover, if the groups to be taken seriously are those with a well-defined and established ethnic, linguistic, or religious identity, even though we know that ethnic identity is socially constructed,[45] does it mean that a group whose identity clearly exhibits its artificial origins should not be recognized, even though it is strongly endorsed by its members? The point to be stressed here is that no definitive list of necessary and sufficient conditions can be easily

---

[44] This problem is taken up by Van Dyke, *Human Rights, Ethnicity, Discrimination*, who lists a number of conditions which, however, are based on empirical considerations and do not represent the necessary and sufficient conditions for group rights to be granted.

[45] See S. Tempelman, "Construction of Cultural Identity: Multiculturalism and Exclusion," *Political Studies*, 47, 1999, pp. 17–31.

spelled out, if only because a rigid list would stop many groups from being considered and would lead to the imposition of a uniform national identity. I think that of the above conditions for acknowledging a group's legitimate claim to collective liberty, the first, i.e. the ability of the group to sustain a comprehensive form of life, is really fundamental because it is a pragmatic requirement concerning the reasonable chance of a group to sustain a separate existence. Furthermore, I consider the group's will to lead a separate existence, regardless of the existence or non-existence of past discrimination, and a feeling of estrangement from the majority, to be crucial. In other words, I believe that the fundamental reason for acknowledging collective liberty should not be a normative one, but the fact of group conflict and enmity, whose alternatives are cultural domination, repression, and terrorism.[46] This implies a compromise with liberal democracy and negotiation over the protection of individual rights inside the group. It does not mean giving up normative principles in the face of a threat to law and order, but, rather, acknowledging that part of the liberal habitus is the tendency to meet half way, instead of stubbornly sticking to set principles whatever the consequences.[47] The virtue of tolerance is supposed to provide us with a reason to accept what in the first instance we dislike for the sake of peace and respect for others. But tolerance does not mean giving way to any wrong or crime: the acknowledgment of collective rights of group autonomy does not free the democratic state from the duty to protect human rights within minorities. To sum up: although collective rights cannot be properly justified, in the face of pluralistic conflicts, we must often behave as if they were.[48] In other words, different circumstances, rather than specific normative arguments, point to group rights and collective liberty as solutions for the minority, as opposed to other multicultural policies. And, of course, the solution is risky, because it may eventually bring about the dissolution of the political unit itself.[49]

In conclusion, the reference to group rights, when made in connection with minority groups who do not intend to secede from the larger society but simply to assert their identity more emphatically and achieve

---

[46] In this sense I take a kind of realist position on this issue, according to the classification made by Freeman in "Democracy and Dynamite."   [47] See Rawls, *PL*.

[48] This idea comes from Walzer, "What Rights for Cultural Communities?"

[49] In fact, there are quite a few liberal arguments in favor of secession, including: A. Buchanan, *Secession. The Morality of Political Divorce from Fort Sumner to Lithuania and Quebec* (Boulder, Colo. and Oxford: Westview Press, 1991); D. Gauthier, "Breaking Up: An Essay on Secession," *Canadian Journal of Philosophy*, 24, 1994, pp. 357–72; C. H. Wellman, "A Defence of Secession and Political Self-Determination," *Philosophy and Public Affairs*, 24, 1995, pp. 142–71.

a more substantial form of public recognition, is out of place and introduces undesirable complications in multicultural politics. Claims for public support of particular cultures should be clearly distinguished from the demands of (usually national) minorities which have experienced a past of conquest, oppression and cultural domination, making integration unattainable or undesirable. Minorities consisting of immigrants or defined by sexual preference, gender, or religious creeds, by contrast, aim at integration within the larger society, but on their own terms, without giving up, subsuming, or feeling ashamed of, their cultural or collective identity.

TWO OBJECTIONS TO TOLERATION AS RECOGNITION

Analysis of the various claims and policies making up multiculturalism has been given as a response to a relevant objection to toleration as recognition, one which emphasizes its perverse effects and undesirable consequences for the social unity and for the persistence of common liberal democratic values and political order. We have seen that only some claims making up the politics of recognition can be considered consequences of the public toleration of differences in a proper sense; the commitment to toleration as recognition does not imply that those claims should be satisfied without further argument. I have argued that a commitment to recognition of differences as a step towards full inclusion of members of minorities entails only the acknowledgment that there are grounds for those claims, while the actual solution can be a subject of negotiation. In general, with the exception of claims to collective liberty, all other demands really amount to a quest for inclusion for members of minority groups on terms more favorable than those that have been traditionally offered by liberal democracy. Therefore, the risk of social fragmentation and of tribalism seems misplaced, even when distributive demands are at issue. From a normative viewpoint, distributive questions should be assessed by criteria of distributive justice, while from a pragmatic viewpoint, such questions are no different from the claims advanced by interest or pressure groups, with which democratic politics is accustomed to deal.

Albert Hirschmann has proposed a typology of forms of reactionary rhetoric that are directed against social reform and change. The forms of rhetoric in this typology comprise arguments about the perverse effects of any reform; of jeopardy to social stability and peace; and of the ultimate futility of any attempt at intentional improvement of social structure. I have so far responded to the objection of perversity, and partly to that of jeopardy. The two further objections I am going to consider fit the third type of argument against social reform: that of futility. I will then have covered all the basic rhetorical models used by conservative thinking.

One objection points out that toleration as recognition belongs just to symbolic politics, like all forms of identity politics. Symbolic politics is viewed in sharp contrast with real politics, and while the former is fed by gestures, rites, provocation, and assertions, the second is made up of coalitions, common interests, strategic plans, and attainable goals. The first can be understood as stemming from frustration and exasperation, but it is sterile: it is an expressive action which has no place in real politics, and which, on the contrary, increases social conflict, resentment, and suspicion among social groups.[50] This objection is based, first, on the implicit belief that real politics consists of political participation, organizations, and distributive claims, while matters of social consideration and respect are either politically irrelevant or politically unattainable; and, second, on the view that symbolic politics, as an end in itself, leads nowhere and creates nothing.

   I have tried to argue that recognition of differences and identities is a real political issue which has to do with the difficult process of the inclusion of people belonging to long-standing or recent minorities. Those whose collective identity has been excluded from public visibility or from inclusion in social norms cannot become full citizens and functioning social actors: recognition of differences becomes an important step in order to reverse the feeling of humiliation and shame suffered by those who are despised and oppressed because of their membership in a particular group. The goal to be attained is public respect and consideration, which contribute to an individual's ability to function as a citizen, and make good use of their rights, resources, and opportunities. In this respect, identity politics is symbolic, yet very real. I think that intentional humiliation is just another form of deprivation, not unlike an insufficient income or lack of education, and can deeply affect people's well-being and activities. And if humiliation is non-contingent because it derives from membership in certain groups, then it is a political problem – or, more precisely, a matter of justice. If it were no more than a part of gesture politics, why would it be so strenuously opposed by those who

---

[50] This objection is made by Walzer in "Minority Rites."

are its objects? If symbolic politics is such a trivial matter, why should it be resisted by the majority and, moreover, why should this very same objection not apply to majorities? In fact, not only is symbolic politics very real indeed, but identity politics includes a number of non-symbolic social transformations, including distributive policies, as I have shown above. But, granting that the symbolic politics of recognition is real, is it also a worthwhile goal? No, according to this objection, because, first, demands for recognition of differences are not usually met, and, second, symbolic politics does not lead to coalitions, organizations, and common interests. I think that all these negative claims are contingent and do not give us good reasons to reject the demands for recognition.

It is more difficult to answer the objections put forward by those who think that recognition can be attained only as a by-product of strategies explicitly pursuing other ends.[51] If this position is correct, identity politics is intrinsically inconsistent. Recognition cannot be given directly, but only by means of specific measures which stand for recognition; but this very fact is already taken into account in the argument for recognition which I have outlined. Toleration of differences, transformations of public conventions, protection against offensive behavior, public support for cultures: all these measures count as forms of recognition. Nevertheless, identity politics is not inconsistent: that recognition can be achieved only as a side-effect of specific measures does not imply that it cannot be pursued intentionally, albeit indirectly. Indeed, as I have emphasized, public toleration can work as recognition only if it is sustained by the appropriate reasons, otherwise it could be no more than non-interference. Thus there is nothing inconsistent in an identity politics in which the goal of recognition is intentionally pursued.

However the objection against recognition as a futile instance of symbolic politics has a point worth mentioning. My argument for toleration as recognition is basically addressed to political authorities and to society's majority, in order to show that public toleration of differences is grounded on strong reasons deriving from principles of justice, for the inclusion on an equal footing of members of oppressed groups. This objection, on the other hand, is addressed to individuals from minority groups, in order to show the genuine risks associated with identity

---

[51] This position is not explicitly intended as a criticism of the politics of recognition, but can be derived from a general argument, made by Jon Elster, on states of affairs which are intrinsically desirable, but cannot be achieved by an intentional design except as by-products, such as happiness (J. Elster, *Sour Grapes* [Cambridge: Cambridge University Press, 1983]). Since I hold that recognition is always the by-product of some other action, it seems that Elster's argument can apply here.

politics, especially if it becomes an alternative to the more traditional democratic participation. Recognition of different identities is supposed to remove obstacles which prevent people from feeling like, being respected, and functioning as full citizens, but it does not resolve all the material and educational disadvantages linked to membership of certain groups. Moreover, its goal should be the full inclusion of members of minority groups; in this respect, the politics of recognition should carefully balance its claims in order to prevent the assertion of identities from becoming an end in itself. Thus it is an open question whether identity politics pursued beyond a certain point or in certain circumstances might not become counterproductive. But this is properly a matter of political evaluation which cannot be settled by any normative theory.

The second objection from futility is theoretically more intriguing: it points out that recognition of different identities can indeed be attained, and inclusion into full citizenship can be realized, but that its value for the newly included may well be much less than expected. If the full status of citizenship de facto excludes minorities, the social standing enjoyed by the majority is a positional good, implying an ability to exercise hegemony over societal standards. Recognition of differences and inclusion of minorities will open up the status of citizenship to previously excluded groups, which will bring about a redrawing of social norms in a non-exclusionary way. At the same time, the universalization of citizenship will tend to cancel its positional value: everyone will be a full citizen, but it will be less valuable. In this sense, the politics of recognition is doomed to failure: when the intended goal is achieved, its value disappears.[52] The hoped-for result – that members from oppressed groups would finally relate to their collective identities and cultures in just the same way as people of the majority have always done, choosing what to pick up and what to dismiss, and feeling unconsciously confident about societal standards – appears to be an impossible dream, because the special sense of power linked to the status of citizenship is, in the end, lost. The expression "*civis romanus sum*" would mean nothing: there would no longer be anything to be proud of if everyone was a *civis romanus*. Identity politics, therefore, is a useless waste of energy, which can have perverse effects on social stability, exciting the

---

[52] See the analysis of this dynamic, which is implicit in positional goods, by Fred Hirsch, *Social Limits to Growth* (London: Routledge and Kegan Paul, 1977).

majority's resentment without bringing about what is expected. All things considered, the politics of minorities would be better if they concentrated on universalistic programs of distributive justice, or even on affirmative action programs; members of minorities should aim at getting more resources and opportunities for disadvantaged individuals, leaving aside the issue of recognition and consideration. When a visible and significant proportion of a minority group becomes successful in certain social spheres, then consideration and recognition will spontaneously follow.

This argument against the politics of recognition, however, fails to consider that the respect paid to any individual, whatever his or her collective identity, will be judged according to the ideal of the white, Christian, heterosexual male – i.e. according to the social norm. And this is neither a just nor a stable form of inclusion. The problem of cultural domination – that is, the exclusive hegemony over societal standards and public conventions by the majority – cannot easily be pushed off the agenda of social justice. But neither can the positional value of citizenship status be ignored.

On the one hand, exclusive hegemony over societal standards is an unjust privilege of majorities which leads to the exclusion or the unequal inclusion of minority groups into democratic citizenship. And there is no justification for preserving such a privilege, given the importance of inclusion as a precondition for individuals to function both as social actors and as full citizens. Inclusion is here used in the comprehensive sense of enjoying citizenship rights, making full use of them, and being recognized as full members in the political and social community. In order to promote comprehensive inclusion, the politics of recognition has been devised as a strategy, starting from the public toleration of differences. On the other hand, public recognition of differences, even if stabilized and complete, will not result in the prestige and social status that majorities have so far enjoyed. It will be a case of having it more, and enjoying it less. Nevertheless, inclusion is a necessary condition for a peaceful and civil coexistence of different social and cultural groups, and, though less valuable the more generalized it becomes, it cannot be given up: the solution cannot be one which allows the lack of public recognition and the persistent marginalization and invisibility of minority groups to continue. Rather, the awareness of this inflationistic process can teach social groups and their representatives or activists to be more disenchanted in identity politics and to invest their energies and expectations more wisely. For example, it can teach them to draw distinctions between what can and what cannot be subject to negotiation. If identity politics is considered from this standpoint, toleration as recognition, and its direct implications, is likely to be acknowledged as non-negotiable, while other forms of recognition will be considered open to political negotiations.

Conclusion

The concept of toleration includes a whole range of meanings: forbearing, putting up with, permitting, accepting, recognizing. Consequently, its value is uncertain: although intolerance is generally regarded as bad and wrong and a tolerant society is generally seen as desirable, as one characterized by openness, understanding, and respect for diversity, sometimes toleration is considered as a form of weakness, questionable complacency, and indulgence, or is equated to indifference. Broadly speaking, toleration is wrong if it permits injustice; it is a necessary evil if it means acquiescing in error; it is a virtue if it promotes mutual respect and social cooperation and allows people to deal with conflicts peacefully. Depending therefore on their general view of tolerance, some people argue that the scope of toleration should be restricted, others that it should be widened, while yet others maintain that contemporary theory and society ought to leave toleration behind and to move on to equal rights, anti-discrimination, and multiculturalism.

Given that the concept of toleration allows for such divergent conceptions, it would seem reasonable for a theoretical work on toleration to begin by mapping out the concept and taking sides between the various conceptions. Yet I have not approached the subject in this way. I have taken instead what I would call a pragmatic perspective: I have begun exploring the questions which are usually regarded as relevant to toleration, and asked which ones raise genuine problems of toleration in our world. The distinction between genuine and trivial questions of toleration is crucial for the argument I have been developing. Genuine questions of toleration are ones that are, at the same time, significant, hence politically relevant, and yet in some sense indeterminate in their solution – at least according to established theories of toleration. Genuine questions of toleration are those which cause some scholars to think that toleration is insufficient to deal with a number of conflicts within contemporary pluralism and that there is an asymmetry between instances of intolerance and cases where toleration properly applies.[1] In that case, one could adopt a well-defined conception of toleration, as the attitude implying a double negation: first, a negative appraisal of some forms of behavior or practices of others, and second, a decision not to interfere with it. In this way, toleration, or better, in this restricted version, tolerance, occupies its small, but distinctive space within the range of possible attitudes and measures for coping with diversity.[2] I can see the point of such strategy, a point of theoretical clarity and neatness. Yet, it seems to me that adopting such a restricted definition, and entrusting the most relevant and divisive cases of intolerance to other categories, deprives us of the possibility of understanding why we actually and properly use the concept "intolerance" when questions of identity are at stake. Moreover, restricting the meaning of tolerance in that way implies also confining one's attention to trivial cases, that is to cases which the traditional doctrine of toleration is well equipped to deal with. That does not mean that such cases are easily solved in practice, but rather that their practical difficulty is to be ascribed to our failure to live up to the virtue and the ideal of toleration; in principle, however, the theory provides us with a clear solution. By contrast, genuine cases appear to lack a clear solution, insofar as the guidelines provided by the theory appear insufficient or unsatisfactory, too simplistic, or unduly reductive. This is the point of departure of my work: instead of leaving tolerance behind and looking for some other category or strategy to face up to these cases, I have tried to make sense of them as issues of toleration, but, in so doing, I have had to revise and expand the conception of toleration beyond the limits set by the traditional doctrines. Thus the argument for toleration as recognition starts as a reflection on the nature of genuine questions of toleration, and on the reason why common views, usually associated with liberal theories, are not satisfactory. I propose toleration as recognition first of all as an interpretive framework to help us to understand the genuine questions that arise in the contemporary world, to account for the underlying claims made by the agents involved in these problematic situations, and to grasp what is properly at stake. What I hold to be crucial when genuine questions of toleration are at issue is the contested public appearance and visibility of members of oppressed or excluded groups. The concept of toleration allows us to detect the asymmetry of

---

[1] The suggestion of an asymmetry between intolerance and toleration was advanced by Dario Castiglioni at the conference "The Culture of Toleration," Exeter, 6–8 April 2000.

[2] This is the position expressed by Preston King "The Concept of Toleration," lecture at the conference "The Culture of Toleration," Exeter, 6–8 April 2000.

power between majorities and minorities and the special kind of power which the majority can wield over social standards, standards so deeply rooted that they have been embodied in political institutions without our even being aware of it. Recognition of this fact allows us to adopt the special vantage point from which we can effectively use the concept of toleration. Adopting the standpoint of toleration as recognition allows us to unveil the power of majorities and its embodiment in institutions which is disguised if we stick to concepts such as neutrality, equal treatment, and equal rights. Also it allows us to grasp the special role played by toleration within a theory of justice: a proper understanding of toleration allows us to see directly that intolerance is a form of injustice, and that the kind of justice that could be attained by the full implementation of the demands of toleration would exceed that associated with a mere study of distributive mechanisms. In addition toleration as recognition points to other goods linked with the capability to be a fully functioning social and political agent. This capability is definitely impaired if someone experiences daily humiliation because his or her appearance or mode of life is socially despised and politically invisible. Toleration as recognition is aimed at making people, whatever their differences and identities, feel at ease with themselves, and at ease with their choice to identify with certain differences. Lastly, under my interpretation, not only does toleration constitute an important component of a theory of justice, but it is also a central part of the politics of identity. In this respect, many liberal objections can be anticipated, and I have tried to respond to some of these, but I have also tried to stress that the commitment to recognition is derived from a commitment to fulfilling what ought to be the proper liberal understanding of the demands of justice.

The argument of toleration as recognition applies both when confronting issues of public acceptance of differences linked to minority identities, and when confronting issues of restraining forms of behavior and practices, especially practices by the majority in society, which are seen as specially offensive to a group that was previously oppressed and discriminated against. As its direct implication, moreover, the argument extends to the issue of the revision of the standards governing a society so as to make room for the differences which have been recognized as part of the "normal" range of social options. Chapters 4, 5, and 6 are examples of such different applications of the argument to social and political issues of the three kinds just mentioned.

The theoretical path I have followed is definitely less neat than a purely conceptual analysis of the virtue of toleration could provide. I have discarded neatness in favor of a wider interpretive conception with higher normative ambitions. I have tried to make sense of the common understanding of that which is intolerable in our world, and I have sought for a response to real contemporary problems which goes beyond the usual boundaries of toleration. Still, the reference to toleration allows us to appreciate the aspect of power asymmetries among social groups, and the less than impartial role of liberal governments and political institutions, operating under the pretense of neutrality. The unfulfilled promise of liberal neutrality is not a reason, in my view, to abandon it and its underlying ideal, i.e. non-discrimination and fairness with reference to people's collective identities. Toleration as recognition is presented as an appropriate reinterpretation of neutrality and as a further step toward the fulfillment of the ideal of equality of respect which I hold to be a fundamental trait of a decent and just society.[3]

---

3 The obvious reference is to the work of Avishai Margalit, *The Decent Society*, Oxford University Press, Oxford, 1996. There is a difference between Margalit's position and mine, because he believes that the decent society is a second-best goal for a society falling short of justice, while I believe that decency is the trait of justice referred to the way people are regarded.

Bibliography

Ackerman, B., *Social Justice in the Liberal State*, New Haven: Yale University Press, 1980.
"What is Neutral about Neutrality?" *Ethics*, 93, 1983, pp. 372–90.
Alexander, L. and Schwarzschild, M., "Liberalism, Neutrality of Welfare vs. Equality of Resources," *Philosophy and Public Affairs*, 16, 1987, pp. 85–110.
Altmann, A., "Liberalism and Campus Hate Speech: A Philosophical Examination," *Ethics*, 103, 1993, pp. 302–17.
Apel, O. A., "Plurality of the Good? The Problem of Affirmative Tolerance in a Multicultural Society from an Ethical Point of View," *Ratio Juris*, 10, 1997, pp. 199–222.
Audi, R., "The Separation of Church and State and the Obligation of Citizenship," *Philosophy and Public Affairs*, 18, 1989, pp. 258–96.
Bainton, R. H., *Studies in the Reformation*, Boston: Beacon Press, 1963.
Barber, J. B., "Unconstrained Conversation: Neutral or Otherwise," *Ethics*, 93, 1982–3, pp. 330–47.
Barry, B., *The Liberal Theory of Justice*, Oxford: Clarendon Press, 1973.
"How Not to Defend Liberal Institutions," in R. B. Douglass, G. R. Mara, and H. S. Richardson, eds., *Liberalism and the Good*, London: Routledge, 1990, pp. 44–58.
Culture and Equality. An Egalitarian Critique of Multiculturalism, Cambridge: Polity Press, 2000.
Baubock, R., "Group Rights for Cultural Minorities: Justification and Constraints," *European Forum on Citizenship*, Florence: EUI, 1996.
Beaume, E. M., "The Limits of Toleration in Sixteenth Century France," *Studies in the Renaissance*, 16, 1966, pp. 250–65.
Becker, L. C., "Places for Pluralism," *Ethics*, 102, 1992, pp. 707–19.
Bellamy, R., "Defining Liberalism: Neutralist, Ethical and Political," *ARSP*, Beiheft, 36, 1996, pp. 23–43.
Bellamy, R. and Hollis, M., eds., *Pluralism and Liberal Neutrality*, London: Frank Cass, 1999.
Bencivenga, E., *Oltre la tolleranza*, Milan: Feltrinelli, 1991.
Benhabib, S., "Democracy and Identity. In Search of the Civic Polity," *Philosophy and Social Criticism*, 24, 1998, pp. 85–100.

Benn, S. I. and Gaus, G. F., "The Liberal Conception of the Public and the Private," in S. I. Benn and G. F. Gauss, eds., *Public and Private in Social Life*, London: Croom Helm, 1983, pp. 31–65.

Berlin, I., *Four Essays on Liberty*, Oxford: Oxford University Press, 1969.

Blasius, M., "An Ethos of Lesbian and Gay Existence," *Political Theory*, 20, 1992, pp. 642–72.

Bobbio, N., "Le ragioni della tolleranza," in P. C. Bori, ed., *Eguali e diversi nella storia*, Bologna: Il Mulino, 1986, pp. 243–57.

"Tolleranza e verità," *Lettera internazionale*, 15, 1988, pp. 16–18.

Boudon, R., *Effets perverses et ordre social*, Paris: Presses Universitaires de France, 1977. In English: *The Unintended Consequences of Social Action*, London: Macmillan, 1982.

Buchanan, A., *Secession. The Morality of Political Divorce from Fort Sumner to Lithuania and Quebec*, Boulder, Colo. and Oxford: Westview Press, 1991.

Buchanan, J. and Tullock, G., *The Calculus of Consent*, Ann Arbor: University of Michigan Press, 1962.

Caney, S., "Antiperfectionism and Rawlsian Liberalism," *Political Studies*, 63, 1995, pp. 248–64.

"Liberal Legitimacy, Reasonable Disagreement, and Justice," in R. Bellamy and M. Hollis, eds., *Pluralism and Liberal Neutrality*, London: Frank Cass, 1999, pp. 19–36.

Castellion, S., *Concerning Heretics: Whether They Are To Be Persecuted and How They Are To Be Treated* [1553], New York: Columbia University Press, 1935.

Cavalli-Sforza, L. and F., *Chi siamo. La storia della diversità umana*, Milan: Mondadori, 1993.

Chaplin, J., "How much Cultural and Religious Pluralism Can Liberalism Tolerate?" in J. Horton, ed., *Liberalism, Multiculturalism and Toleration*, London: Macmillan, 1993, pp. 32–49.

Cohen, B., "An Ethical Paradox," *Mind*, 76, 1967, pp. 250–9.

Cohen, M., Nagel, T., and Scanlon, T., eds., *Equality and Preferential Treatment*, Princeton: Princeton University Press, 1977.

Connor, W., *Ethnonationalism. The Quest for Understanding*, Princeton: Princeton University Press, 1994.

Conover, P. J. and Searing, D. D., "Citizens and Members: Dilemmas for Accommodation for Cultural Minority," mimeo, Bordeaux, 1995.

Crawford, J., ed., *The Rights of the Peoples*, Oxford: Oxford University Press, 1988.

Crick, B., "Toleration and Tolerance in Theory and Practice," *Government and Opposition*, 6, 1971, pp. 144–71.

Crowder, J., "Pluralism and Liberalism," *Political Studies*, 42, 1994, pp. 293–305.

Day, J. P., *Liberty and Justice*, London: Croom Helm, 1987.

De Marneffe, P., "Liberalism, Liberty and Neutrality," *Philosophy and Public Affairs* 19, 1990, pp. 253–74.

Dench, G., *Minorities in the Open Society: Prisoners of Ambivalence*, London: Routledge and Kegan Paul, 1986.

De-Shalit, A., "National Self-Determination: Political, Not Cultural," *Political Studies*, 44, 1996, pp. 906–20.

Devlin, P., *The Enforcement of Morals*, Oxford: Oxford University Press, 1959.

Diggs, B. J., "The Common Good as Reason for Political Action," *Ethics*, 83, 1972–3, pp. 283–93.

Douglass, R. B., Mara, G. R., and Richardson, H. S., eds., *Liberalism and the Good*, London: Routledge, 1990.

Dworkin, A., *Men Possessing Women*, New York: Periggee, 1980.

Dworkin, G., "Non-Neutral Principles," *Journal of Philosophy*, 71, 1974, pp. 491–506.

"Equal Respect and the Enforcement of Morality," *Social Philosophy and Policy*, 7, 1990, pp. 180–93.

Dworkin, R., "Liberalism," in S. Hampshire, ed., *Private and Public Morality*, Cambridge: Cambridge University Press, 1978, pp. 113–43.

Taking Rights Seriously, London: Duckworth, 1981.

"Fondamenti filosofici per la neutralità liberale," in S. Maffettone ed., *L'idea di giustizia*, Naples: Guida, 1983, pp. 57–71.

A Matter Of Principle, Cambridge, Mass.: Harvard University Press, 1985.

Life's Dominion: An Argument about Abortion, Euthanasia and Individual Freedom, New York: Knopf, 1993.

"Women and Pornography," *New York Review of Books*, October 1993, pp. 36–42.

Elster, J., *Sour Grapes*, Cambridge: Cambridge University Press, 1983.

Erasmus, Desiderius, *In Praise of Folly* [1511], Princeton: Princeton University Press, 1970.

Eskridge, W. N., *The Case for Same-Sex Marriage*, New York: The Free Press, 1996.

Ettelrick, P., "Since When is Marriage a Path to Liberation?" in W. Bubenstein, ed., *Lesbians, Gays and the Law*, New York: The New Press, 1993, pp. 401–5.

Ezorsky, G., *Racism and Justice: The Case for Affirmative Action*, Ithaca: Cornell University Press, 1991.

Feinberg, J., *Social Philosophy*, Prentice Hall, Englewood Cliffs, 1973.

Ferraresi, F., *Threats to Democracy*, Princeton: Princeton University Press, 1996.

Fishkin, J. S., "Can There Be a Neutral Theory of Justice?" *Ethics*, 93, 1982–3, pp. 348–56.

Fiss, O., "Groups and the Equal Protection Clause," *Philosophy and Public Affairs*, 5, 1975, pp. 107–77.

Fitt, G., "Toleration in Northern Ireland," in S. Mendus and D. Edwards, eds., *On Toleration*, Oxford: Clarendon Press, 1987, pp. 62–82.

Fitzmaurice, D., "Liberal Neutrality, Traditional Minorities and Education," in J. Horton, ed., *Liberalism, Multiculturalism and Toleration*, London: Macmillan, 1993, pp. 50–69.

Flathman, R. E., "Egalitarian Blood in Skeptical Turnips?" *Ethics*, 93, 1982–3, pp. 357–66.

Toward a Liberalism, Ithaca: Cornell University Press, 1989.

Forst, R., ed., *Toleranz*, Frankfurt: Campus Verlag, 2000.

Frazer, N., "From Distribution to Recognition? Dilemmas of Justice in a Post-Socialist Era," *New Left Review*, 212, 1995, pp. 68–93.

Freeman, M., "Democracy and Dynamite: The People's Right to Self-Determination," *Political Studies*, 44, 1996, pp. 746–61.

Galeotti, A. E., "Individualism, Social Rules, Tradition," *Political Theory*, 15, 1987, pp. 163–81.

"Individualismo metodologico e liberalismo," *Biblioteca della libertà*, 96, 1987, pp. 24–47.

"L'insorgenza delle regole e dell'ordine nella teoria sociale di F. A. Hayek," *Working Papers*, Politeia, Milan: Bibliotechne, 1987.

"Intervista a Michael Walzer," *Notizie di Politeia*, 1988.

"La questione della tolleranza," *Working Papers*, Politeia, Milan: Bibliotechne, 1990.

"Citizenship and Equality: The Place for Toleration," *Political Theory*, 21, 1993, pp. 585–605.

La tolleranza. Una proposta pluralista. Naples: Liguori, 1994.

"La differenza: politica, non metafisica," in S. Maffettone and S. Veca, eds., *Filosofia, politica e società*, Rome, Donzelli, 1995, pp. 19–35.

"Questioni di giustizia e questioni di tolleranza," *Filosofia e questioni pubbliche*, 1, 1995, pp. 64–78.

"Tolérance et justice sociale," in J. Affichard and J. B. de Foucauld, eds., *Pluralisme et équité*, Paris: Esprit, 1995, pp. 103–19.

"Contemporary Pluralism and Toleration," *Ratio Juris*, 10, 1997, pp. 223–35.

Multiculturalismo. Filosofia politica e conflitto identitario, Naples: Liguori, 1999.

"Neutrality and Recognition," in R. Bellamy and M. Hollis, eds., *Pluralism and Liberal Neutrality*, London: Frank Cass, 1999, pp. 37–53.

"Do We Need Toleration as a Moral Virtue?" *Res Publica*, forthcoming.

Galston, W., *Justice and the Human Good*, Chicago: University of Chicago Press, 1980.

Liberal Purposes, Cambridge: Cambridge University Press, 1991.

Gauthier, D., "Breaking Up: An Essay on Secession," *Canadian Journal of Philosophy*, 24, 1994, pp. 357–72.

Gianni, M., "Le 'fait' du multiculturalisme: Quelques implications concernant la théorie de la citoyenneté," mimeo, Geneva, 1994.

Gibbard, A., *Wise Choice, Apt Feelings*, Cambridge, Mass.: Harvard University Press, 1990.

Goodin, R. and Reeve, A., eds., *Liberal Neutrality*, London: Routledge, 1987.

Gostin, L., ed., *Civil Liberties in Conflict*, London: Routledge, 1988.

Gray, J., "Where Pluralists and Liberals Part Company," *International Journal of Political Studies*, 6, 1999, pp. 17–36.

Green, L., "Internal Minorities and their Rights," in W. Kymlicka, ed., *The Rights to Minority Cultures*, Oxford: Oxford University Press, 1995, pp. 256–72.

Greenawalt, K., *Religious Convictions and Political Choice*, Oxford: Oxford University Press, 1988.

Gutmann, A., "Communitarian Critics of Liberalism," *Philosophy and Public Affairs*, 14, 1985, pp. 308–22.

Gutmann, A., ed., *Multiculturalism and "The Politics of Recognition,"* Princeton: Princeton University Press, 1993.

Gutmann, A. and Thompson, D., "Moral Conflict and Political Consensus," *Ethics*, 101, 1990, pp. 64–88.

Democracy and Disagreement, Cambridge, Mass.: Harvard University Press, 1996.

Habermas, J., "Reconciliation through the Public Use of Reason: Remarks on John Rawls's *Political Liberalism*," *Journal of Philosophy*, 92, 1995, pp. 109–31.

The Inclusion of the Other, Cambridge: Polity Press, 1998.

Hare, R., "Abortion and the Golden Rule," *Philosophy and Public Affairs*, 4, 1975, pp. 201–22.

Harel, A., "The Boundaries of Justifiable Tolerance: A Liberal Perspective," in D. Heyd, ed., *Toleration: An Elusive Virtue*, Princeton: Princeton University Press, 1996, pp. 114–16.

Harrison, G., "Relativism and Tolerance," in P. Laslett and J. Fishkin, eds., *Philosophy, Politics, Society*, Oxford: Blackwell, 1979, pp. 273–90.

Harrison, R., "Tolerating the Offensive," in J. Horton and P. Nicholson, eds., *Toleration: Theory and Practice*, Aldershot: Avebury, 1992, pp. 14–27.

Hart, H. H., *Law, Liberty and Morality*, Oxford: Oxford University Press, 1962.

Haskar, V., *Equality, Liberty and Perfectionism*, Oxford: Oxford University Press, 1979.

Hayek, F. A., *Individualism and Economic Order*, London and Chicago: Routledge and University of Chicago Press, 1948.

The Counter-Revolution of Science, Glencoe, Ill.: The Free Press, 1952.

The Constitution of Liberty, London and Chicago: Routledge and University of Chicago Press, 1960.

Law, Legislation and Liberty, London: Routledge, 1982.

Hegel, G. W. F., *The Phenomenology of Spirit* [1807], Oxford: Clarendon Press, 1970.

Heim, J. C., "The Demise of the Confessional State and the Rise of the Idea of a Legitimate Minority," in *Majority and Minorities*, New York: New York University Press, 1980, pp. 11–23.

Herman, B., "Pluralism and the Community of Moral Judgement," in D. Heyd, ed., *Toleration: An Elusive Virtue*, Princeton: Princeton University Press, pp. 60–80.

Heyd, D., ed., *Toleration: An Elusive Virtue*, Princeton: Princeton University Press, 1996.

Hicks, S. and McDermott. J., eds., *Lesbian and Gay Fostering and Adoption*, London and Philadelphia: Jessica Kinsley, 1999.

Hirsch, F., *Social Limits to Growth*, London: Routledge and Kegan Paul, 1977.

Hirschman, A., "Against Parsimony," *Economics and Philosophy*, 1, 1985, pp. 7–20.

The Rhetoric of Reaction, Cambridge, Mass. and London: Belknap Press, 1991.

Horton, J., "Toleration, Morality and Harm," in S. Mendus and J. Horton, eds., *Aspects of Toleration*, London: Methuen, 1985, pp. 113–35.

"Toleration as a Virtue" in D. Heyd, ed., *Toleration: An Elusive Virtue*, Princeton: Princeton University Press, 1996, pp. 28–43.

Horton, J. ed., *Liberalism, Multiculturalism and Religious Pluralism*, London: Macmillan, 1993.

Horton, J. and Mendus, S., eds., *Toleration, Identity and Difference*, London: Macmillan, 1999.

Horton, J. and Nicholson, P., eds., *Toleration: Theory and Practice*, Aldershot: Avebury, 1992.

Hurka, T., *Perfectionism*, Oxford: Oxford University Press, 1993.

Jackson, J., "Intolerance on the Campus," in J. Horton and P. Nicholson, eds., *Toleration: Theory and Practice*, Aldershot: Avebury, 1992, pp. 28–46.

James, S., "Cittadinanza femminile e indipendenza," in A. E. Galeotti, ed., *Individui e istituzioni*, Turin: La Rosa, 1992, pp. 175–205.

Johnasson, W. and Percy, W., *Outing: Shattering the Conspiracy of Silence*, New York and London: Hawarth Press, 1994.

Jones, P., "Toleration, Harm and Moral Effect," in S. Mendus and J. Horton, eds., *Aspects of Toleration*, London: Methuen, 1985, pp. 136–57.

"The Ideal of the Neutral State," in R. Goodin and A. Reeve, eds., *Liberal Neutrality*, London: Routledge, 1987, pp. 9–38.

Kant, I., *Answer to the Question: What is Enlightenment?* [1783], in *Political Writings*, ed. Hans Reiss, Cambridge: Cambridge University Press, 1991.

The Critique of Practical Reason [1788], ed. Mary Gregory, Cambridge: Cambridge University Press, 1997.

Kaplan, M. B., "Intimacy and Equality: The Question of Lesbian and Gay Marriage," *Philosophical Forum*, 25, 1994, pp. 333–40.

Kilcullen, J., *Sincerity and Truth. Essays On Arnauld, Bayle and Toleration*, Oxford: Clarendon Press, 1988.

King, P., *Toleration*, London: Allen and Unwin, 1976.

"The Concept of Toleration," mimeo, Exeter, 2000.

Koselleck, R., *Kritik und Krise: Eine Studie zur Pathogenese der burgherlichen Welt*, Frankfurt: Suhrkamp Verlag, 1973.

Kraut, R., "Politics, Neutrality and the Good," *Social Philosophy and Policy*, 16, 1999, pp. 315–32.

Kukathas, C., "Are There Any Cultural Rights?" *Political Theory*, 20, 1992, pp. 105–39.

"Cultural Rights Again. A Rejoinder to Kymlicka," *Political Theory*, 20, 1992, pp. 647–80.

Kymlicka, W., *Liberalism, Community and Culture*, Oxford: Oxford University Press, 1989.

Contemporary Political Philosophy, Oxford: Clarendon Press, 1990.

"The Right of Minority Cultures. A Reply to Kukathas," *Political Theory*, 20, 1992, pp. 140–6.

Multicultural Citizenship, Oxford: Oxford University Press, 1995.

"Liberal Nationalism," *European Forum on Citizenship*, Florence: EUI, 1996.

"Social Unity in a Liberal State," *Social Philosophy and Policy Foundation*, USA, 1996.

Kymlicka, W., ed., *The Rights of Minority Cultures*, Oxford: Oxford University Press, 1995.

Larmore, C., *Patterns of Moral Complexity*, Cambridge: Cambridge University Press, 1987.

Leader, S., "Three Faces of Toleration in a Democracy," *Journal of Political Philosophy*, 4, 1996, pp. 45–67.

Lewis, D., *Convention*, Cambridge, Mass.: Harvard University Press, 1969.

Locke, J., *A Letter Concerning Toleration* [1685], ed. J. Horton and S. Mendus, London: Routledge, 1991.

Losano, M., "Contro la società multietnica," *Micromega*, December 1991, pp. 7–16.

Lukes, S., *Moral Conflict and Politics*, Oxford: Clarendon Press, 1991.

"Toleration and Recognition," *Ratio Juris*, 10, 1997, pp. 213–22.

Macedo, S., *Liberal Virtues: Citizenship, Virtues and Community*, Oxford: Clarendon Press, 1990.

MacKinnon, C., *Only Words*, Cambridge, Mass.: Harvard University Press, 1993.

"Sexuality, Pornography and Method: Pleasure under Patriarchy," *Ethics*, 99, 1989, pp. 314–46.

Margalit, A., *The Decent Society*, Oxford: Oxford University Press, 1996.

Margalit, A. and Halbertal, M., "Liberalism and the Right to Culture," *Social Research*, 61, 1994, pp. 491–537.

Margalit, A. and Raz, J., "National Self-Determination," in W. Kymlicka, ed., *The Rights of Minority Cultures*, Oxford: Oxford University Press, 1995, pp. 79–92.

Martiniello, M., *Sortir des ghettos culturels*, Paris: Presses des Sciences Politiques, 1997.

Matsuda, M., "Public Response to Racist Speech: Considering the Victim's Story," *Michigan Law Review*, 87, 1989, pp. 2329–59.

Matsuda, M. and Delgado, C. L., *Words that Wound*, San Francisco: Westview, 1992.

McClure, K., "Difference, Diversity and the Limits of Toleration," *Political Theory*, 18, 1990, pp. 361–91.

Mendus, S., *Toleration and the Limits of Liberalism*, London: Macmillan, 1989.

Mendus, S., ed., *Justifying Toleration*, Cambridge: Cambridge University Press, 1988.

Politics of Toleration: Tolerance and Intolerance in Modern Life, Edinburgh: Edinburgh University Press, 1999.

The Politics of Toleration in Modern Life, Durham, N.C.: Duke University Press, 2000.

Mendus, S. and Edwards, D., eds., *On Toleration*, Oxford: Clarendon Press, 1987.

Mendus, S. and Horton, J., eds., *Aspects of Toleration*, London: Methuen, 1985.

Mereu, I., *Storia dell'intolleranza in Europa*, Milan: Mondadori, 1979.

Mill, J. S., *On Liberty* [1859], ed. H. B. Acton, London: Dent Dutton, 1972.

Miller, D., "Group Identities, National Identities and Democratic Politics," in J. Horton and S. Mendus, eds., *Toleration, Identity and Difference*, London: Macmillan, 1999, pp. 103–25.

Milton, J., *Areopagitica*, ed. R. M. Lea, Oxford: Clarendon Press, 1973.

Modood, T., "Collective Rights: An Unnecessary Complication," *European Forum on Citizenship*, Florence: EUI, 1996.

Montefiore, A., ed., *Neutrality and Impartiality. The University and Political Commitment*, Cambridge: Cambridge University Press, 1975.

Moon, D., *Constructing Community. Moral Pluralism and Tragic Conflict*, Princeton: Princeton University Press, 1993.

Moore, M. S., "Sandelian Antiliberalism," *California Law Review*, 77, 1989, pp. 539–60.

Moruzzi, N., "A Problem with Headscarves. Reply to Galeotti," *Political Theory*, 22, 1994, pp. 653–72.

Mosse, G., *Toward the Final Solution: History of European Racism*, New York: Howard Fertig, 1978.

Nagel, T., "Moral Conflict and Political Legitimacy," *Philosophy and Public Affairs*, 16, 1987, pp. 215–40.

Equality and Partiality, Oxford: Oxford University Press, 1991.

Neal, P., "A Liberal Theory of the Good?" *Canadian Journal of Philosophy*, 17, 1987, pp. 567–81.

Nicholson, P., "Toleration as a Moral Ideal," in S. Mendus and J. Horton, eds., *Aspect of Toleration*, London: Methuen, 1985, pp. 158–73.

Nozick, R., *Anarchy, State and Utopia*, New York: Basic Books, 1974.

O'Neill, J., ed., *Modes of Individualism and Collectivism*, London: Heinemann, 1973.

O'Neill, O., "The Public Use of Reason," *Political Theory*, 14, 1986, pp. 523–51.

Paine, T., *The Rights of Man*, part 1 [1791], in *Political Writings*, ed. Bruce Kuklick, Cambridge: Cambridge University Press, 1989.

Parek, B., "Discourses on National Identity," *Political Studies*, 42, 1994, pp. 492–504.

Perry, M., "Neutral Politics?" *Review of Politics*, 51, 4, 1989, pp. 479–509.

Phillips, A., *Democracy and Difference*, Cambridge: Polity Press, 1993.

Piazza, A., "Biologia senza razze," *Sisifo*, 26 October 1993.

Pizzorno, A., *Le radici della politica assoluta*, Milan: Feltrinelli, 1993.

Pocock, J. G. A., "Religious Freedom and the Desacralization of Politics: From the English Civil Wars to the Virginia Statute," in M. D. Peterson and R. Vaughan, eds., *The Virginia Statute for Religious Freedom*, Cambridge: Cambridge University Press, 1988, pp. 43–73.

Poliakov, L., *Le Mythe Arian*, Paris: Calman-Lévy, 1971.

Popper, K., "Toleration and Intellectual Responsibility," in S. Mendus and D. Edwards, eds., *On Toleration*, Oxford: Clarendon Press, 1987, pp. 17–34.

Post, R. C., "Racist Speech, Democracy and the First Amendment," *William and Mary Law Review*, 32, 1991, pp. 267–388.

Rae, D., *Equalities*, Cambridge, Mass.: Harvard University Press, 1981.

Raphael, D. D., "The Intolerable," in S. Mendus, ed., *Justifying Toleration*, Cambridge: Cambridge University Press, 1988, pp. 137–53.

Rawls, J., *A Theory of Justice*, Oxford: Oxford University Press, 1971.

"Justice as Fairness: Political Not Metaphysical," *Philosophy and Public Affairs*, 14, 1986, pp. 219–51.

"The Idea of an Overlapping Consensus," *Oxford Journal of Legal Studies*, 16, 1987, pp. 1–25.

"The Priority of the Right and Ideas of the Good," *Journal of Philosophy*, 1988, pp. 251–76.

"The Domain of the Political and Overlapping Consensus," *New York University Law Review*, 64, 1989, pp. 233–55.

Political Liberalism, New York: Columbia University Press, 1993.

"Reply to Habermas," *Journal of Philosophy*, 92, 1995, pp. 132–80.

Raz, J., *The Morality of Freedom*, Oxford: Clarendon Press, 1986.

"Autonomy, Toleration and the Harm Principle," in S. Mendus, ed., *Justifying Toleration*, Cambridge: Cambridge University Press, 1988, pp. 155–75.

"Facing Diversity: The Case for Epistemic Abstinence," *Philosophy and Public Affairs*, 19, 1990, pp. 3–46.

Ethics and the Public Domain, Oxford: Clarendon Press, 1994.

"Multiculturalism: A Liberal Perspective," *Dissent*, Winter 1994, pp. 67–79.

Remer, G., "Rhetoric and the Erasmian Defense of Religious Toleration," *History of Political Thought*, 10, 1989, pp. 377–403.

Richardson, H. S., "The Problem of Liberalism and the Good," in R. B. Douglass, G. R. Mara, and H. S. Richardson, eds., *Liberalism and the Good*, London: Routledge, 1990, pp. 1–28.

Riley, J., "Rights to Liberty in Purely Private Matters," part 1: *Economics and Philosophy*, 5, 1989, pp. 1–121; part 2: *Economics and Philosophy*, 6, 1990, pp. 27–64.

Ryan, A., "Hobbes, Toleration, and the Inner Life," in D. Miller and L. Siedentop, eds., *The Nature of Political Theory*, Oxford: Clarendon Press, 1983, pp. 197–218.

"A More Tolerant Hobbes?" in S. Mendus, ed., *Justifying Toleration*, Cambridge: Cambridge University Press, 1988, pp. 37–59.

"Can We Coerce People to be Free?" mimeo, Princeton University, 1992.

Sandel, M., *Liberalism and the Limits of Justice*, Cambridge: Cambridge University Press, 1992.

"Moral Argument and Liberal Toleration. Abortion and Homosexuality," *California Law Review*, 77, 1989, pp. 521–38.

Schauer, F., "The Phenomenology of Speech and Harm," *Ethics*, 103, 1993, pp. 635–53.

Schelling, T., *The Strategy of Conflict*, Cambridge, Mass.: Harvard University Press, 1960.

Schlesinger, A. Jr., *The Disuniting of America*, New York: Norton, 1991.

Schmitt, C., "Der Begriff des Politischen," *Archiv für Sozialwissenschaft und Sozialpolitik*, 53, 1927.

The Concept of the Political, ed. G. Schwab and L. Strauss, New Brunswick: Rutgers University Press, 1976.

Schwartz, W. F., ed., *Justice in Immigration*, Cambridge: Cambridge University Press, 1995.

Schwarz, A., "Moral Neutrality and Primary Goods," *Ethics*, 83, 1972–3, pp. 294–307.

Scoccia, D., "Paternalism and Respect for Autonomy, *Ethics*, 100, 1990, pp. 318–34.

Selfa, L., "What's Wrong with Identity Politics?" in D. Morton, ed., *The Material Queer*, Boulder, Colo.: Westview Press, 1996, pp. 46–8.

Sen, A., "Liberty and Social Choice," *Journal of Philosophy*, 80, 1983, pp. 5–28.

"Rights and Capabilities," in T. Honderich, ed., *Morality and Objectivity*, London: Routledge and Kegan Paul, 1985, pp. 130–48.

"Well-Being, Agency and Freedom," *Journal of Philosophy*, 82, 1985, pp. 169–221.

Inequality Reexamined, Oxford: Oxford University Press, 1992.

Shiffrin, S. H., *The First Amendment: Democracy and Romance*, Princeton: Princeton University Press, 1990.

Shklar, J., *American Citizenship: The Quest for Inclusion*, Cambridge, Mass.: Harvard University Press, 1991.

Sigler, J. A., *Minority Rights. A Comparative Analysis*, Westport, Conn.: Greenwood Press, 1983.

Smith, A., *An Inquiry into the Nature and Causes of the Wealth of Nations* [1776], 2 vols., London: Everyman's Library, 1954.

Stocker, M., "The Schizophrenia of Modern Ethical Theories," *Journal of Philosophy*, 73, 1976, pp. 453–65.

Strasser, M., *Legally Wed: Same Sex Marriage and the Constitution*, Ithaca: Cornell University Press, 1997.

Taguieff, P.-A., *La force du préjugé*, Paris: La Découverte, 1988.

Tamir, Y., *Liberal Nationalism*, Princeton: Princeton University Press, 1993.

"Reflection on the Nature of Collective Rights and Collective Punishment," *European Forum on Citizenship*, Florence: EUI, 1996.

Taylor, C., "The Politics of Recognition," in A. Gutmann, ed., *Multiculturalism and "The Politics of Recognition,"* Princeton: Princeton University Press, 1993, pp. 25–73.

Tempelman, S., "Construction of Cultural Identity: Multiculturalism and Exclusion," *Political Studies*, 47, 1999, pp. 17–31.

Thompson, D. and Gutmann, A., *Democracy and Disagreement*, Cambridge, Mass.: Harvard University Press, 1996.

Thompson, J. J., "A Defense of Abortion," *Philosophy and Public Affairs*, 1, 1971, pp. 47–66.

Tooley, M., "Abortion and Infanticide," *Philosophy and Public Affairs*, 2, 1972, pp. 37–65.

Tuck, R., "Scepticism and Toleration in the Seventeenth Century," in S. Mendus, ed., *Justifying Toleration*, Cambridge: Cambridge University Press, 1988, pp. 21–35.

Van Dyke, V., "Justice as Fairness: For Groups?" *American Political Science Review*, 69, 1974, pp. 607–14.

"The Individual, the State and Ethnic Communities in Political Theory," *World Politics*, 29, 1977, pp. 343–69.

"Collective Entities and Moral Rights: Problems in Liberal Thought," *Journal of Politics*, 44, 1982, pp. 21–40.

Human Rights, Ethnicity, Discrimination, Westport, Conn.: Greenwood Press, 1985.

Vivanti, C., "Assolutismo e tolleranza nel pensiero politico francese del Cinque–Seicento," in L. Firpo, ed., *Storia delle idee economiche, politiche e sociali*, vol. IV, Turin: UTET, 1986, pp. 13–93.

Voltaire, *Traité sur la tolerance. A l'occasion de la mort de Jean Calais* [1763] in *Mélanges*, Paris: Gallimard, 1961.

Waldron, J., "Theoretical Foundations of Liberalism," *Philosophical Quarterly*, 37, 1987, pp. 127–50.

"Toleration and the Rationality of Persecution," in S. Mendus, ed., *Justifying Toleration*, Cambridge: Cambridge University Press, 1988, pp. 61–86.

"Legislation and Moral Neutrality," in R. Goodin and A. Reeve, eds., *Liberal Neutrality*, London, Routledge, 1987, pp. 61–83.

"Autonomy and Perfectionism in Raz' *Morality of Freedom*," *California Law Review*, 62, 1989, pp. 1097–152.

"Superseding Historic Injustice," *Ethics*, 103, 1992, pp. 4–28.

"Minority Culture and the Cosmopolitan Alternative," in W. Kymlicka, ed., *The Rights of Minority Cultures*, Oxford: Oxford University Press, 1995, pp. 93–129.

Wall, S., *Liberalism, Perfectionism and Restraint*, Cambridge: Cambridge University Press, 1988.

Walzer, M., *Spheres of Justice*, New York: Basic Books, 1983.

"New Tribalism," *Dissent*, spring 1992, pp. 164–71.

What it Means to be an American, Padua: Marsilio, 1992.

"Minority Rites," *Dissent*, Summer 1996, pp. 53–5.

On Toleration, New Haven: Yale University Press, 1997.

"What Rights for Cultural Communities?" mimeo, Turin, 2000.

Warnock, M., "The Limits to Toleration," in S. Mendus and D. Edwards, eds., *On Toleration*, Oxford: Clarendon Press, 1987, pp. 123–39.

Weale, A., "Toleration, Individual Differences and Respect for Persons," in S. Mendus and J. Horton, eds., *Aspects of Toleration*, London: Methuen, 1985, pp. 16–35.

Weber, M., *Science as a Vocation* and *Politics as a Vocation*, in *Selections in Translation*, ed. W. G. Runciman, Cambridge: Cambridge University Press, 1978.

Wissenschaft als Beruft [1904], Berlin: Dunker und Humblot, 1975.

Wellman, C. H., "A Defense of Secession and Political Self-Determination," *Philosophy and Public Affairs*, 24, 1995, pp. 142–71.

Weston, K., *Family We Choose: Lesbians, Gays, Kinship*, New York: Columbia University Press, 1991.

Williams, B., "Space Talk: The Conversation Continued," *Ethics*, 93, 1982–3, pp. 367–71.

"Toleration: An Impossible Virtue," in D. Heyd, ed., *Toleration: An Elusive Virtue*, Princeton: Princeton University Press, 1996, pp. 18–27.

"Toleration: A Political or Moral Question?" *Diogenes*, 44, 1996, pp. 35–48.

Wilson, A., ed., *A Simple Matter of Justice*, London: Cassel, 1995.

Wintemute, R., *Sexual Orientation and Human Rights*, Oxford: Clarendon Press, 1996.

Wolf, S., "Two Levels of Pluralism," *Ethics*, 102, 1992, pp. 785–98.

Wong, D. B., 1992, "Coping with Moral Conflict and Ambiguity," *Ethics*, 102, 1992, pp. 763–84.

Young, I., *Justice and the Politics of Difference*, Princeton: Princeton University Press, 1990.

Democracy and Deliberation, Cambridge, Mass.: MIT Press, forthcoming.

Zincone, G., *Da sudditi a cittadini*, Bologna: Il Mulino, 1992.

Index